ACADEMIC ASSOCIATES   TEE Study

Biology

Third Edition

Featuring:

Trial Tests

Course Objectives

Revision Activities

TEE Style Questions

Detailed Answers

Glossary

Peter Walster

First Published 1996
Second Edition 1997
Third Edition 2001

©   Academic Associates

ACN   075 259 871

Apart from any fair dealing for the purposes of private study, research, criticism or review, as permitted under the Copyright Act, no part of this publication may be reproduced by any process without written permission of the publisher.

National Library of Australia

ISBN   0 9577061 7 0

Typesetting and Layout by:
Techtype

Cover Design:
Cave Design

Printed by:
Australian Print Group

Acknowledgments:

Grateful thanks to:

- Alison, Catherine, James and Joanna Walster for their support and understanding.
- Phillip Richardson for his thorough editing.
- Mike and Rita Lucarelli for their encouragement, ideas and support.
- Tarin Rowe, Techtype, for her attention to detail and her efficiency.
- Geoff Meyer for his advice and help with the electron micrographs.

TO THE STUDENT

This revision guide has been written specifically for the TEE Biology Course taught in Western Australia. It covers the core objectives outlined for the course by the Curriculum Council of W.A.

The guide is divided into five sections.

- Revision Questions
- Revision Question Answers
- Trial Tests
- Trial Test Answers
- Glossary

Revision Questions and Answers

Each of the Modules 1 to 4 is subdivided into two sections. Module 0 is one section. Each section begins with a list of the core objectives. Read these carefully and think about what each objective means. The review questions which follow are designed to make you think and write about each objective.

It is recommended that you do these questions after you have covered the section in your lessons. Complete them fully and make corrections to your answers using the answers provided. When you have done this you will have a good summary from which to revise your work. This should enable you to apply the biological principles embodied in these answers to new situations which you will encounter in tests and examinations.

Trial Test and Answers

There are nine trial tests - one for Module 0 and two for each of the other Modules 1 to 4.

Short answers are required. They are very comprehensive and cover the course more thoroughly than would multiple choice or extended answer type questions.

The time allocations are suggested as a guide. Try to work quickly through them as you would in an examination. The marks allocation is based on many years teaching and marking experience. The answers are more detailed than is generally required. However, compare your answers carefully with those given, firstly to make corrections to your own where necessary and secondly to see how you might improve on your own answers.

Glossary

While learning this subject you should be developing a vocabulary which is peculiar to biology. The words listed are particularly relevant to the year twelve biology course. The list does not contain all the words you have encountered in your biology studies but it should provide an opportunity to check the meanings of many new words that you are likely to encounter this year.

It is essential that, if you are going to understand what you read about biology and if you are going to be able to communicate your ideas to others, you learn the vocabulary of the subject.

Biology is a fascinating subject. I hope this book helps you to understand it better and to succeed in your biology examinations and tests.

PREFACE TO THIRD EDITION

The Curriculum Council has made only minor changes to the Biology syllabus since this study guide was extensively revised in 1997. The only new objective to be added has been the last one in Module 0.

The third edition has improved graphics and layout which should make this edition easier for the student to use.

PETER WALSTER

Head of Science
Perth Modern Senior High School   November 2000

CONTENTS

Module 0	INTRODUCTION TO SCIENTIFIC METHODS		
	Review Questions		1
	Answers to Review Questions		8
Module 1	THE CELL (Part 1)		
	Review Questions		10
	Answers to Review Questions		19
Module 1	THE CELL (Part 2)		
	Review Questions		22
	Answers to Review Questions		28
Module 2	THE ORGANISM (Part 1)		
	Review Questions		30
	Answers to Review Questions		39
Module 2	THE ORGANISM (Part 2)		
	Review Questions		42
	Answers to Review Questions		50
Module 3	THE SPECIES (Part 1)		
	Review Questions		53
	Answers to Review Questions		61
Module 3	THE SPECIES (Part 2)		
	Review Questions		64
	Answers to Review Questions		69
Module 4	ECOSYSTEMS (Part 1)		
	Review Questions		71
	Answers to Review Questions		79
Module 4	ECOSYSTEMS (Part 2)		
	Review Questions		82
	Answers to Review Questions		88

TRIAL TESTS

Test 1	Module 0	92
Test 2	Module 1 (Part 1)	97
Test 3	Module 1 (Part 2)	105
Test 4	Module 2 (Part 1)	112
Test 5	Module 2 (Part 2)	122
Test 6	Module 3 (Part 1)	133
Test 7	Module 3 (Part 2)	140
Test 8	Module 4 (Part 1)	145
Test 9	Module 4 (Part 2)	150

SOLUTIONS TO TRIAL TESTS

Test 1	Module 0	157
Test 2	Module 1 (Part 1)	159
Test 3	Module 1 (Part 2)	162
Test 4	Module 2 (Part 1)	164
Test 5	Module 2 (Part 2)	167
Test 6	Module 3 (Part 1)	171
Test 7	Module 3 (Part 2)	173
Test 8	Module 4 (Part 1)	175
Test 9	Module 4 (Part 2)	176

GLOSSARY 179

Module 0 – Introduction to Scientific Method

SYLLABUS CHECKLIST

You should be able to:

- ✔ 0.1 Define biology and give specific examples of areas of study encompassed by that term.
- ✔ 0.2 Recall that in seeking solutions to problems and answers to questions biologists use scientific methodology.
- ✔ 0.3 Observe phenomena and describe, measure and record these as data.
- ✔ 0.4 Distinguish between observations and inferences.
- ✔ 0.5 Locate, interpret and summarise information relevant to an investigation.
- ✔ 0.6 Formulate hypotheses and make predictions based on them.
- ✔ 0.7 Design, carry out and write a report of a scientific investigation.
- ✔ 0.8 Distinguish between independent and dependent variables in a controlled experiment.
- ✔ 0.9 Identify and explain the importance of the controlled and experimental variables in scientific investigations.
- ✔ 0.10 Explain why sample size, randomly selected samples, replicates and repeat procedures are important in scientific investigations.
- ✔ 0.11 Display the relevant motor skills required to carry out scientific investigations appropriate to course objectives.
- ✔ 0.12 Classify, collate and display both first and second hand data.
- ✔ 0.13 Use diagrams, graphs, flow charts and physical models as visual representations of phenomena and relationships arising from the data.
- ✔ 0.14 Analyse and draw conclusions from simple data.
- ✔ 0.15 Examine and evaluate investigative procedures that may be carried out in the school laboratory.
- ✔ 0.16 Distinguish between an hypothesis, a generalisation, and a theory, and give biological examples of each of these.
- ✔ 0.17 Use internationally accepted names and symbols for primary and derived units of measurement relevant to biology.
- ✔ 0.18 Understand that the use of animals for scientific purposes has ethical and social implications.

REVIEW QUESTIONS

1. Distinguish between the studies 'botany' and 'zoology'.

   _____

   _____

2. How is scientific methodology unique?

   _____

   _____

3. List the senses used in obtaining 'observations'. In each case give an example of a phenomenon which could be observed using that sense.

4. How is an *observation* different from an *inference*? Give two examples of each.

5. Construct a table which you might use to tally the weight distribution of populations of fish of four species found at a particular location.

6. What is meant by:
   (i) An hypothesis; _____

   (ii) A prediction. _____

7. Give (i) an example of an hypothesis, and (ii) a prediction based on that hypothesis.

    (i) _____

    _____

    _____

    (ii) _____

    _____

    _____

8. Under what headings would you present a report of a *scientific investigation*?

    _____

    _____

9. (i) What is a variable? _____

    _____

    (ii) Give 10 examples of variables. _____

    _____

    _____

    _____

    _____

    _____

10. Define each term below.

    (i) Dependent variable. _____

    _____

    _____

    _____

    (ii) Independent variable. _____

    _____

    _____

    _____

11. Using your hypothesis in question 7, name:
    (i) the dependent variable; _____
    (ii) the independent variable. _____

12. The following is a description of a simple experiment carried out to test a particular hypothesis.

"Two batches of 1000 bean seeds were planted in the same soil type in nearby localities. One batch (X) was played classical music for 1 hour each day. The other batch (Y) was not subjected to any music at all. The dry weight of a randomly selected sample of each batch was measured each week for several months from germination to maturity."

(i) What hypothesis was this experiment designed to test?
_____
_____

(ii) How was the experiment controlled?
_____
_____

(iii) Why were so many bean seeds (1000) used in each batch?
_____
_____

(iv) a) What was the 'independent variable' in this experiment? _____
 b) What was the 'dependent variable'? _____
 c) List four other variables which should have been controlled in this experiment.
_____
_____

(v) a) What is meant by the 'dry weight' of a sample?
_____

 b) Why use 'dry weight' instead of 'total weight' of the sample?
_____

(vi) Why were the samples chosen 'randomly'?
_____
_____

(vii) Explain why the procedure may have been repeated by other scientists.
_____
_____

4

13. The following measurements were obtained from a series of samples taken at weekly intervals beginning one week from seed germination.

   Music: 50 g , 30 g , 80 g , 150 g , 175 g
   No Music: 45 g , 31 g , 83 g , 155 g , 180 g

   (i) Present this data in an appropriate table.

   (ii) Draw a graph to show the effect that music has on bean growth.

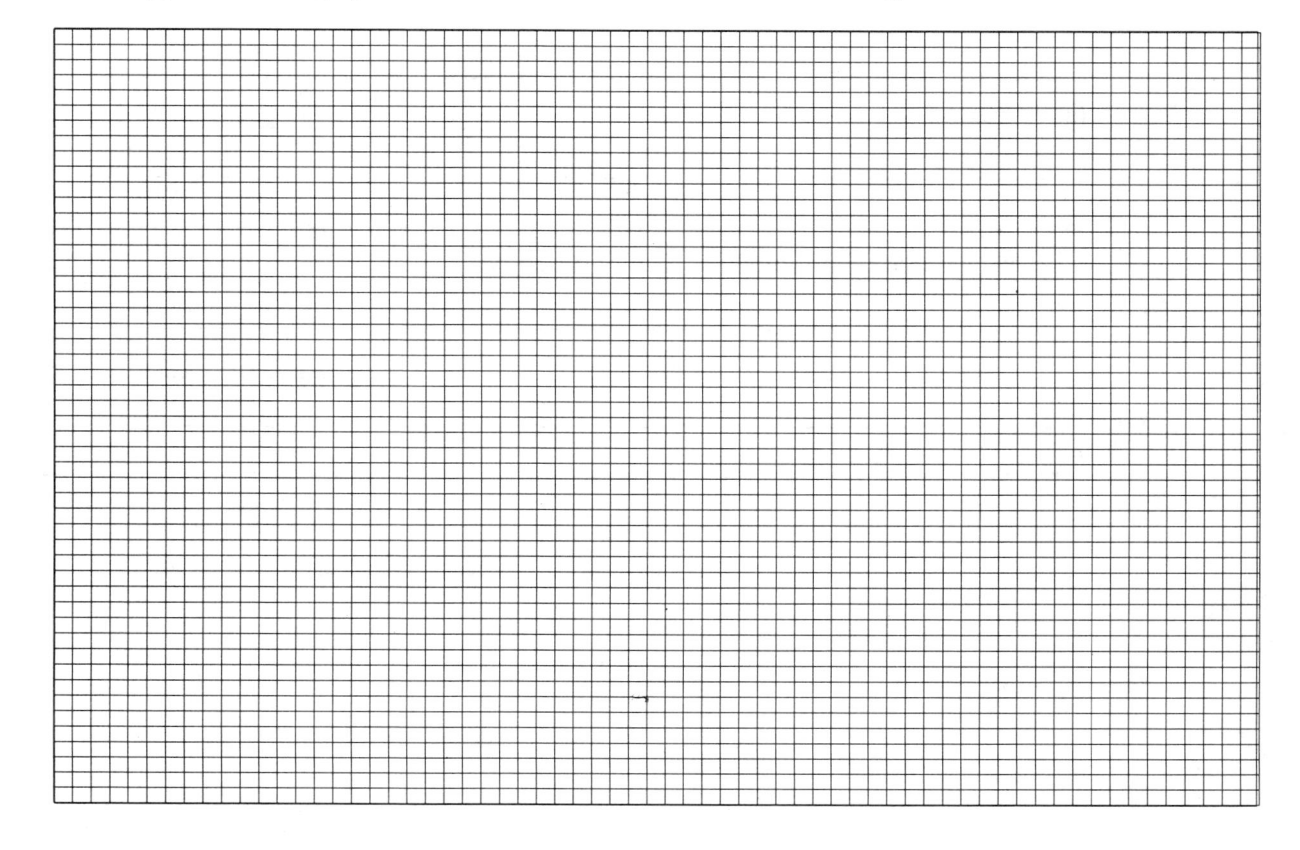

14. Does the data above support the hypothesis you have given in question 12(i)? _____ Justify your answer. _____
    _____
    _____

15. (i) How might you improve the design of the above experiment? List a few ways.
    _____
    _____
    _____
    _____

    (ii) Would you be confident, from this experiment, of the effect that music has on other plants? Explain your answer.
    _____
    _____
    _____

16. What is a:
    (i) generalisation; _____
    _____
    _____
    _____

    (ii) theory? _____
    _____

    Give an example from biology of each of the above.
    (iii) _____
    _____
    _____

    (iv) _____
    _____
    _____

17. Some units which are commonly used in biology are listed in the table below. Complete this table by adding those names or numbers which have been omitted.

Note: S.I. refers to the "System International d' Unites", a system of measures adopted by the international scientific community which should be used in scientific work.

S.I. units for length, mass, time and temperature are metres, grams, seconds and degrees Celsius respectively. For some factors derived from these - area, volume and energy the S.I. units are square metres, cubic metres and joules respectively.

Quantity	Unit	Symbol	SI Equivalents
length	metre	m	N/A
	centimetre	_____	0.01 m
	millimetre	_____	_____
	_____	µm	0.000001 m
area	hectare	_____	10,000 m²
	_____	m²	N/A
volume	cubic metre	_____	N/A
	_____	cm³	_____
volume (liquid)	_____	L	_____
	millilitre	_____	_____
mass	tonne	_____	_____
	_____	kg	N/A
	gram	_____	_____
	_____	mg	_____
temperature	degrees Celsius	_____	N/A
energy/amount of heat	megajoule	_____	_____
	kilojoule	_____	_____
	joule	_____	N/A

ANSWERS TO REVIEW QUESTIONS – Module O

1. Botany is the study of plants and plant life. Zoology is the study of animals and animal life.

2. Scientific methodology uses controlled experiments which are designed to test hypotheses in seeking the truth.

3. Sight - visible light enables humans to see objects.
   Touch - surfaces are recognised by texture and temperature.
   Hearing - sounds within the audible range of 30 - 40,000 Hz can be detected.
   Smell - minute quantities of water soluble substances can be detected in the atmosphere.
   Taste - substances which are water soluble stimulate receptors in our tongue.
   Note:
   1. While we may make observations with these senses, other animals may detect stimuli which we cannot and vice versa.
   2. We are not limited by our senses in making observations. We have developed instruments capable of measuring changes in the environment which are outside our sense capabilities, eg. we can use instruments such as Geiger counters to measure radiation levels.

4. An observation is just what we sense.
   egs. 1. "The plant is bending towards the window as it grows."
   2. "The Tuart is the largest native tree on Perth's coastal plain."
   An inference is an explanation of an observation.
   egs. 1. "The plant grows towards the window because it needs light."
   2. "The Tuart is adapted better than other native trees (eg. Jarrah, Marri) to the sandy soils of Perth's coastal plain."

5.

		WEIGHT OF FISH (at Point Pothole)			
		0 - 5 g	6 - 10 g	11 - 15 g	16 - 20 g
F I S H S P E C I E S	A	~~||||~~ 1	1		
	B	1	11	~~||||~~	11
	C	1	1		
	D	1	~~||||~~ ~~||||~~	1	

(Note: This is **one** way of presenting the data. You need not include any data in your table.)

6. (i) **An hypothesis**: A testable educated guess which is an attempt to explain some phenomenon.
   (ii) **A prediction**: An educated guess as to what might happen in the future.

7. (i) "That the fish species A in question 5 is the most numerous of the four fish species studied at Point Pothole."
   (Note: This is an educated guess because we know that smaller fish are generally more numerous - we can also test the hypothesis.)
   (ii) **If** species A is the most numerous species at Point Pothole **then** we should find a greater proportion of species A in fish nets used to catch fish at Point Pothole.

8. Title
   Aim   (Normally involves testing an hypothesis.)
   Equipment   (Diagrams included.)
   Procedure   (Method - listed in logical steps.)
   Results   (Data - presented in tables and graphs.)
   Conclusions (Analysis which reflects on the aim. Comment on whether or not the hypothesis is supported.)

9. (i) A variable: a factor which may change.
   (ii) Temperature, pH, humidity, time, altitude, windspeed, wind direction, level of carbon dioxide, level of oxygen, length of daylight, intensity of light, pressure.

10. Dependent variable: the variable we are interested in finding out about - we do not control the dependent variable.
    Independent variable: the variable we deliberately change in order to measure any possible effect on the dependent variable.

11. Dependent variable: number of fish, species A caught.
    Independent variable: total number of fish caught.

12. (i) "That classical music promotes the growth of beans."
    (ii) It was controlled by using batch Y - batch Y was treated in every way the same as batch X but with one variable, the music, omitted from its environment. It could therefore be compared to X and any differences in growth attributed to the music.
    (iii) Using many bean seeds helps to improve reliability. The results should be more typical of what to expect. It eliminates error which may be due to sick or abnormally slow growing beans.
    (iv) a) Independent variable: presence or absence of classical music.
    b) Dependent variable: dry weight of bean seeds.
    c) Soil type, soil temperature, bean type (variety), amount of water used, regularity of watering, amount of light received, wind (protection).

12. (v) a) A sample placed in a 'slow' oven (so that it is not burnt to a cinder). The water content of the plant gradually evaporates leaving just the organic matter. This can provide a good measure of plant growth.
    b) 'Total weight' (before heating) includes both the organic matter in the plant and also its water content. Water content may vary because of prevailing weather conditions and soil water content. A better measure of a plant's accumulation of sugar, starch, protein, etc is its 'dry weight'.
  (vi) Samples are chosen randomly to avoid bias. (It may be in the interests of the biologist's back to carry only small plants back to the laboratory - but they might not reflect the normal growth.)
  (vii) Repetition is necessary to confirm results. A hypothesis cannot be accepted as true unless experiments based on that hypothesis consistently support it by providing similar results.

13. (i) Table: Dry Weight of Bean Seedling Samples with and without Music taken at weekly intervals from germination.

Time since germination (weeks)	Weight of Bean Sample (g) Music	Weight of Bean Sample (g) No Music
1	50	45
2	30	31
3	80	83
4	150	155
5	175	180

    Note: Independent variable (time) in left column, dependent variable (weight) in right column(s).

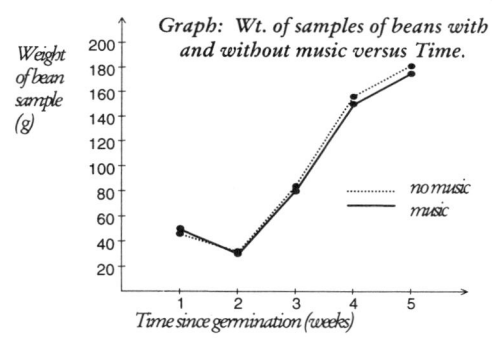

    Graph: Wt. of samples of beans with and without music versus Time.

14. No. It does not because the plants show little difference in their growth weights.

15. (i) Repeat the experiment several times. Use different varieties of bean. Continue the experiment beyond 5 weeks. Measure the productivity of the beans in terms of the weight of bean seeds they produce. Use even larger samples. Play different types of music. Vary the loudness. Use different soils.
   (ii) No. Unless other plant species were tested it would not be justified to generalise. Before a generalisation about the effect of music on plant growth can be made, many other plant species should be tested.

16. (i) A generalisation is a statement about situations which may or may not have been tested. For example we may make the generalisation that "All living things contain DNA." While we have much evidence to support this generalisation there are numerous species of living things which have not yet been studied at all. Many haven't even been given a scientific name. However, because many many organisms have been tested, the generalisation is acceptable.
  (ii) A theory is an hypothesis for which a significant amount of supporting evidence has been gathered.
  (iii) Plants need light to produce glucose.
  (iv) Life evolved on earth from simple inorganic and organic compounds.

17.

Quantity	Unit	Symbol	SI Equiv.
length	metre	m	N/A
	centimetre	cm	0.01 m
	millimetre	mm	0.001 m
	micrometres	μm	0.000001 m
area	hectare	ha	10,000 m²
	sq. metre	m²	N/A
volume	cubic metre	m³	N/A
	cubic centimetre	cm³	0.000001 m³
volume (liquid)	litre	L	0.001 m³
	millilitre	mL	0.000001 m³
mass	tonne	t	1,000 kg
	kilogram	kg	N/A
	gram	g	0.001 kg
	milligram	mg	0.000,001 kg
temperature	degrees Celsius	°C	N/A
energy/ amount of heat	megajoule	MJ	1,000,000 J
	kilojoule	kJ	1,000 J
	joule	J	N/A

Module 1 – The Cell (Part 1)

SYLLABUS CHECKLIST

You should be able to:

- 1.1 Explain the relationship between a eukaryotic cell and its external environment.
- 1.2 Explain the significance of the SA : volume and its importance to the survival of the cell.
- 1.3 Identify from diagrams and photomicrographs, the following cell structures: cytoplasm, plasma membrane, cell wall, nucleus, nucleolus, nuclear membrane, vacuoles, chloroplasts, ribosomes, endoplasmic reticulum, mitochondria, golgi bodies, centrioles, cilia, flagella.
- 1.4 Describe the functioning of plasma membrane, cell wall, nucleus, vacuoles, chloroplasts, ribosomes, endoplasmic reticulum, mitochondria, golgi bodies, centrioles, cilia, flagella.
- 1.5 Provide evidence that the continued survival of the cell depends on the presence of the nucleus.
- 1.6 Use a monocular microscope to observe plant and animal cells and estimate their dimensions.
- 1.7 Investigate single cell responses to environmental stimuli.
- 1.8 Use staining techniques to facilitate observation of specific structures and identification of chemicals in plant and animal cells (general principles).
- 1.9 Investigate the effect on cells of exposure to various solutions and from this infer the structure of the membrane.
- 1.10 Compare and contrast the passive and active processes by which substances move across cell membranes (diffusion, osmosis, active transport, pinocytosis, phagocytosis, endo/exocytosis).

REVIEW QUESTIONS

1. What factors (list six), in the external environment of a cell, could affect its survival. After each factor briefly explain **why** it is important.

    (i) _____ , _____

    _____

    _____

    (ii) _____ , _____

    _____

    _____

    (iii) _____ , _____

    _____

    _____

Module 1 – The Cell (Part 1)

(iv) _____ , _____

(v) _____ , _____

(vi) _____ , _____

2. Describe the relationship between the surface area and the volume of a cell.

3. What advantage might a small cell living in an aquatic environment have over a larger cell living in the same place?

4. Label the diagram of the cell shown using the following labels; cytoplasm, plasma membrane, cell wall, nucleus, nucleolus, nuclear membrane, vacuole, chloroplast, ribosome, endoplasmic reticulum, mitochondrion and Golgi body.

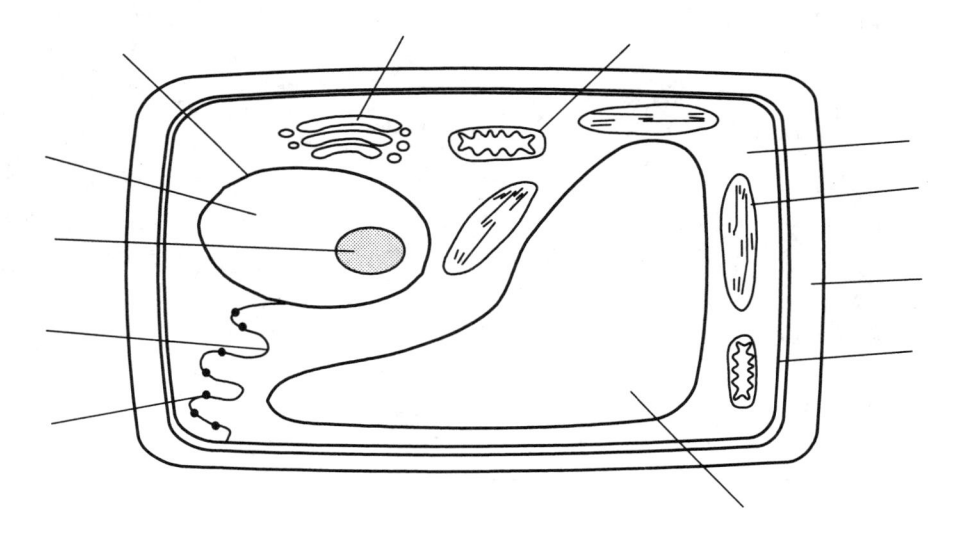

5. What is the function of each of the following organelles?

(a) plasma membrane: _____
(b) cell wall: _____
(c) nucleus: _____
(d) vacuole: _____
(e) chloroplast: _____
(f) ribosome: _____
(g) endoplasmic reticulum: _____
(h) mitochondrion: _____
(i) Golgi body: _____
(j) centriole: _____
(k) cilia: _____
(l) flagellum: _____

6. The figure below was taken from an electron micrograph of animal tissue (original magnification 20,000 ×).

(i) Write the names of the parts labelled.

a _____   b _____
c _____   d _____

(ii) Using the scale shown below the figure, estimate the size of the organelle b.

_____

6.

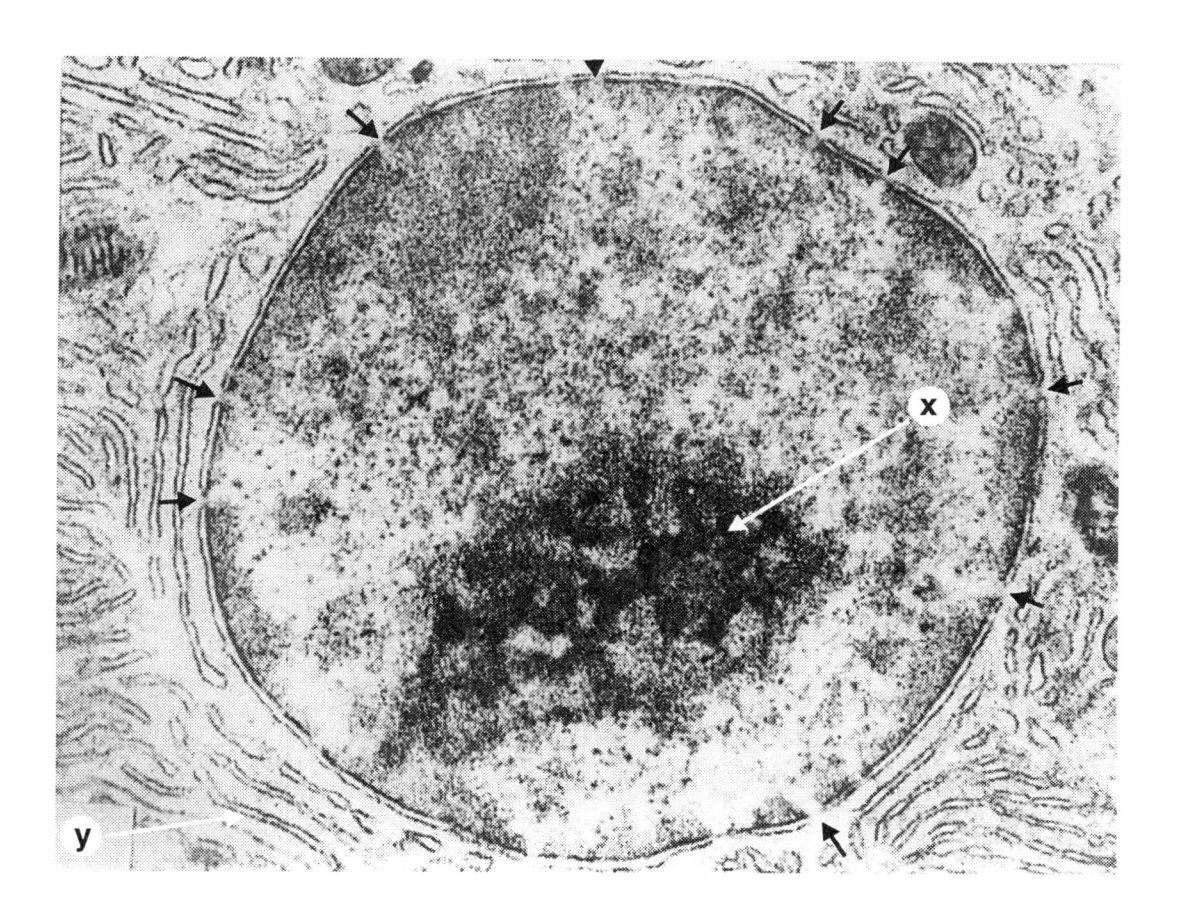

This electron micrograph shows a cell nucleus (the large spherical structure occupying most of the area).

(iii) To what are the small arrows on the diagram pointing? _____

(iv) Name the darker region in the nucleus, marked X. _____

(v) Name the lines outside the nucleus, marked Y. _____

(vi) What two features of the nuclear membrane are evident from this electron micrograph?
_____
_____

7. Write the correct spelling of the plural of the following organelles in question 5.

(c) _____   (g) _____

(h) _____   (k) _____

(l) _____

Biology Study Guide

8. Cells require a nucleus for their survival. Describe an experiment which demonstrates this fact.

_____
_____
_____
_____
_____
_____
_____
_____
_____
_____

9. Label the monocular microscope shown below and beside each label indicate briefly what the part is used for.

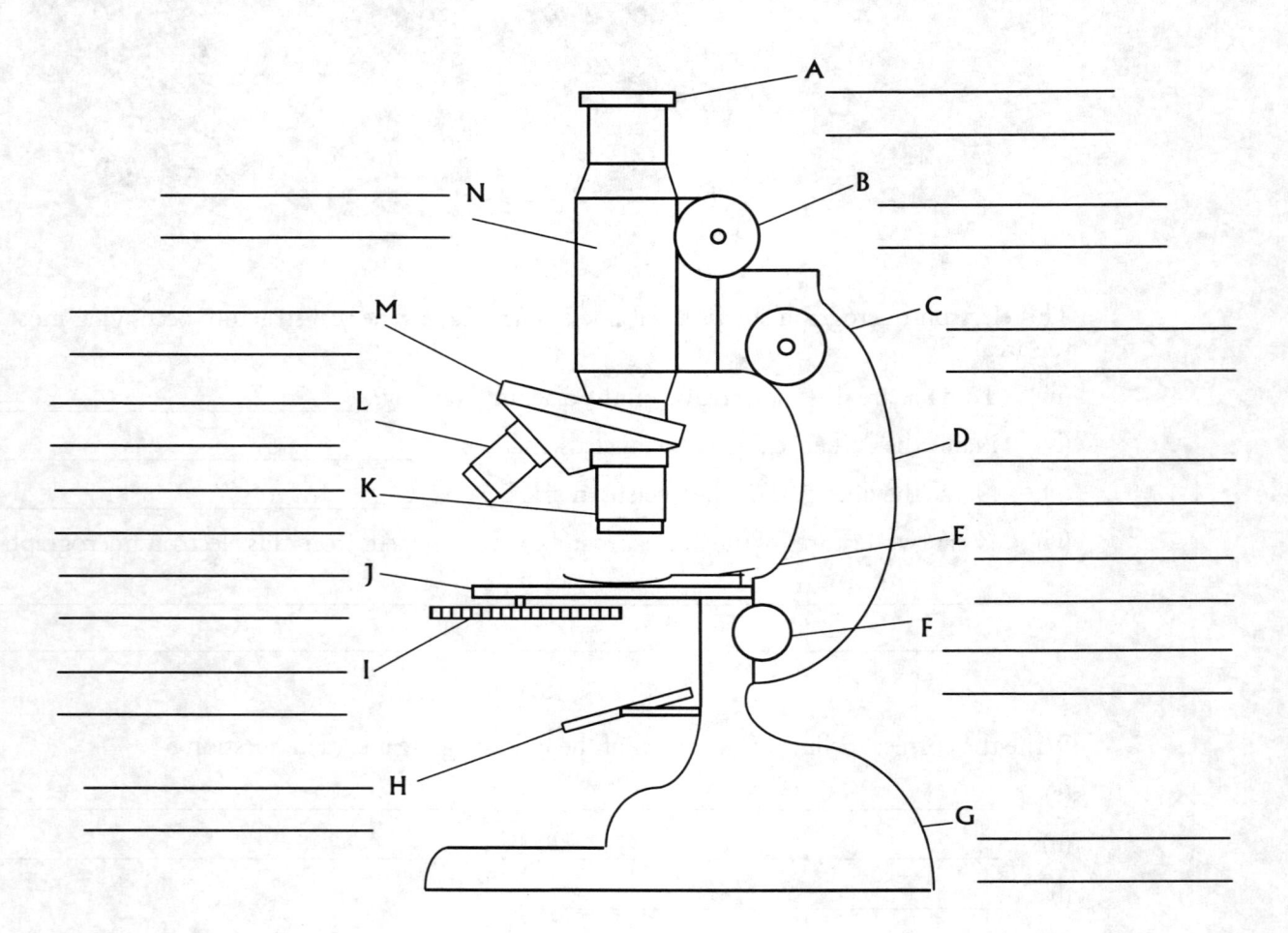

10. A student has made up a slide of a piece of 1 mm graph paper and observes this with her microscope. Using an ocular of 10x and an objective of 4x, she sees the image of the graph paper as shown below.

(a) What was the magnification used above? _____

(b) Estimate the diameter of the field of view at this magnification:

   (i) in mm _____ (ii) in µm _____

Using the same microscope, the student changed the objective to 10x. Draw lines on the circle below to indicate, approximately, the new image that she would observe.

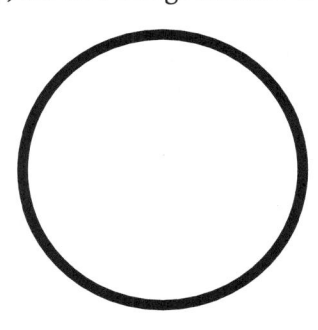

(c) Estimate the diameter of the field of view on this second magnification:

   (i) in mm _____ (ii) in µm _____

(d) If, when using the second magnification later in the day, she observed an organism which she drew carefully (shown below) estimate the:

   (i) length _____ mm or _____ µm

   (ii) width _____ mm or _____ µm

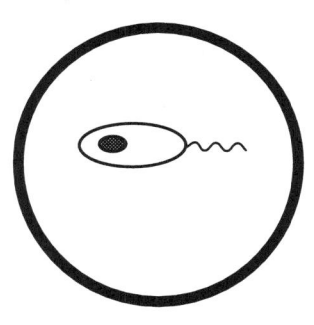

11. If you were asked to use a light microscope to determine whether a cell belonged to that of a plant or an animal, what would you look for on/in the cell?

_____

12. List three environmental stimuli which might affect a motile microorganism and discuss how each stimuli may affect the organism ie. a possible response.

    (i) _____   _____

    (ii) _____   _____

    (iii) _____   _____

13. Describe an experiment you could carry out to determine whether or not any one of your predicted responses in question 12 was correct.

    _____
    _____
    _____
    _____
    _____
    _____
    _____
    _____
    _____
    _____
    _____

14. (i) Why are stains often used on microscope slides of cells?

    _____
    _____

    (ii) For what classes of compounds are the stains commonly used? _____ ,
    _____ , _____ , _____

    (iii) On the diagram of the plant cell below, mark in clearly where each of these classes of compounds is likely to be in significant quantities.

15. What are the two main chemical constituents of cell membranes?

   (i) _____ (ii) _____

   Explain how and why alcohol and detergent affect cell membranes.

   (i) alcohol _____

   _____

   (ii) detergent _____

   _____

16. Using the diagram below, discuss the "fluid mosaic" model of the cell membrane. You will need to label the diagram first.

   EXTRA CELLULAR SURFACE

   INTRA CELLULAR SURFACE

   (i) _____ (ii) _____ (iii) _____ (iv) _____ (v) _____ (vi) _____

   _____
   _____
   _____
   _____
   _____
   _____
   _____
   _____
   _____
   _____
   _____
   _____
   _____

17. (i) Which of the following processes are active means by which substances move across cell membranes: diffusion, osmosis, active transport, pinocytosis, phagocytosis, exocytosis.

   _____

   (ii) Explain why these are active. _____

   _____

(iii) Which processes are passive? _____

_____

(iv) Explain why these are passive. _____

_____

(v) Which two processes are examples of endocytosis? _____

_____

18. Describe clearly what is meant by:
   (a) diffusion _____

   _____

   (b) osmosis _____

   _____

   (c) active transport _____

   _____

   (d) pinocytosis _____

   _____

   (e) phagocytosis _____

   _____

19. How is diffusion different from osmosis?

   _____
   _____
   _____

20. How is pinocytosis different from phagocytosis?

   _____

ANSWERS TO REVIEW QUESTIONS – Module 1 – Part 1

1. (i) Temperature: Enzymes function best at an optimum temperature. A cell's intra-cellular enzymes will be denatured if the temperature goes beyond their tolerance. They will work too slowly if the temperature becomes too low.
   (ii) pH: Enzymes within the cell also function best at an optimum pH.
   (iii) Osmotic Pressure: This is determined by the relative amounts of water and solutes. If extra-cellular fluid is very dilute and the cell absorbs too much water by osmosis, this may dilute the cytoplasm too much, or even cause animal cells to lyse. If the extra-cellular fluid is too concentrated dehydration of the cell may occur.
   (iv) Glucose levels: For heterotrophic cells this is often an essential food. Insufficient glucose may lead to a lack of necessary energy.
   (v) Nitrogenous Wastes: These are generally toxic and must be removed eg. uric acid, ammonia, urea.
   (vi) Level of CO_2: As with nitrogenous wastes, CO_2 needs to be removed. Rising levels of CO_2 increase acidity - carbonic acid forms when CO_2 dissolves in water. This generally reduces enzyme activity.

2. As the volume increases the surface area increases also but relatively more slowly. Therefore as the volume increases the S.A. : vol. becomes smaller.

3. Diffusion of oxygen and food to the centre of the small cell will be quicker than the diffusion to the centre of a larger cell. The diffusion of wastes will also be more efficient in a smaller cell. This is a direct result of a high S.A. : Volume.

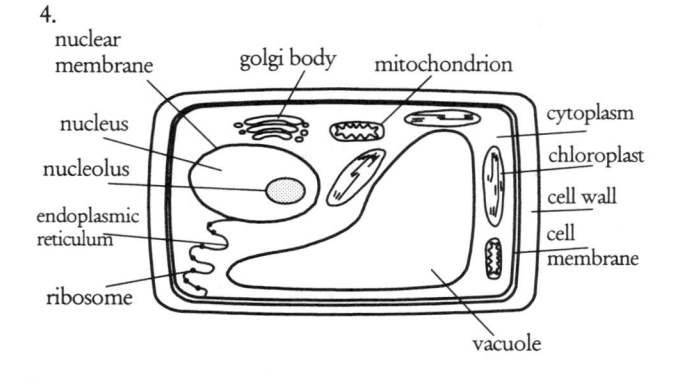

4. [Diagram of plant cell with labels: nuclear membrane, golgi body, mitochondrion, cytoplasm, chloroplast, cell wall, cell membrane, vacuole, ribosome, endoplasmic reticulum, nucleolus, nucleus]

5. (a) plasma membrane: selectively permeable - allows some things to enter or leave freely, actively transports when necessary, contains the fluid of cytoplasm.
   (b) cell wall: provides plant cell with support and protection.
   (c) nucleus: contains DNA which indirectly controls the activities of the other cell parts.
   (d) vacuole: large plant vacuole stores water and some mineral ions.
   (e) chloroplast: contains chlorophyll for photosynthesis, converts light energy to chemical energy.
   (f) ribosome: site for protein synthesis.
   (g) endoplasmic reticulum: membranous canal system for transport of substances within the cytoplasm, especially from nucleus to cell membrane.
   (h) mitochondrion: site for aerobic stage of respiration.
   (i) Golgi body: collecting and packaging centre for substances synthesised by cell.
   (j) centriole: forms spindles in cell division (not found in higher plant cells).
   (k) cilia: hair like structures which help propel many single celled organisms. Also found lining trachea in humans helping to remove dust by carrying mucus from lungs.
   (l) flagellum: long thread-like organelle - moves to propel some cells (eg. sperm and some protozoa and algae).

6. (i) (a) golgi body (b) mitochondrion
       (c) nucleus/nuclear membrane
       (d) nucleus/nucleoplasm

   (ii) size of $b = \dfrac{2}{2.5} \times 1\ \mu m = 0.8\ \mu m$

   (iii) nuclear pores
   (iv) nucleolus
   (v) endoplasmic reticula
   (vi) It has pores, it is a **double** membrane.

7. (c) nuclei   (g) endoplasmic reticula
   (h) mitochondria (k) cilia (cilium is the singular)
   (l) flagella

8. Amoeba can be divided so that two live fragments are formed each enclosed in cell membranes. One fragment contains the nucleus, the other no nucleus. The fragment with the nucleus lives whereas the non-nucleated fragment may live for several days but then dies.

9.

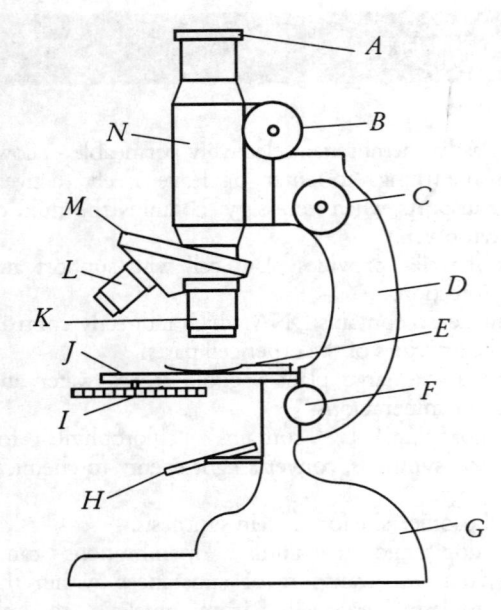

(A) Ocular (lens through which image is magnified.
(B) Coarse adjustment (for large movements of body tube in rough focusing)
(C) Fine adjustment (for final focusing).
(D) Arm (used for carrying).
(E) Clip (holds slide in place).
(F) Inclination joint (for tilting body tube).
(G) Base (provides stable support).
(H) Mirror (reflects light through aperture in wheel diaphragm).
(I) Wheel diaphragm (controls the amount of light passing through object).
(J) Stage (supports slide).
(K) High power objective (increases magnif-ication).
(L) Low power objective (lesser magnif-ication).
(M) Revolving nosepiece (moves objectives to change magnification).
(N) Body tube (allows light to pass up to ocular).

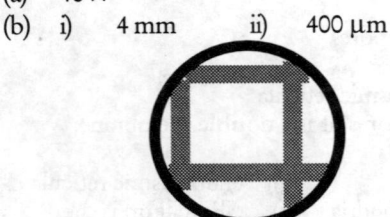

10. (a) 40 ×
    (b) i) 4 mm ii) 400 μm

    (c) i) $4 \times \dfrac{40}{100} = 1.6$ mm
        ii) $4000 \times \dfrac{40}{100} = 1600$ μm
    (d) i) length (body not including flagellum)
           = 0.64 mm and 640 μm
        ii) width = 0.27 mm and 270 μm

11. Presence of cell wall, large vacuole, chloroplasts. (These would indicate a plant cell.)

12. (i) light, may move away from/to light
    (ii) oxygen, may respire more rapidly
    (iii) heat, may move away from heat

13. **Hypothesis**: Amoeba will move towards light source.
    Prediction: If a beam of light is directed through a container which has amoeba in it, then these organisms will move towards the beam.
    Method:
    1) Set up two aquaria both with equal numbers of amoeba under the same conditions of temperature, water quality, size, water level and keep each the same.
    2) Place aquaria in a darkened room.
    3) Direct a beam of light at one aquaria (this is the experimental set up).
    4) Leave the other aquaria with no light (the control).
    5) Periodically remove samples of water from the same parts of both aquaria to determine the location of amoeba.
    Results: If the amoeba in the experiment consistently accumulate around the light beam, while those in the control are randomly distributed in their aquarium, these results would support the hypothesis.

14. (i) Most microorganisms are transparent and colourless. The stains highlight various organelles and inclusions.
    (ii) carbohydrates (starch, glucose, lignin, cellulose), proteins, lipids, nucleic acids.
    (iii)

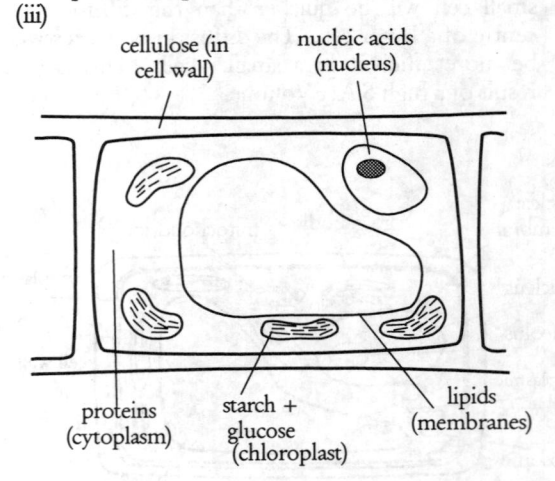

    cellulose (in cell wall), nucleic acids (nucleus), proteins (cytoplasm), starch + glucose (chloroplast), lipids (membranes)

15. (i) lipids (ii) proteins
    (i) Alcohol breaks down cell membranes. This is because it dissolves lipids.
    (ii) Detergent breaks down cell membranes. This is because it emulsifies lipids.

16. Labels
    (i) bilipid layer (with lipids showing both hydrophobic and hydrophilic regions)
    (ii) protein (with a central hydrophilic region which allows ions and some molecules to pass through)
    (iii) protein (with shaded hydrophobic and unshaded hydrophilic regions) - passes through entire membrane
    (iv) branching carbohydrate attached to protein (forming a glycoprotein)
    (v) small protein not spanning entire membrane
    (vi) branching carbohydrate attached to a lipid (forming a glycolipid)

    The "fluid mosaic" model proposes that the cell membrane is made up of two layers of lipid. Proteins "float" in the lipids, some extend right across the membrane (and may form channels through which substances pass) and some proteins do not extend right through the membrane but float on either the external or internal surface of the membrane.

17. (i) Active transport, pinocytosis, phago-cytosis, exocytosis.
    (ii) These are called "active" processes because they require energy provided by the cell.
    (iii) Diffusion and osmosis.
    (iv) These are passive because no energy needs to be supplied **by the cell**. The particles move because they have kinetic energy and move down a concentration gradient.
    (v) pinocytosis and phagocytosis

18. (a) Diffusion: movement of particles in a liquid or gas from an area in which they are more concentrated to an area in which they are less concentrated.
    (b) Osmosis: movement of solvent (water) through a membrane from an area where the solvent (water) is in greater concentration (or solutes are in lesser concentration) to an area where the solvent is less concentrated (or solutes are in greater concentration).
    (c) Active transport: movement of substances by the cell membrane against a concentration gradient. This process requires carrier molecules and energy which is supplied by ATP.
    (d) Pinocytosis: this is the ingestion of fluid by a cell which occurs when an invagination (or infold) of the membrane envelopes the fluid, enclosing it in a vacuole within the cytoplasm.
    (e) Phagocytosis: similar to pinocytosis but a pseudopod forms, engulfing solid particles which are enclosed within cytoplasmic vacuoles until digested by lysosomes.

19. Diffusion may or may not take place through cell membranes. It may be assisted by the membrane, if it does occur through the membrane. Osmosis is the diffusion of the solvent through the membrane. (In living things the solvent is water.)

20. Pinocytosis involves an infold and the ingestion of fluid (eg. drop of oil).
    Phagocytosis involves a pseudopod and the ingestion of solid particles (eg. a bacterium).

Module 1 – The Cell (Part 2)

SYLLABUS CHECKLIST

You should be able to:

- 1.11 Describe the structure of DNA at the level of major structural components (sugar, phosphate and nitrogenous bases) and state that the sequence of nitrogenous bases stores genetic information.
- 1.12 Describe and name the sequence of phases of mitosis.
- 1.13 Explain the need for DNA replication in the cell cycle.
- 1.14 Investigate the actions of enzymes and describe their functions.
- 1.15 Account for the properties of enzymes with reference to the 'lock and key' hypothesis for enzyme action.
- 1.16 Discuss the effect of temperature and pH on the rates of enzyme-controlled reactions.
- 1.17 Describe anaerobic and aerobic respiration in terms of sites at which they occur, requirements and products including wastes.
- 1.18 Compare and contrast aerobic and anaerobic respiration in terms of requirements for oxygen, amount of ATP produced and waste products in plants and animals.
- 1.19 Discuss why ATP is important for cell functioning.
- 1.20 Describe photosynthesis in terms of raw materials, role of chloroplasts, energy transfer to carbohydrates, products.
- 1.21 Compare and contrast the roles of photosynthesis and respiration in transferring energy between cells and their environments.

REVIEW QUESTIONS

1. The following diagram represents a short segment of DNA.

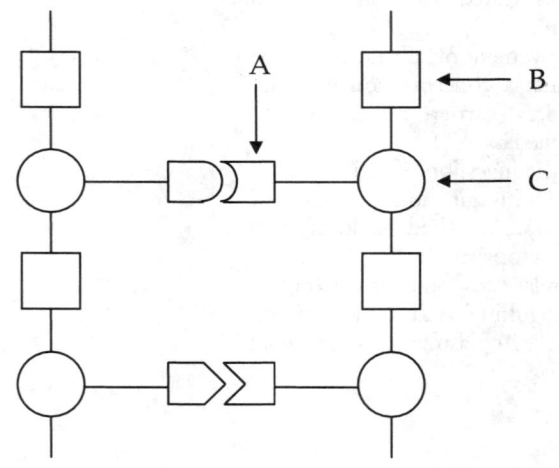

   Name the substances labelled A, B and C.

   A _____

   B _____

   C _____

2. If a small part of the molecule is isolated it could be represented by:

   (i) What is this unit called: _____ and (ii) where might it be found in this separated form? _____

3. Explain briefly why the *sequence* of nitrogenous bases in DNA is important.

   _____
   _____

4. The following diagrams show various stages of *mitosis*. They are in a jumbled order. Along side each diagram write the name of the phase and describe what is occurring during the phase.

   A) _____

   B) _____

   C) _____

   D) _____

   E) _____

5. List the order in which these phases would occur.

   _____ _____ _____ _____ _____

6. (i) In the sequence shown above what is the number of chromosomes in the 'parent' cell?
   _____

   (ii) How many pairs of chromosomes does it have? _____

   (iii) How many chromosomes does each of the daughter cells have? _____

   (iv) How many pairs of chromosomes does each daughter cell have? _____

   (v) What, therefore, is the **total** number of chromosomes in the daughter cells? _____

7. (i) Since the total number of chromosomes in the daughter cells is twice that of the parent cell, explain how this doubling in the number of chromosomes has come about.

   _____
   _____
   _____
   _____
   _____

   (ii) At what stage in the sequence does this replication of chromosomes occur?
   _____

   (iii) Explain concisely why the replication is necessary.
   _____
   _____
   _____
   _____

8. (i) What is an "enzyme"?
   _____
   _____
   _____

   (ii) Outline the 'lock and key' hypothesis which has been proposed to explain how enzymes function.
   _____
   _____
   _____
   _____
   _____
   _____

(iii) Why are enzymes required only in small quantities?

_____
_____
_____

(iv) What is the 'active site' on the enzyme?

_____
_____
_____

(v) Describe the effect that **temperature** has on enzyme action.

_____
_____
_____
_____

(vi) What other environmental changes may change enzyme activity?

_____

9. (i) What is aerobic respiration? _____

_____

(ii) Show the net reaction using a simple word equation.

_____

(iii) What is anaerobic respiration? _____

_____

(iv) Show a simple word equation for anaerobic respiration:
   a) in animals; _____
   b) in plants. _____

10. Complete the table below to contrast the two processes in question 9 above.

	Aerobic Respiration	Anaerobic Respiration
Site of occurrence		
Requirements for oxygen		
Products in plants		
Products in animals		
Amount of ATP produced from 1 molecule of glucose		

11. Since glucose is the starting substance in both plants and animals, explain why the products of anaerobic respiration are different in plants and animals.

12. (i) What is ATP and why is it important in the cell?

    (ii) List four cell processes which rely on ATP as a source of energy.

13. (i) Write a word equation for the breakdown of ATP in releasing useful energy for the cell.

    (ii) How and where are the material products of the breakdown of ATP recycled by the cell?

14. (i) Complete the simple word equation for photosynthesis.

    water + _____ ⟶ _____ + _____

    (ii) In order for this reaction to proceed, what other requirements must be met?
    _____

    (iii) Where does this process occur in a eukaryotic cell? _____

    (iv) Explain the need for each requirement.

    light _____
    _____

    water _____
    _____

    enzymes _____
    _____
    _____

    carbon dioxide _____
    _____

    chlorophyll _____
    _____

    ADP and P _____
    _____

15. (i) How are photosynthesis and respiration related? _____
    _____
    _____

    (ii) What is the energy relationship between the environment and photosynthesis?
    _____
    _____
    _____

    (iii) What is the energy relationship between the environment and respiration?
    _____
    _____
    _____

ANSWERS TO REVIEW QUESTIONS – Module 1 – Part 2

1. A nitrogenous base
   B phosphate group
   C ribose sugar

2. (i) nucleotide
   (ii) found in nucleoplasm

3. The sequence of nitrogenous bases in DNA is important because it provides a code which determines the sequence of amino acids in the proteins the cell can synthesise.

4. A) telophase – cell has divided, new nuclear membranes grow to enclose each cluster of chromosomes. Centrioles have duplicated. Chromosomes unravel to form chromatin.
   B) anaphase – chromatids are drawn to opposite sides of the cell – when separated they are called chromosomes. In plants a new cell wall begins to form between the two groups of chromosomes.
   C) early prophase – chromosomes shorten and thicken ("condense") – become visible (under microscope) – two chromatids are held together at centromere.
   D) mid prophase – centrioles moving to opposite sides of nucleus, spindles – network of fibres.
   E) metaphase – chromosomes are arranged across the 'equator' of the cell, each chromosome has a spindle attached at its centromere.

5. early prophase, mid prophase, metaphase, anaphase, telophase.

6. (i) four   (ii) two
   (iii) four (iv) two   (v) eight

7. (i) During the interphase each chromosome makes a copy of itself (the DNA 'unzips' along its entire length and free nucleotides move to the exposed nitrogenous bases). This is called replication.
   (ii) Before the chromosomes condense – during interphase.
   (iii) Because each of the two daughter cells must have the complete set of chromosomes to be identical to the parent cell.

8. (i) An enzyme is an organic catalyst, a protein which speeds up (or in some cases slows down) a particular chemical reaction.
   (ii) Every enzyme has a unique three dimensional shape. On the surface of the enzyme is a particular part of that shape onto which another molecule (the substrate) can be held. The enzyme holds the substrate while the chemical reaction occurs. The changed molecule (the product) is released, leaving the enzyme unchanged. The enzyme can therefore be compared to a key and the substrate a lock (the key remains unchanged).
   (iii) Because they are not changed by the reaction and are reused in the cell's metabolism many times before they denature.

8. (iv) The 'active site' or 'catalytic site' is the place on the enzyme onto which the substrate fits.
   (v) Temperature alters the three dimensional shape of the enzyme molecule - it therefore alters the shape of the active site and affects the enzyme's efficiency (like a melting key). If the enzyme is heated too strongly, its shape is changed irreversibly - it is denatured.
   (vi) Enzymes are sensitive to pH and their activity is also affected by the concentration of both the reactants and the products.

9. (i) Respiration which requires oxygen.
   (ii) Glucose + oxygen → carbon dioxide + water + energy.
   (iii) Respiration which does not require oxygen.
   (iv) Animals: glucose → lactic acid + energy
   Plants: glucose → alcohol + carbon dioxide + energy

10.

	Aerobic Respiration	Anaerobic Respiration
Site	first in cytoplasm then in mitochrondrion	in cytoplasm
Requirements for oxygen	oxygen required	oxygen not required
Products in plants	carbon dioxide + water (+ energy)	carbon dioxide + alcohol (+ energy)
Products in animals	carbon dioxide + water (+ energy)	lactic acid (+ energy)
ATP produced from 1 glucose molecule	36 - 38 molecules of ATP	2 molecules of ATP

11. Plants and animals share many enzymes in common. However those involved in the later stages of anaerobic respiration are different and therefore the products formed are different.

12. (i) ATP is adenosine triphosphate, a molecule consisting of adenosine (a nitrogenous base linked to a sugar molecule) and three phosphate groups.

   adenosine   phosphate   third bond

   It is important because it stores chemical energy in the third phosphate bond, which can be released and used within the cell.
   (ii) anabolism (egs. photosynthesis, protein synthesis)
   movement of organelles (egs. cilia, flagella)
   active input or output (egs. active transport, endocytosis, exocytosis)
   cell division (egs. mitosis and meiosis)
   cytoplasmic streaming
   nerve impulses (movement of ions)

13. (i) ATP → ADP + P + energy
    (ii) ADP + P are reconverted back to ATP in both the mitochondria and in chloroplasts by the provision of energy from respiration and sunlight respectively.
    ADP + P + energy → ATP

14. (i) water + carbon dioxide → glucose + oxygen
    (ii) Chlorophyll, light energy, enzymes, ADP and P must be present.
    (iii) in chloroplasts
    (iv) **Light** - provides the energy to produce ATP, the energy in ATP is then used to synthesise glucose.
    Water - this is a raw material (its hydrogen is used in building the glucose and its oxygen released).
    Enzymes - photosynthesis, like respiration takes place in many stages with many intermediate compounds formed before the final products (glucose and oxygen). Each stage is controlled by a specific enzyme.
    Carbon dioxide - raw material, the carbon is used in the glucose and the other organic compounds formed from it.
    (iv) **Chlorophyll** - pigment which absorbs light energy and transfers it to the ATP.
    ADP and P - used to make ATP.

15. (i) The products of photosynthesis (glucose + oxygen) are the raw materials of respiration and the products of respiration (carbon dioxide + water) are the raw materials for photosynthesis.
    (ii) Photosynthesis relies on the light energy from the sun.
    (iii) Respiration releases energy, most of this energy is lost to the environment as heat energy.

Module 2 – The Organism (Part 1)

SYLLABUS CHECKLIST

You should be able to:

✔ 2.1 Explain why plants and animals need to obtain matter and energy from their environments.

✔ 2.2 Explain why living organisms only survive within limits to the range of variations in internal conditions with respect to:
- carbon dioxide
- oxygen
- glucose
- wastes
- temperature
- salts, and
- water.

✔ 2.3 Describe the connection between type of diet and the amount of nitrogenous waste.

✔ 2.4 Describe the different types of nitrogenous waste produced by animals from different vertebrate groups (ammonia from fish and amphibia, uric acid from reptiles and birds, urea from mammals).

✔ 2.5 Relate the different toxicity, solubility and the need for rapid removal of different nitrogenous wastes from different vertebrate groups to the amount of water available in their environment.

✔ 2.6 Explain the relationship between temperature and metabolic rate.

✔ 2.7 Explain the advantages and limitations of ectothermy and endothermy and state in which animal groups each occurs.

✔ 2.8 Describe and explain the relationship between metabolic rate and body size in terms of surface area per unit volume and heat loss in endotherms.

✔ 2.9 Explain the process of endothermy in terms of balance between heat gain (and heat production) and heat loss.

✔ 2.10 Explain some special adaptations of endotherms and ectotherms which live in extremely hot and extremely cold habitats.

✔ 2.11 Describe and discuss the stimulus-response-negative feedback model and its role in understanding temperature regulation in endotherms and ectotherms. (No detail of nervous systems, nerves, endocrine systems and hormones.)

REVIEW QUESTIONS

1. (i) What do plants take from their surroundings?

   _____
   _____

   (ii) Why are these materials taken in by the plant?

   _____
   _____
   _____
   _____

(iii) How is the energy which is absorbed, used by the plant?

_____

_____

_____

2. (i) What do animals take from their surroundings?

_____

_____

(ii) Explain why they need to absorb each of these things.

_____

_____

_____

_____

_____

_____

_____

3. Explain why the level of each of the following factors must be kept within limits in living organisms or within their environment.

(i) carbon dioxide _____

_____

(ii) oxygen _____

_____

(iii) glucose _____

_____

(iv) salt _____

_____

(v) water _____

_____

(vi) urea _____

_____

(vii) temperature _____

Biology Study Guide

4. How do multicellular animals **respond** to an excess of the following within their bodies?

   (i) carbon dioxide _____
   _____
   _____

   (ii) salt _____
   _____

   (iii) water _____
   _____

   (iv) heat _____
   _____

5. How might an animal respond to having too little of the following in its body cells?

   (i) oxygen _____
   _____
   _____

   (ii) glucose _____
   _____
   _____

   (iii) heat _____
   _____
   _____

   (iv) water _____
   _____
   _____

6. What might be the consequences of **a single celled organism** absorbing an excess of -

   (i) water? _____
   _____

   (ii) carbon dioxide? _____
   _____

   (iii) heat? _____
   _____

7. In mammals the liver removes excess glucose from the blood storing it as glycogen. The liver also plays a part in the metabolism of nitrogenous compounds like amino acids.
    (i) How does the liver deal with surplus amino acids that are absorbed from the digestive tract and enter the mammal's blood?
    _____
    _____

    (ii) What happens to the products produced from amino acids by the liver?
    _____
    _____

8. (i) What type of animal has a high protein diet?
    _____
    _____

    (ii) How does this diet affect the animal's excretory products?
    _____
    _____

    (iii) Explain how an animal with a high intake of protein and a low intake of fat and carbohydrate obtains sufficient energy from its diet.
    _____
    _____

9. (i) In what form do most aquatic organisms (e.g. fish, amphibians, invertebrates) excrete waste nitrogen?
    _____

    (ii) Why do most terrestrial animals (e.g. mammals, birds, reptiles, insects) not use this substance to remove nitrogen wastes?
    _____
    _____
    _____

10. Birds and reptiles (also terrestrial snails and insects) excrete their excess nitrogen as a semi-solid whitish paste.
    (i) What is this nitrogen compound called?
    _____

    (ii) What special properties make it particularly suited for excretion by these animals?
    _____
    _____
    _____

11. (i) Below is a list of three nitrogen waste types which are excreted by various vertebrates. Give at least one example of an animal group which excretes the particular waste.

   a) Ammonia _____

   b) Urea _____

   c) Uric acid _____

   (ii) Which of these waste types requires the least energy to produce and which requires the most energy to produce? Explain your answer.

   _____
   _____
   _____
   _____
   _____

12. (i) What is "metabolism"? _____
   _____
   _____
   _____

   (ii) Why is metabolism affected by temperature? _____
   _____
   _____
   _____
   _____

   (iii) Explain why tropical fish can tolerate higher temperatures than fish from colder regions.
   _____
   _____
   _____

   (iv) What is the advantage of -

   a) a high metabolic rate? _____

   b) a low metabolic rate? _____

   (v) Give examples of animals which utilise each rate and briefly state how the particular animal benefits.

   a) _____
   _____
   _____
   _____

   b) _____
   _____
   _____
   _____

13. (i) Define each of the following terms and give two examples of animals which show each.
    a) Endothermy _____
    _____
    _____

    b) Ectothermy _____
    _____
    _____

(ii) Briefly explain why ectothermic animals generally have lower food energy requirements than endothermic animals of similar size.
_____
_____
_____

(iii) Why does the metabolic rate of an ectothermic animal decrease with a decrease in its external temperature?
_____
_____
_____

(iv) Describe three different ways by which an ectothermic animal may increase its body temperature.
_____
_____
_____

14. What is meant by the term 'homeostasis'?
_____
_____

15. Calculate the surface area and the volume of the three cubes shown below. Enter your answers in the table and then calculate the surface area per cubic centimetre for each cube.

Cube	Surface Area (cm^2)	Volume (cm^3)	S.A. / cubic cm (cm^2 / cm^3)
1			
2			
3			

Use the results in the table to answer the following questions:

    (i)   Which cube has the greatest surface area per cubic centimetre? _____

          Which has the smallest surface area per cubic centimetre? _____

    (ii)   What generalisation could be made from this table? _____

_____

    (iii)   If all three cubes were heated to the same temperature and then placed in a cold room, which cube would lose heat most rapidly per cubic centimetre to the surrounding atmosphere?

_____

    (iv)   Explain the consequences of your answers to (ii) and (iii) to endothermic animals which live in cold climates.

_____

_____

_____

16.   (i)   In order to maintain a constant body temperature, mammals and birds must balance heat gain and heat loss. Show this in a simple word equation.

_____

    (ii)   How does heat enter the body of an animal?

_____

_____

    (iii)   Describe how heat is produced within an animal's body.

_____

_____

    (iv)   How is heat lost from the animal's body?

_____

_____

17.   Animals that are adapted to live in extremes of temperature, both high and low, have adaptations which involve:
        (i)   control of heat production
        (ii)   control of heat loss
        (iii)   control of heat gain.

Give two examples of each of these adaptations indicating in each case an animal which possesses the particular adaptation.

    (i)   _____

_____

    (ii)   _____

_____

(iii) _____

18. How might a mammal respond to -
    (i) a sudden rise in its body temperature? _____

    e.g. _____
    (ii) a drop in its body temperature? _____

    e.g. _____

19. Describe each of the following adaptation types and give two examples of each.
    (i) Physiological _____

    (ii) Structural / Anatomical _____

    (iii) Behavioural _____

20. Define each of the following terms related to animal function.
    (i) stimulus _____

    (ii) receptor _____

    (iii) sensory neuron _____

(iv) coordinating centre _____
_____
_____

(v) motor neuron _____
_____
_____

(vi) effector _____
_____
_____

(vii) response _____
_____
_____

(viii) negative feedback _____
_____
_____

21. Distinguish between external and internal stimuli, give two examples of each.

(i) external stimuli _____
_____
_____

(ii) internal stimuli _____
_____
_____

22. Illustrate the idea of a system controlled by negative feedback, by completing the diagram below with a specific example.

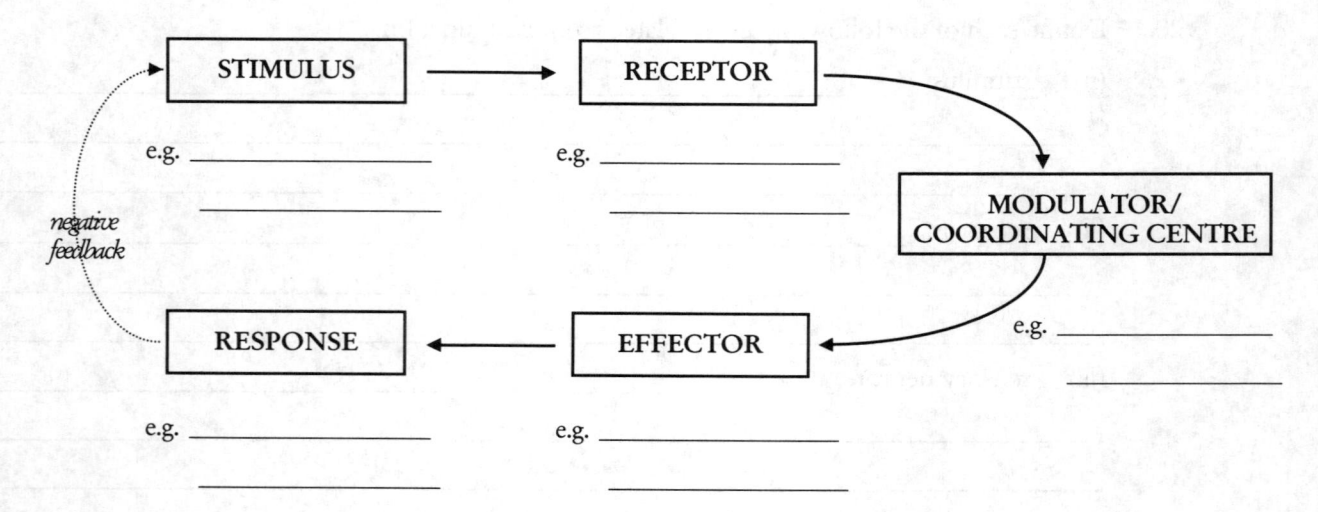

```
         STIMULUS  ───────▶  RECEPTOR
           ▲                     │
           │                     │
  e.g. _____        e.g. _____        ▼
       _____             _____   MODULATOR/
  negative                             COORDINATING CENTRE
  feedback
                                            e.g. _____
         RESPONSE ◀─────── EFFECTOR              _____

  e.g. _____        e.g. _____
       _____             _____
```

38

ANSWERS TO REVIEW QUESTIONS – Module 2 – Part 1

1. (i) Plants take carbon dioxide, water, light energy, mineral ions and when necessary oxygen from their surroundings.
   (ii) Carbon dioxide, water and light energy are required for photosynthesis. Mineral ions are used as co-factors (assisting enzymes) and in the synthesis of many organic compounds using glucose as the starting compound.
   (iii) The light energy absorbed by the plant is converted to chemical energy.

2. (i) Animals take food (mainly organic matter), water and oxygen and some heat energy from their surroundings.
   (ii) **Food** is used as a source of energy. It is also a source of the raw materials needed for growth e.g. amino acids needed for protein synthesis. It also provides vitamins, some of which are co-enzymes (assisting enzymes).
   Water is used as a medium in which all the essential metabolic reactions take place. It is essential in the dilution of nitrogenous wastes. It may also be used to help cool the organism. Important in transporting materials.
   Oxygen - needed for aerobic respiration which provides the organism's energy.

3. (i) Carbon dioxide: too much CO_2 causes a lowering of the pH in the organism's internal environment. This may interfere with enzymes' actions.
   (ii) Oxygen: the organism needs the oxygen level to be kept within limits so that the rate of respiration is fairly constant.
   (iii) Glucose: glucose concentrations also control the rate of respiration. Too little glucose would restrict energy production, therefore reducing growth rates and activity. Too much glucose can cause osmotic pressure outside cells to rise, dehydrating body cells.
   (iv) Salt: too little salt may cause the organism to become too hydrated, too much salt may cause the body cells to become dehydrated. Sodium ions are also essential for various metabolic processes, especially used in nerve cells.
   (v) Water: the level of water in the organism must be sufficient to allow metabolic processes to occur at required rates. Too little water may lead to some reactions occurring too rapidly, whilst too much water is likely to reduce the overall rates of metabolism.
   (vi) Urea: this is a nitrogenous compound which is toxic in larger concentrations. It is therefore eliminated by excretion.
   (vii) Temperature: organisms function at an optimum temperature. Their enzymes are best suited to the temperature of their internal environment.

4. (i) Excess CO_2 - the organisms will excrete CO_2 through gills or lungs or by diffusion from outer tissue.
   (ii) Excess salt - excreted using kidneys or equivalent structures.
   (iii) Excess water - lost with wastes, e.g. in urine. (Contractile vacuoles in single-celled animals pump excess water out.) (Water lost in sweating and breathing is not related to excretion of excess water.)
   (iv) Excess heat - lost through behavioural mechanisms, i.e. moving to a cool place
   - lost by vasodilation of surface vessels, by hair/feathers lying flat on skin,
   - lost by sweating from skin or evaporation of water from mouth and lungs.

5. (i) Too little oxygen: reduce aerobic respiration therefore reduce activity / increase breathing rate / switch to anaerobic respiration
   (ii) Too little glucose: reduce respiration - reduce activity / increase breakdown of stored glycogen to glucose / use other compounds as a source of energy, e.g. fats and proteins / ingest more glucose
   (iii) Too little heat: move to a warmer place / increase rate of metabolism, i.e. produce more heat / shiver / reduce heat loss by vasoconstriction of surface vessels, fluffing up feathers or hair / reduce exposed surface area
   (iv) Too little water: seek water to drink / reduce loss in wastes, e.g. produce concentrated urine

6. (i) Single-celled organism: plant - becomes turgid / animal - may lyse / contractile vacuole's rate of contractions increases.
   (ii) Carbon dioxide - increase lowers the pH - slows down activity of enzymes.
   (iii) Heat - may denature enzymes and cause the death of the cell (unless it has enzymes suited to high temperatures).

7. (i) The liver breaks down excess amino acids, converting them, first to ammonia, then to urea and carbohydrates. This process is called deamination.
   (ii) The urea is excreted.
   The carbohydrates may be used as a source of energy.

8. (i) Animals which eat other animals i.e. carnivorous e.g. eagle, dingo, numbat.
   (ii) Animals with a high protein intake produce larger amounts of nitrogenous wastes e.g. ammonia, urea, uric acid.
   (iii) The energy is obtained from the carbohydrate produced in the deamination of excess proteins.

9. (i) ammonia - lost dissolved in water
    (ii) Ammonia being very toxic must be greatly diluted with water to make it less poisonous when excreted. Terrestrial animals need to conserve water. Therefore, losing nitrogen waste in this form would be too expensive in terms of water loss.

10. (i) Uric acid.
    (ii) It is less toxic than urea and ammonia. It is also much less soluble than urea. Because of these properties it may be lost with little water. Birds save weight in excreting uric acid as they are required to carry less water than would be needed if urea was to be excreted.

11. (i) a) fish (also tadpoles, coelenterates)
       b) mammals (also adult frogs)
       c) birds, reptiles (also insects)
    (ii) Ammonia requires the least energy.
    Uric acid requires the most.
    Uric acid ($C_5H_4O_3N_4$) is a more complex compound than ammonia (NH_3). Therefore its synthesis (uricogenesis) requires more energy.

12. (i) Metabolism: This is the sum of all the chemical reactions which occur in an organism. The chemical reactions include both anabolism (synthesis) and catabolism (break down). Photosynthesis and respiration are part of metabolism.
    (ii) Temperature affects the rate of chemical reactions. Low temperatures generally slow down reactions. High temperatures generally increase reaction rates. However, since many metabolic reactions are controlled by enzymes, they generally occur at a temperature which is dependent on the enzyme involved.
    (iii) Tropical fish possess enzymes which function at optimum temperatures which are higher than those at which the enzymes possessed by fish from colder regions function.
    (iv) a) A high metabolic rate results in a rapid growth rate and rapid movement.
       b) A low metabolic rate requires less food intake, less waste - energy is conserved.
    (v) a) Birds and mammals - because their metabolic rate is high, the amount of heat they produce is great. This enables them to live and remain active in cold climates.
       b) Fish, amphibians, reptiles may have slow metabolic rates when the temperature is low. This conserves energy and therefore the animal is not forced to find food in cold conditions, when food might be scarce. Some mammals and birds which hibernate also utilise this conservation of energy.

13. (i) a) The capacity of an animal to maintain a relatively constant body temperature independent of the surrounding temperature. This is achieved by varying the rate at which heat is produced within the animal's body e.g. mammals, birds.
       b) The condition in which an animal's body temperature is largely determined by the temperature of the surrounding environment. The animal uses external sources of heat (e.g. sun) to increase its body temperature when necessary e.g. fish, amphibians, reptiles, invertebrates.
    (ii) Because ectothermic animals use external sources of heat energy, for example to increase body heat they may bask in the sun, they do not require the use of food energy. Therefore they have lower food energy requirements than endothermic animals. Endotherms use food to produce the heat necessary to maintain a constant temperature when their body temperature exceeds that of the environment.
    (iii) As the external temperature drops, so too does the internal temperature of an ectotherm. Chemical reactions slow down as temperature is reduced. Therefore the ectotherm's metabolism slows down with a fall in temperature.
    (iv) To increase its body temperature an ectothermic animal may move into a warmer part of its environment (e.g. shade to sun), increase activity (e.g. bees move rapidly to generate heat in the hive), change the orientation of its body to maximise heat gain from the sun (i.e. lie at right angles to the sun's rays).

14. Homeostasis is the maintenance of fairly constant conditions within the body of an organism (despite changes to the external conditions or the activity of the organism).

15.

Cube	S.A. (cm^2)	Vol. (cm^3)	S.A. per cm^3 (cm^2 / cm^3)
1	6	1	6
2	24	8	3
3	54	27	2

   (i) Cube 1 (it has 6 cm^2 / cm^3)
   Cube 3 (it has 2 cm^2 / cm^3)
   (ii) Provided the shape remains constant, the S.A. per unit volume becomes smaller.
   (iii) The smaller cube, as it has a greater S.A. per cm^3 exposed to the cold atmosphere.
   (iv) Endothermic animals must maintain a constant body temperature. To minimise heat loss and thereby conserve energy, they must have a small surface area per unit volume (or a small S.A. : vol ratio). Therefore they need to be larger rather than smaller.

16. (i) Heat gain + Heat production = Heat loss
    (ii) Heat enters as:
    - warm food and drink
    - radiation from sun's energy
    - conduction from atmosphere, water or soil.
    (iii) Heat is produced:
    - metabolism (many chemical reactions release heat).
    (iv) Heat is lost:
    - by radiation from body to the surroundings
    - conduction to surroundings
    - wastes (faeces, urine)
    - evaporation of sweat, moisture from lungs and skin.

17. (i) Control of Heat Production:
- Increased or decreased movement of limbs e.g. many insects warm their bodies up before flight by vigorously moving their wings.
- Increased or decreased rate of metabolism e.g. mammals increase metabolism when heat loss to the environment increases.
- Shivering e.g. mammals generate extra heat by these rapid involuntary muscle contractions.

(ii) Control of Heat Loss:
- Vasodilation (dilation of blood vessels close to skin) reduces heat loss from the blood e.g. humans).
- Vasoconstriction (constriction of blood vessels close to skin) increases heat loss from the body e.g. humans.
- Erection of hair follicles or feathers - fluffing up hair or feathers increases the depth of air trapped in a layer around the body, this reduces heat loss e.g. birds, mammals.

(iii) Control of Heat Gain:
- Animals may move to a warmer/cooler part of its environment to increase/ decrease heat gain. e.g. fish may move closer to surface
- Animals bask in the sun to increase heat gain. e.g. lizards and snakes
- Animals utilise the heat given off by decomposing plants. e.g. some ants build nests using thousands of twigs

18. (i) Sudden rise in body temperature: mammal increases rate of heat loss (e.g. sweating, licks fur, panting, vasodilation of surface vessels, hairs/feathers lie flat). Reduces activity. Seeks shade.

(ii) Sudden drop in body temperature: mammal increases heat production and/or reduces heat loss e.g. increased rate of metabolism, vasoconstriction of surface vessels and hairs/feathers raised.

19. (i) Physiological adaptations: adaptations which involve the way in which an organism's body functions in order to survive e.g. an increased metabolic rate compensates for extra heat loss in cold weather in endotherms. Termites have protozoa within their digestive tracts which digest cellulose for them.

(ii) Structural adaptations: adaptations which involve the shape and size of particular organs which assist an organism to survive e.g. Black Cockatoos' beaks are adapted to feed on particular woody fruit.

(iii) Behavioural adaptations: adaptations which involve a change in the way an organism acts e.g. an echidna may raise its spines in response to an attack by a predator.

20. (i) Stimulus: a change in an organism's internal or external environment which is detected and brings about a response.

(ii) Receptor: organ, tissue or cell which is sensitive to specific changes in the animal's environment and which sends impulses to a co-ordinating centre when these changes are acted upon.

20. (iii) Sensory neuron: special nerve cell or neuron which sends impulses from the receptor to the co-ordinating centre. Often also detects stimuli (i.e. acts as receptor).

(iv) Co-ordinating centre: usually part of the central nervous system, i.e. in the brain or spinal cord, which on receiving impulses from the receptor, interprets this information and sends impulses to effector/s.

(v) Motor neuron: special nerve cell which carries impulses from the co-ordinating centre to effectors.

(vi) Effector: organ, tissue or cell which receives impulses via the motor neuron from the co-ordinating centre and responds to them.

(vii) Response: the action which the effector carries out as a result of a stimulus.

(viii) Negative feedback: when the response carried out as a result of a stimulus reduces the stimulus.

21. (i) An external stimulus is a change which occurs in an organism's external environment and which is detected, e.g. temperature, light.

(ii) An internal stimulus is a change which occurs and is detected in the organism's internal environment, e.g. blood sugar level, water level (osmotic pressure) of blood.

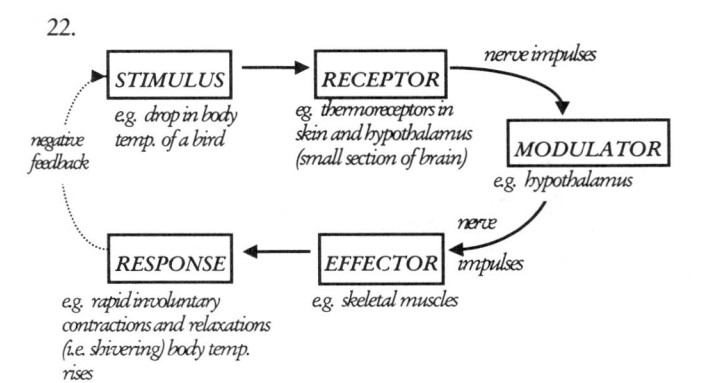

22.

```
STIMULUS → RECEPTOR → MODULATOR
e.g. drop in body    e.g. thermoreceptors in    e.g. hypothalamus
temp. of a bird      skin and hypothalamus
                     (small section of brain)
    ↑                                            ↓
negative                                        nerve
feedback                                        impulses
    ↑                                            ↓
RESPONSE ← EFFECTOR
e.g. rapid involuntary    e.g. skeletal muscles
contractions and relaxations
(i.e. shivering) body temp.
rises
```

Note: This is only one of several responses that the bird's body would make. Other responses include vasodilation of blood vessels close to skin, fluffing up of feathers and in the long term an increase in thyroxine levels (a hormone which increases metabolic rate) in the blood stream.

Module 2 – The Organism (Part 2)

SYLLABUS CHECKLIST

You should be able to:

- 2.12 Interpret quantitative data on water loss or gain by osmosis, with emphasis on the movements: of both salt and water organisms which occur in saline and fresh water habitats.
- 2.13 Compare the movements of salt and water between marine and freshwater fish and their environments.
- 2.14 Present a water balance for animals from terrestrial habitats, showing how water is gained and removed from their bodies.
- 2.15 Discuss the structural and physiological adaptations of angiosperms for transporting water and nutrients (stomata, root hair cells, xylem tissue, leaves, roots and supporting tissue) and sugar (phloem tissue).
- 2.16 Describe factors affecting (and) the ways to measure the water loss from terrestrial plants in different conditions.
- 2.17 Compare the adaptive structural features and the physiological mechanisms which enable different plants to exploit habitats with different levels of water availability and different temperatures.
- 2.18 Explain the effect of stomatal regulation of water loss in plants on CO_2 uptake.
- 2.19 Explain how auxins are involved in response of plants to light.

REVIEW QUESTIONS

1. (i) Define the term 'osmosis'. _____

   (ii) Why is osmosis important to living cells? _____

2. (i) Organisms which live in salt water must have adaptations to prevent dehydration of their cells due to osmosis. List three such special features.

2. (ii) Organisms which live in fresh water have a problem caused by too much water diffusing into their cells by osmosis. List three adaptations which assist them to overcome this problem.

_____

_____

_____

_____

_____

_____

3. How does a terrestrial animal -
   (i) gain water? _____
   _____
   (ii) lose water? _____
   _____

4. What special adaptations do animals which live in hot, dry environments possess to prevent them from dehydrating?

_____

_____

_____

_____

_____

5. How might a mammal respond to -
   (i) excessive water within its body? _____
   _____
   e.g. _____
   (ii) dehydration? _____
   _____
   e.g. _____

6. Describe the structure of:
    (i) a stoma _____
    _____
    _____

    (ii) a root hair cell _____
    _____
    _____

    (iii) xylem tissue _____
    _____
    _____

    (iv) phloem tissue _____
    _____
    _____
    _____
    _____

7. How does each of the above help the plant obtain/retain/transport water?
    (i) stoma _____
    _____
    _____

    (ii) root hair cell _____
    _____
    _____

    (iii) xylem tissue _____
    _____
    _____

8. (i) What is the function of phloem tissue? _____

(ii) List the differences between xylem and phloem tissue.

9. The diagram below shows a magnified transverse section through a leaf blade.

Name each part and describe how it contributes to the plant's survival.

A _____

B _____

C _____

D _____

E _____

F _____

10. Discuss the nature, location and function of the following plant cell types.
    (i) Parenchyma _____
    _____
    _____

    (ii) Sclerenchyma _____
    _____
    _____

    (iii) Collenchyma _____
    _____
    _____

11. A terrestrial plant generally loses water by evaporation to the atmosphere.
    (i) What climatic factors affect this rate of water loss?
    _____
    _____
    _____

    (ii) What features of the plant itself affect this rate?
    _____
    _____
    _____
    _____

    (iii) The rate of loss can be measured experimentally. Name an instrument which is commonly used and briefly describe how it is used.
    _____
    _____
    _____
    _____

12. How does the leaf's shape normally maximise photosynthesis?
    _____
    _____
    _____
    _____

13. (i) Temperature may vary from freezing to hot during one twenty four hour period in many terrestrial environments. Why do most plant cells not tolerate freezing conditions?

_____
_____
_____

(ii) Discuss one adaptation angiosperms may have to cope with this problem.

_____
_____
_____

(iii) Extreme heat may also kill plant cells. What adaptations do plants living in hot areas have to cope with extreme heat? (Discuss two such adaptations.)

(a) _____
_____

(b) _____
_____

14. Excessive loss of water may cause an herbaceous plant to wilt. How may each of the following help such plants to reduce water loss?

(i) Stomata _____
_____
_____

(ii) Hairs on leaves _____
_____
_____

(iii) Waxy leaves _____
_____
_____

(iv) Leaf shape _____
_____
_____
_____

(v) Leaf orientation _____
_____
_____
_____
_____

(vi) Leaf size _____
_____
_____
_____
_____

(vii) Phyllodes (modified petioles) _____
_____
_____
_____
_____

15. What is the general name given to plants which are adapted to live in hot dry environments?
_____
_____

16. Discuss three ways in which the root system of a plant may be adapted to obtain water in an arid climate.

(i) _____
_____
_____

(ii) _____
_____
_____

(iii) _____
_____
_____

17. When an angiosperm begins to lose water at a rate greater than the rate at which water is being taken up by its roots -

    (i) what visible evidence often shows that water loss has exceeded water gain?

    (ii) how does the plant respond?

    (iii) what effect does this change have on its rate of photosynthesis?

    (iv) how does this affect the plant's general growth rate?

18. A growing plant has a strong tendency to grow towards light.

    (i) What is this response called?

    (ii) Name the chemicals that cause this response to occur.

    (iii) Explain how these chemicals bring about the response.

ANSWERS TO REVIEW QUESTIONS – Module 2 – Part 2

1. (i) Osmosis is the diffusion of a solvent (usually water) across a selectively permeable membrane.
   (ii) Living cells contain intra-cellular fluid containing water and dissolved solutes. Cells are surrounded by extra-cellular fluid which may be the fluid between cells in a multicellular organism or the water in a marine or freshwater environment in a unicellular organism. Water therefore is likely to diffuse either into or out of living cells depending on the concentration difference between the intracellular fluid and the extracellular fluid.

2. (i) - Specialised cells in the gills of many marine fish pump salt ions out.
   - Salt ions are excreted in the urine of marine fish.
   - Sharks maintain an ion concentration within their bodies which equals the surrounding salt water. Sharks retain a high level of urea rather than excreting it. They have a high tolerance to urea through enzymes which are not denatured by a high urea concentration.
   (ii) - Rigid cell walls in plants prevent too much water diffusing into the cells as the cells swell but do not burst.
   - Waxy cuticles in some insects make them waterproof.
   - Freshwater fish produce copious quantities of dilute urine.

3. (i) Water is gained through drinking, in food and as a product of the respiration of carbohydrates.
   (ii) Water is lost through excretion (e.g. urine), in faeces, sweat, evaporation from skin and lungs.

4. Animals living in hot dry environments may prevent dehydration by:
   - nocturnal behaviour
   - aestivating during summer
   - excreting less urine (diet may be restricted to carbohydrate with little protein intake)
   - utilising the water produced in carbohydrate respiration
   - obtain water from seeds which have been stored in moist burrows
   - reabsorbing more water from urine (kidneys are more efficient at reabsorption of water)
   - tolerance to high urea concentration in blood.

5. (i) Excessive water: animal loses more water in wastes (e.g. more dilute urine produced). Higher contractile vacuole rate of contractions (e.g. freshwater protozoa).
   (ii) Dehydration: animal develops a thirst and/or produces wastes which are drier.
   (e.g. concentrated urine, dry faecal pellets)

6. (i) A stoma: tiny opening in the epidermis of a leaf, it is a gap between two specialised epidermal cells, called guard cells.
   (ii) A root hair cell: a specialised root epidermal cell which has an elongated process which increases its surface area.
   (iii) Xylem tissue: dead cells which stand end to end, with their common upper and lower cell walls missing, the column forms a straw-like structure up which water and mineral ions may pass.
   (iv) Phloem tissue: live elongated cells, called sieve elements arranged end to end to form a long sieve tube. Each sieve element has end walls called sieve plates which have numerous pores which allow materials (soluble products of photosynthesis) to pass from one sieve element to the next. These materials move along fine cytoplasmic filaments which pass through the pores. On the side of each sieve element is attached a companion cell which unlike the sieve element has a nucleus and more organelles. The companion cell probably controls the activities of the sieve element and sucrose moves freely along cytoplasmic filaments which connect them. Phloem tissue is not lignified but is strengthened by accompanying fibres.

7. (i) A stoma may open or close depending on the shape of its guard cells. When the guard cells are turgid, the aperture is large, when they are flaccid the aperture is reduced. The aperture determines the rate at which water is transpired from the leaf and therefore the rate at which it is transported. When closed it helps the plant to retain water.
   (ii) A root hair cell has a large process which absorbs water and minerals from between soil particles. The root hairs increase the surface area of the root available to absorb water. They increase the rate at which water is obtained.
   (iii) Xylem tissue form a connection between the root cells and the leaf cells. They transport water (and minerals) from the roots to the leaves.

8. (i) Phloem tissue transports sucrose and amino acids from the leaves to other parts of the plant where they are either stored or used. (This movement from leaves to roots, etc is called translocation. If these organic compounds are stored then moved via phloem to other sites (e.g. during periods of rapid growth), this is called retranslocation.)
   (ii) Xylem - consists of dead cells
   - cell walls are lignified
   - continuous
   - carries water and minerals from the soil to the leaves i.e. only upwards
   Phloem - consists of live cells
   - cell walls are not lignified
   - smaller than xylem in diameter
   - move soluble organic materials both up and down the plant

9. A Waxy cuticle: helps to reduce rate of water loss. If a plant loses too much water its cells die.
    B Upper epidermal tissue: secrete waxy cuticle, are transparent allowing light to reach palisade cells, provide protective covering and enclose other leaf cells. Contains few stomata.
    C Palisade mesophyll cell layer: tightly packed column shaped cells which have an increased number of chloroplasts. Most of the leaf's photosynthesis takes place here.
    D Spongy mesophyll cell layer: cells which because of their asymmetrical shapes, form large air spaces in the lower section of the leaf. The spaces allow gases to readily diffuse to and from the palisade layer. Spongy mesophyll cells also have some chlorophyll and therefore photosynthesise.
    E Lower epidermal tissue: typically contain a greater number of stomata to allow gaseous exchange between the atmosphere and the intercellular spaces of the spongy mesophyll.
    F Guard cells: two sausage shaped cells which control the size of the stoma. Control aperture of stoma and therefore rate of water loss from plant.

10. (i) Parenchyma: thin walled cells, forming packing tissue in a plant. Found in central (pith) and outer (cortex) areas of stems and in the centre of some leaves. They often store starch.
    (ii) Sclerenchyma: thick walled cells formed from parenchyma cells when their walls are thickened and lignified. Help to support and strengthen the plant. Two types of sclerenchyma include fibres (found in xylem tissue) and sclereids (found in woody seed coats and stem cortex).
    (iii) Collenchyma: living cells which have walls which are thickened at the corners. Help to support young plant stems and leaves.

11. (i) **Atmospheric humidity**: higher humidity reduces evaporation rate
         Temperature: increased temperature increases evaporation rate
         Wind speed: increased wind speed increases evaporation rate
    (ii) - density of stoma on leaf surface
         - location of stoma i.e. only underside of leaf, only upper surface or on both sides
         - amount of waterproof wax on leaf surfaces
         - shiny hairs on leaves may reduce evaporation
         - stoma may be deeply recessed into leaf
         - stoma may only be open at night in some plants, carbon dioxide is taken in during the night for photosynthesis during the day
         - reduced leaf surface e.g. sheoak has long cylindrical leaves
         - some leaves roll up to reduce surface exposed to atmosphere
         - leaves which hang vertically are not exposed to the full intensity of the sun during the middle of the day when evaporation is at its greatest
    (iii) A **potometer** may be used to measure the rate of transpiration from a plant.
         A leafy shoot is placed in the apparatus as shown below.

11. (iii) (cont)

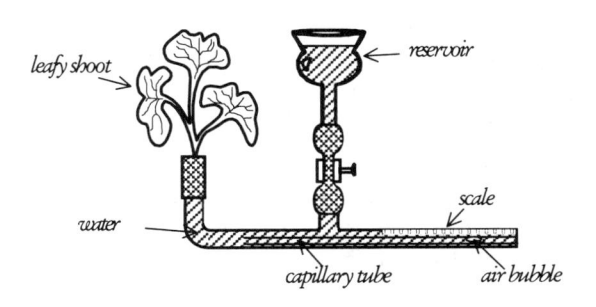

The rate at which the air bubble moves to the left (in this diagram) is dependent on the rate at which water evaporates from the leaves on the shoot.

12. Most leaves are flat and thin. The flat surface is presented towards the sunlight and therefore absorbs a greater amount of light energy. The thinness of the leaf ensures rapid gas exchange between the palisade layer and the atmosphere. Carbon dioxide can reach the palisade layer very quickly by diffusion because of the short distance and the air filled intercellular spaces.

13. (i) Plant cells do not tolerate freezing conditions generally because as their cytoplasm, which is largely water, freezes it expands. The expansion leads to the fracture of their cell walls, formation of ice crystals which rupture membranes and irreparable damage to the plant including a loss of support.
    (ii) Some plant cells have proteins in their cytoplasm which lower the freezing point of their cytoplasm. This means that while the temperature may be well below 0°C, their cytoplasm does not freeze but remains liquid.
    (iii) Plants living in extremely hot conditions may - (a) possess tiny hairs on their leaves which reflect heat; (b) be a whitish green colour to reflect heat.

14. (i) Stomata: close to reduce water loss. May be located on the underside of the leaf only (not in the upper epidermis) so that they are protected from the sun and therefore less water is lost from them.
    (ii) Hairs on leaves: apart from reflecting heat, also trap a layer of humid air and reduce water loss because this reduces the evaporation rate.
    (iii) Waxy leaves: because it is impermeable, wax prevents the loss of water from the leaf. Most leaves have this coating on the upper epidermis (which makes the leaf look darker on that side), the side which faces the sun.
    (iv) Leaf shape: often leaves are narrow and reduced in area, reducing the heat absorbed (but also reducing light absorbed and therefore their rate of photosynthesis).
    (v) Leaf orientation: leaves sometimes hang vertically, so that at the hottest time of the day, when the sun is overhead, they are receiving the least amount of heat (and light).

14. (vi) Leaf size: often leaves are greatly reduced in size so that less heat is absorbed but at a cost to the plant's growth rate. The leaves of some plants are reduced to a spine which does not photosynthesise but may only function as a protective prickle. Photosynthesis is then carried out by the stem alone. (e.g. cacti)
    (vii) Phyllodes: a leaf stalk (petiole) which is flattened and looks like a leaf. It carries out photosynthesis whereas the leaf is likely to be reduced to a prickle. (e.g. most wattles)

15. Xerophytes. (Plants that are capable of surviving almost total dehydration are sometimes called xeromorphs. A halophyte is able to live in salty soil.)

16. (i) Root system may be extensive i.e. cover a huge volume of the ground below the plant.
    (ii) Root system may have adventitious roots which grow extensively just below the surface of the soil to take advantage of the dew.
    (iii) Root system may have a very long tap root which penetrates deep into the ground to the water table below.

17. (i) The plant may begin to wilt. If herbaceous, it may bend over as its leaves and stem lose their turgidity.
    (ii) The stoma close (as the guard cells also wilt) and evaporation from the leaves is greatly reduced.
    (iii) As the stoma are closed little atmospheric carbon dioxide can enter the leaves, thus photosynthesis may slow then cease.
    (iv) As the plant is unable to carry out photosynthesis, its growth rate will be reduced. This accounts for the slow growth of many plants which live in arid conditions.

18. (i) Positive phototropism.
    (ii) Auxins.
    (iii) If light is directed at one side of a growing shoot auxins, produced by cells in its apical meristem, move down the shaded side of the shoot. The auxins cause the cells in the growing region of the shoot along its side to expand. This bends the shoot in the direction of the light.

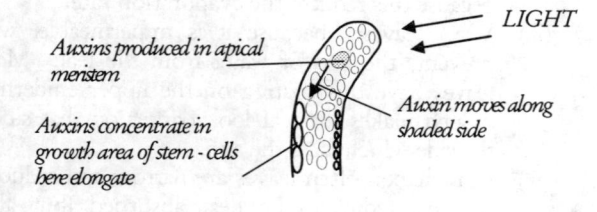

Auxins produced in apical meristem

Auxins concentrate in growth area of stem - cells here elongate

Auxin moves along shaded side

LIGHT

The auxin moves by diffusion from cell to cell along the shaded side.

Module 3 – The Species (Part 1)

SYLLABUS CHECKLIST

You should be able to:

✔ 3.1 Describe characteristics of a species which are determined by heredity, environmental factors, and the interaction of heredity and environmental factors.

✔ 3.2 Give a functional definition of a gene and explain the relationship between genes and chromosomes.

✔ 3.3 Define the terms 'allele', 'homologous chromosomes', 'haploid' and 'diploid' numbers.

✔ 3.4 State that in reproduction, genes may be passed on from parents to offspring and that aspects of the reproductive processes determine the inheritance patterns.

✔ 3.5 Describe the process of meiosis with reference to pairing of homologous chromosomes, attachment of chromosomes to spindle fibres, halving of chromosome number and effect on variation in gametes (names of phases not required).

✔ 3.6 Contrast the effects of sexual and asexual reproduction on heritable variation in species and relate this to survival in a changing or stable environment.

✔ 3.7 Define the terms 'autosome' and 'sex chromosome' and explain how the sex of the individual is determined at fertilisation.

✔ 3.8 Distinguish between phenotypes and genotypes (homozygous and heterozygous), and describe how the expression of an allele may be affected by the presence of an alternative allele carried on the homologous chromosome (complete dominance and recessiveness).

✔ 3.9 Predict the frequencies of genotypes and phenotypes in offspring from monohybrid crosses (autosomal and sex-linked).

✔ 3.10 Explain how a test cross, using the homozygous recessive individual, can be used to reveal the genotype of another individual.

✔ 3.11 Interpret genetic patterns of inheritance as shown in pedigree charts and use these to explain how genes are inherited (dominant/recessive autosomal, sex-linked).

REVIEW QUESTIONS

1. Make a list of 5 features of a named animal which are:

   (i) determined primarily by its heredity; _____
   _____
   _____
   _____
   _____

(ii) determined by both its heredity and environmental factors. _____
_____
_____
_____

2. (i) What do genes do? _____
_____

(ii) Where are genes found? _____

(iii) What are chromosomes? _____
_____
_____

3. Define:
(i) allele _____
_____

(ii) homologous _____
_____

(iii) haploid number _____
_____

(iv) diploid number _____
_____
_____

4. (i) Explain why a zygote with forty chromosomes probably contains twenty maternal and twenty paternal chromosomes.
_____
_____
_____

(ii) Following the answer in 4(i) above, about how much DNA is acquired from each parent?
_____

5. (i) The following sequence shows a cell undergoing **meiosis**. In the spaces provided, describe what is occurring in and to the cell.

MEIOSIS

① _____

② _____

③ _____

④ _____

⑤ _____

⑥ _____

⑦ _____

⑧ _____

In the example above:
- (ii) How many chromosomes did the parent cell contain? _____
- (iii) How many chromosomes do each of the gametes contain? _____
- (iv) What is the total number of chromosomes in the four daughter cells? _____
- (v) How do you account for the apparent increase in the total number of chromosomes?

_____

- (vi) Why must the gametes contain less chromosomes than the parent cell?

_____

6. (i) Distinguish between sexual and asexual reproduction.
___

Give two examples of each.
___

(ii) How do the offspring of each type of reproduction compare with their parents?
asexual ___

sexual ___

(iii) Explain why organisms which live in a stable environment often use asexual reproduction.
___

(iv) Sexual reproduction is 'favoured' by those organisms which live in changing, unstable environments. Why is it a more advantageous means of reproduction in these environments?
___

7. (i) Define: autosome ___

: sex chromosome ___

(ii) Briefly explain how an organism's sex is normally determined at fertilisation.

8. Explain the following terms, using examples to illustrate the answer.
   (i) phenotype

   (ii) genotype

   (iii) homozygous

   (iv) heterozygous

   (v) dominant

   (vi) recessive

   (vii) co-dominant

9. (i)   A cross between homozygous green podded peas (GG) and homozygous yellow podded peas (gg) produces offspring which are all green podded. Explain this result.

(ii) If two of the green podded offspring were crossed what proportion of each genotype and therefore each phenotype would be likely in their progeny? Show how you arrive at your answer.

(iii) A family with a history of colour blindness (an x-linked recessive trait) has the pedigree shown below.

KEY

○ } normal
□ }

◍ } colour-
▨ } blind

b ≡ colour blind gene

B ≡ normal gene

[Write the possible genotypes for each individual in the spaces provided.]

(iv) If individuals 1 and 2 in generation III have children, what is the probability of each of the following genotypes in their offspring?

X^bY _____

X^BY _____

X^BX^B _____

X^BX^b _____

X^bX^b _____

10. A breeder of rabbits needs to find out if a rabbit, which is not an albino, is homozygous or heterozygous for hair colour. (ie. She wishes to find out if the rabbit has the genotype AA or Aa, where 'A' is the gene for normal hair and 'a' the gene for albinism.). Explain how she might find out using a 'test cross'.

11. For each of the pedigrees below, determine the most likely mode of inheritance (ie. whether sex linked or autosomal and whether dominant or recessive). Explain how you arrived at your answer in each.

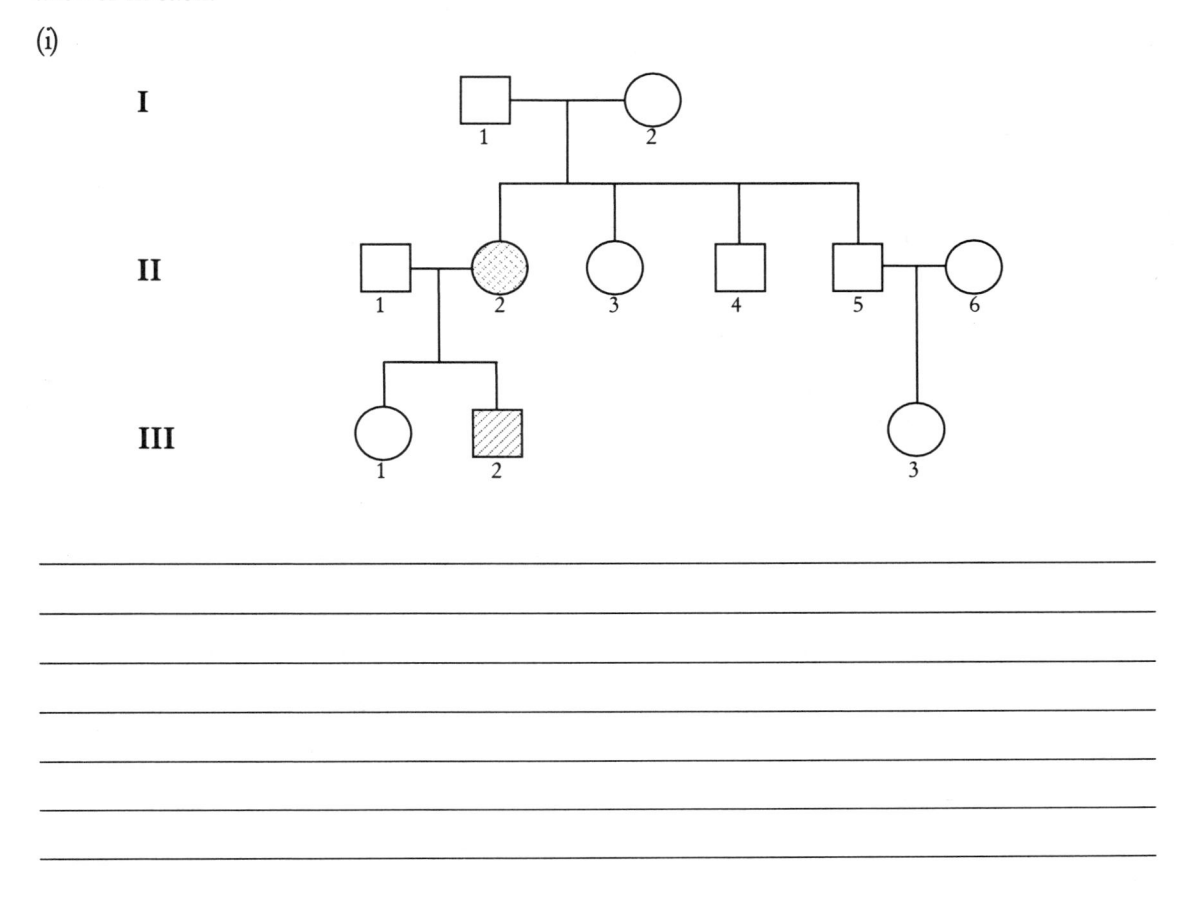

(i)

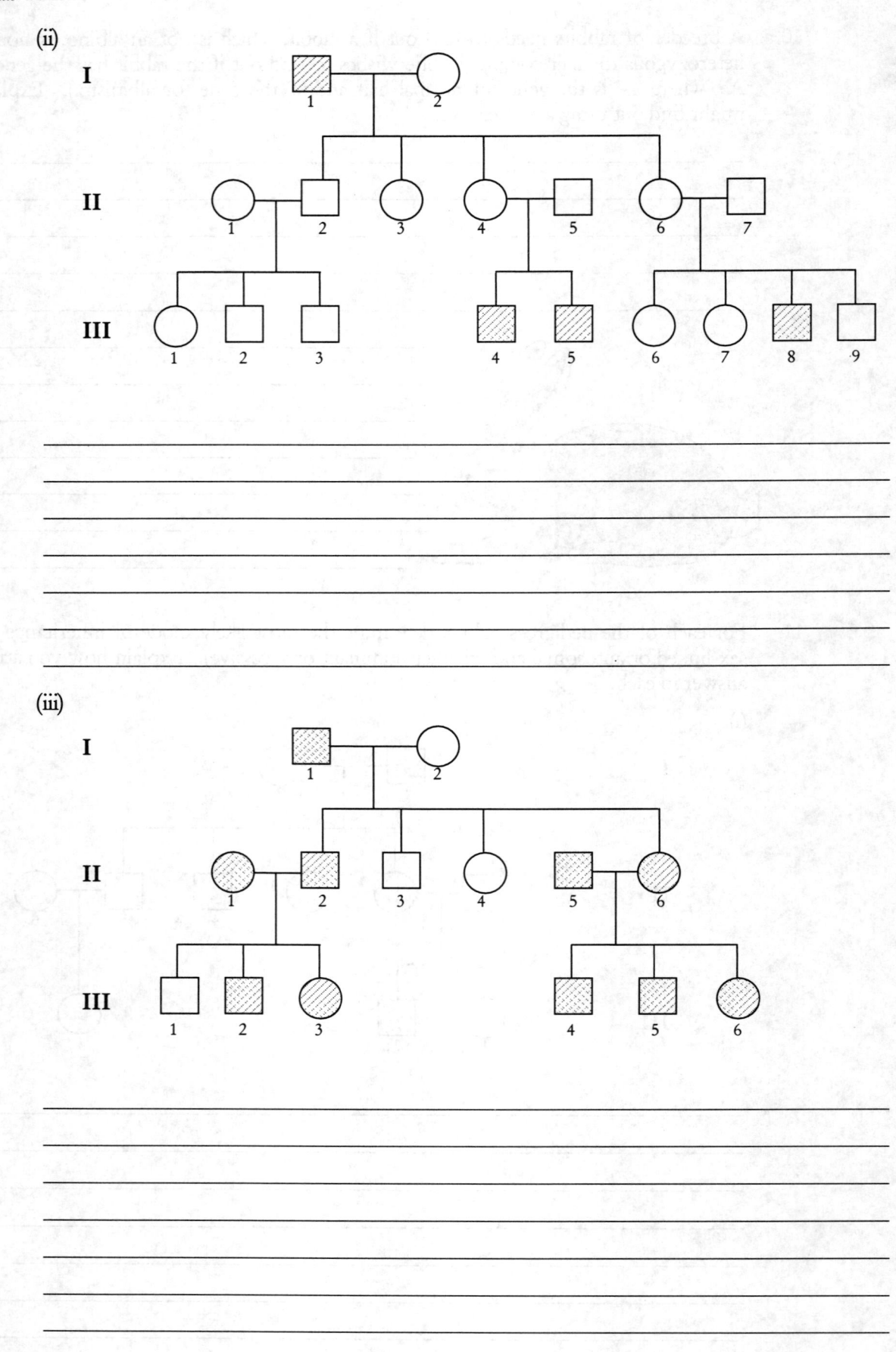

(ii)

I
1 2

II
1 2 3 4 5 6 7

III
1 2 3 4 5 6 7 8 9

_____
_____
_____
_____
_____
_____
_____

(iii)

I
1 2

II
1 2 3 4 5 6

III
1 2 3 4 5 6

_____
_____
_____
_____
_____
_____
_____

ANSWERS TO REVIEW QUESTIONS – Module 3 – Part 1

1. eg. dog
   (i) heredity: maximum number of teeth, eye colour, head shape, number of legs, hair length.
   (ii) heredity and environment: intelligence, weight, size, resistance to disease, wear on teeth, claw length.

2. (i) Genes control the type of proteins which an organism's cells synthesise. They therefore control the structure and chemistry of its cells.
   (ii) Genes are found as part of chromosomes. There are generally thousands of genes making up each chromosome.
   (iii) Chromosomes are made up mainly of tightly coiled DNA, which is a double strand of nucleotides which forms a double helix.

3. (i) Allele: an alternative form of a gene. eg. if one gene codes for eye colour, one allele may code for brown eyes, another allele may code for blue eyes.
   (ii) Homologous: refers to matching chromosomes. ie. chromosomes which carry genes for the same traits at the same loci. They are generally the same length and when they replicate the chromatids are attached at the same position by the centromere.
   (iii) Haploid number: a number equal to half the normal number of chromosomes of a normal body cell, contains only one of each homologous pair. eg. sperm and ova are haploid.
   (iv) Diploid number: the number of chromosomes in a complete set, contains all homologous chromosomes. eg. zygote and all subsequent body cells generally (except gametes).

4. (i) A zygote results from the fusion of gametes. Generally each gamete is haploid, ie. it contains half the normal number of chromosomes. In the example, the sperm would therefore contain twenty and the ovum twenty chromosomes. When these fuse the zygote would contain forty chromosomes.
   (ii) About the same amount of DNA is acquired from each parent. (In humans the male offspring inherit slightly more from their mother as she contributes a longer 'X' chromosome while the father only contributes a shorter 'Y' chromosome).

5. (i) 1. At this stage chromosomes are not visible. Chromosomes replicate (each copy is called a chromatid), chromatids are attached by a centromere (protein molecule).
   2. Chromosomes appear, each chromosome is recognisable as a pair of chromatids - begin to shorten and thicken. Centrioles move towards opposite "poles" of nucleus, begin to form spindles. Chromosomes pair with homologous partner. Nuclear membrane disintegrates.

5. (i) (cont)
   3. Homologous chromosome pairs arranged together across the "equator" of cell. Each chromosome attached at its centromere to spindle fibres.
   4. Spindles draw homologous chromosomes apart. Whole cell begins to constrict around the "equator".
   5. Whole cell divides. New nuclear membranes appear around separated chromosomes. Each cell contains only one of each homologous pair (but it consists of two chromatids). Centrioles duplicate and move towards opposite poles once again. Nuclear membranes disintegrate.
   6. Individual chromosomes arrange themselves on spindles across cell equator.
   7. Spindles separate chromatids, as centromeres are divided. A copy of each chromosome moves towards the opposite pole.
   8. New nuclear membranes appear. Each cell has one copy of each homologous chromosome in its nucleus. Four 'daughter' cells formed from single 'parent' cell.
   (ii) four (two pairs)
   (iii) two (one of each homologous pair)
   (iv) eight
   (v) Each chromosome was replicated (duplicated) in the interphase, before the first division.
   (vi) Two gametes fuse to form the zygote. The zygote then undergoes mitosis to form a multicellular organism. If the species is to maintain a constant number of chromosomes before fertilisation takes place the number of chromosomes must be reduced in the gamete (and then restored in the zygote when fertilisation has occurred).

6. (i) Sexual reproduction involves the fusion of two haploid nuclei, one from a paternal gamete and one from a maternal gamete.
   Asexual reproduction does not involve fertilisation, there is no fusion of gametes. Part of a single organism forms the offspring.
   egs. sexual: angiosperms, birds
   egs. asexual: bacteria - binary fission, hydra - budding
   (ii) Asexual offspring are genetically identical to their parent. They therefore show little difference to their parent and offspring show little variation amongst themselves.
   Sexual offspring are rarely identical to their parents. They have a combination of the genes of both parents and because of the great variety of possible combinations, the offspring show great variation.
   (iii) If the environment is stable, organisms which are adapted to it, produce offspring which are the same as themselves and are therefore also adapted to the same unchanging environment.

6. (iv) When the environment is unstable and changes periodically, an organism which produces a variety of different offspring is likely to be reproductively successful because at least some of the variants may tolerate a change in the environment and survive to reproduce themselves.

7. (i) Autosome: a chromosome which does not influence the sex of the organism.
   Sex chromosome: a chromosome which contains some genes which determine the sex of the organism.
   (ii) - In humans, a male produces sperm containing twenty two autosomes and either an x or a y sex chromosome.
   - The proportion of these two types of sperm is about 50% of each.
   - A female produces eggs all of which carry twenty two autosomes and an x chromosome.
   - At fertilisation it is equally likely that either a sperm carrying an x or a sperm carrying a y chromosome will fuse with the egg carrying an x chromosome.
   - Therefore, it is equally likely that the resulting zygote will acquire an xx combination or an xy combination of sex chromosomes. ie. the probability of the zygote being female is the same as being male.
   (ii) Note: In other mammals the inheritance of sex is similar though the number of autosomes varies. In birds the sperm are all similar whereas the ova are of two types. Therefore, in birds, it is the type of egg which determines the sex of the fledgling.

8. (i) Phenotype: often refers to the appearance of the organism. However, it can also be used to describe physical makeup that is not seen eg. blood type, expression of a genotype. The phenotype is also influenced by the environment.
   (ii) Genotype: the genes for a trait that an organism possesses in its cells. They may or may not be expressed eg. Tt.
   (iii) Homozygous: when cells contain the same alleles for a particular characteristic eg. TT or tt.
   (iv) Heterozygous: when cells contain two different alleles for a particular characteristic eg. Tt.
   (v) Dominant: when one allele masks the presence of another. When one allele determines the resulting character in a heterozygous organism that allele is said to be dominant. eg. If Tt is tall, then T is described as dominant.
   (vi) Recessive: the allele which is hidden or plays no part in the resulting character in a heterozygous organism. eg. If Tt is tall, then t is described as a recessive allele.
   (vii) Co-dominant (or Incompletely dominant): in the heterozygous organism, neither allele is dominant but both are expressed in the heterozygote. eg. If RR is red and WW white, the heterozygote RW is pink.

9. (i) If parents genotype is GG × gg
   parents gametes   G   g
   ∴ offspring's genotype: Gg
   Since offspring's phenotype: all green, therefore, gene G (green) is dominant to gene g (yellow).
   (ii) F_1 cross, phenotypes: green × green
   F_1 genotypes: Gg × Gg
   F_1 gametes: (½G + ½g) × (½G + ½g)
   ∴ F_2 genotypes: ¼GG + ½Gg + ¼gg
   ∴ F_2 phenotypes: ¾green + ¼yellow

   (You may prefer to work this out using a Punnett square which is acceptable.)

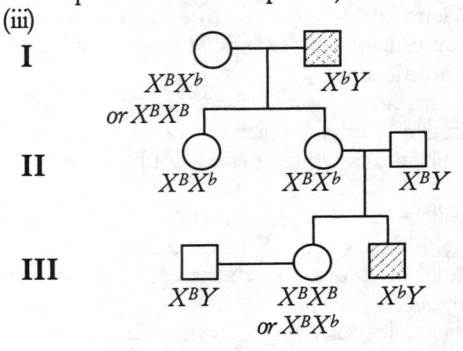

   (iii)
   I $X^B X^b$ or $X^B X^B$ $X^b Y$
   II $X^B X^b$ $X^B X^b$ $X^B Y$
   III $X^B Y$ $X^B X^B$ or $X^B X^b$ $X^b Y$

   (iv) If III 2 is $X^B X^B$ then
   $P(X^b Y) = 0$
   $P(X^B Y) = ½$
   $P(X^B X^B) = ½$
   $P(X^B X^b) = 0$
   $P(X^b X^b) = 0$

III 1 \ III 2	X^B	X^B
X^B	$X^B X^B$	$X^B X^B$
Y	$X^B Y$	$X^B Y$

   If III 2 is $X^B X^b$ then
   $P(X^b Y) = ¼$
   $P(X^B Y) = ¼$
   $P(X^B X^B) = ¼$
   $P(X^B X^b) = ¼$
   $P(X^b X^b) = 0$

III 1 \ III 2	X^B	X^b
X^B	$X^B X^B$	$X^B X^b$
Y	$X^B Y$	$X^b Y$

10. The 'test cross' means crossing the organism of the dominant phenotype with an organism with the recessive phenotype (ie. homozygous recessive organism).
    Here we want to discover whether the organism is AA or Aa, so we cross it with aa (an albino). This is called the 'test cross'.
    If the animal is AA, then the cross will be:

	A	A
a	Aa	Aa
a	Aa	Aa

    ∴ all the offspring will have genotype Aa
    ∴ all will appear with normal colour.

    If the animal is Aa, then the cross will be:

	A	a
a	Aa	aa
a	Aa	aa

    ∴ ½ the offspring will have genotype Aa, ½ will have genotype aa.
    ∴ ½ will be normal colour and ½ will be albino.

    If after producing many offspring no albinos result, the test cross suggests that the animal is probably homozygous. However, if just one albino offspring results, the animal must be heterozygous.

11. (i) Since I 1 and I 2 give rise to II 2, the shaded characteristic must be recessive. If it were dominant I 1 or I 2 would have to have the condition.
Since II 2 is female it cannot be sex linked, because if it were I 1 would have the characteristic.
Therefore it is recessive and autosomal.

(ii) It is recessive because, for example, II 4 and II 5 do not show condition but III 4 and III 5 do. It may also be sex linked as only males in the pedigree inherit the condition.
I 1 may therefore have genotype
X^bY where b ≡ condition
None of his sons would have the condition, if I 2 has the genotype X^BX^B. All his daughters II 3 II 4 and II 6 would be "carriers" X^BX^b. III 4, III 5 and III 8 could then be X^bY.
∴ The most likely mode of inheritance is recessive and sex linked.

(iii) This condition is dominant, because II 1 and II 2 both have the condition but III 1 does not. It cannot be recessive.
It is not sex-linked because II 2 would have to be X^BY (where B is the dominant gene), and he would have to have acquired the X^B from I 2 (his mother), then she would have to be either X^BX^B or X^BX^b which she clearly is not (as she does not show the condition).
It is dominant and autosomal.

Module 3 – The Species (Part 2)

SYLLABUS CHECKLIST

You should be able to:

- 3.12 State that mutation provides the raw material for evolutionary change.
- 3.13 Describe examples which illustrate natural selection in action e.g. peppered moth, antibiotic resistance in bacteria, insecticide resistance.
- 3.14 Discuss the factors which alter allele frequencies.
- 3.15 Describe examples of selective forces/pressures in the environment which have contributed to evolutionary change.
- 3.16 Describe how selection pressures may become so great that species become extinct.
- 3.17 Describe how natural selection and isolation of population can contribute to the development of new species.
- 3.18 Describe the concept of evolution and briefly outline the evidence that supports this concept.
- 3.19 Describe how conservation strategies can reduce selection pressure on species at risk of extinction.

REVIEW QUESTIONS

1. What is a mutation?

2. Why are most mutations harmful to the organism?

3. What are the most likely causes of mutations?

4. How is **artificial** selection different from **natural** selection?

5. What is meant by a 'selection pressure'?

6. In each of the examples of natural selection below name the selection pressure.
   (i) British peppered moth _____
   (ii) bacteria developing a resistance to an antibiotic _____
   (iii) mosquito populations tolerant to pesticide _____

7. **How** might allele frequencies in a population change?

8. The mechanism of natural selection involves four steps.

   (i) Inherited variation exists due to (list 4 causes)
   _____
   _____
   _____

   (ii) A small proportion of offspring reach maturity. The high mortality rate is due to
   _____
   _____

   (iii) Certain members of a species are more successful in particular environments. This is because
   _____
   _____
   _____

   (iv) The characteristics of the whole population change to suit the environment. This is because
   _____
   _____
   _____
   _____

9. The ability of populations to survive environmental changes may depend on
   _____
   _____
   _____
   _____
   _____

10. A new species may arise from an isolated population over a period of time. This is due to a combination of _____ and _____.

11. Populations may be isolated due to barriers. Name three barriers which may isolate organisms.
    (i) _____
    (ii) _____
    (iii) _____

12. When barriers between isolated populations are removed, what are three possible outcomes?

    (i) _____

    (ii) _____

    (iii) _____

13. If isolated populations become genetically so different they are unable to interbreed, they form separate -

    _____ .

14. What is meant by referring to two species' 'common ancestry'?

    _____
    _____
    _____

15. Give an example of 'adaptive radiation' or 'speciation'.

    _____
    _____

16. Eukaryotic cells may have been formed by the symbiotic union of prokaryotic cells. What evidence is there for this hypothesis?

    _____
    _____
    _____
    _____

17. What is evolution? _____

    _____
    _____
    _____

18. Using examples, show how each of the following areas may support the theory of evolution.

    (i) Comparative anatomy. _____

    _____
    _____

    (ii) Distribution studies. _____

    _____

(iii) Embryology. _____
_____
_____

(iv) DNA and Protein Analysis. _____
_____
_____

(v) Palaeontology. _____
_____
_____

19. (i) What factors determine **where** an animal or plant species lives?
_____
_____

(ii) Describe how a change in one or more of these factors may affect the organism.
_____
_____
_____

20. (i) What is meant by **extinction** of a species?
_____
_____

(ii) What may cause extinction?
_____
_____

21. (i) What conservation strategies can be employed to avoid extinction?
_____
_____
_____

(ii) Give one example of the use of a conservation strategy which appears to have been successful.
_____
_____

ANSWERS TO REVIEW QUESTIONS – Module 3– Part 2

1. A mutation is a random change to a gene or a number of genes or a whole chromosome. If the change occurs in gametes it can be inherited by offspring. If the change occurs in a somatic cell, it is not inherited. However, the latter mutation could still be harmful, as it is in the case of cancer.

2. Because mutations are random and occur to genes or chromosomes in normal healthy cells they have an extremely high probability of making the gene or chromosome less functional.

3. Mutations are caused by chemicals (eg. mustard gas, some pesticides, some drugs), radiation (eg. x-rays, radioactivity) and sudden rises in temperature.

4. Artificial selection occurs when man selects particular varieties of plants or animals which suit his purposes, eg. grapes which are seedless, and promotes the growth and proliferation of the selected variety.
   Natural selection occurs when a particular variety of plant or animal is able to survive better in nature, because it has adaptations which give it a competitive advantage over other varieties of the same species. The variety is more likely to survive and reproduce - passing the competitive advantage on to its offspring.

5. A species' survival is always dependent on many factors in its environment. The presence of particular predators, diseases and competitors all impact on its likelihood of survival. A 'selection pressure' refers to any one of the variable factors which may affect the survival of a species, eg. predatory birds affect the chances of survival of moth species, the predatory bird is a 'selection pressure' on the moth species.

6. (i) predatory bird
   (ii) antibiotic
   (iii) pesticide spray

7. The cause of change in allele frequencies in large populations is usually natural selection. Certain genes are favoured, eg. the gene for white colour in small mammals is likely to be favoured in an alpine environment (because white snow provides a white animal with camouflage from predators). If a population with a range of colours (dark brown to white) but with mostly normal brown colour were to migrate to an alpine environment, the change in environment (with the change in selection pressures) would result over time in a greater proportion of white genes in the population. The "gene pool" would change over several generations such that a greater proportion of white genes would occur. Other alleles would be selected against and so they would become less frequent.

8. (i) - Crossing over during meiosis producing new combinations;
   - Random assortment of chromosomes during meiosis;
   - Random fertilisation of gametes; and
   - Mutations.
   (ii) There is competition for scarce resources in nature, (eg. food, shelter, mates), disease and predators.
   (iii) They have inherited particular genes which give them an advantage in competition with others of the same species.
   (iv) Those organisms with favoured genes are more likely to live and to reproduce in greater numbers, than others. Their offspring inherit their favourable genes. The gene pool changes so that a greater proportion of the genes are favourable genes.

9. The range of variation in the population. If there is a great number of different types in a population, then some of these variants might survive and flourish in the new environment. If there is little variation in the population, a significant change is likely to cause the population to become extinct because none of the population is able to tolerate the change.

10. Mutations and natural selection.

11. (i) Water - channels, sea, rivers.
    (ii) Mountains.
    (iii) Deserts.
    or Behaviour.

12. (i) The isolated populations may interbreed (where isolation has been short).
    (ii) The isolated populations may interbreed at the boundaries to produce a third hybrid population.
    (iii) No interbreeding occurs - speciation has occurred.

13. Species. (This process is called speciation or adaptive radiation.)

14. Common ancestry - two species have evolved from one species.

15. The finches on the Galapagos Islands.

16. Eurkaryotic cells contain organelles such as mitochondria and chloroplasts. Both these organelles contain DNA and are capable of dividing. Mitochondria resemble prokaryotic bacteria and chloroplasts single celled algae.

17. Evolution - the formation of new varieties and species of organisms from already existing organisms. This is a gradual process which may take millions of years to become apparent.

18. (i) Comparative anatomy. eg. the limbs of mammals are built on the same basic plan. This suggests that a common ancestor possessed this limb structure.

   (1 bone, 2 bones, many small bones, 5 digits)

   (ii) Distributional studies: the location of present day and recently extinct large flightless birds, eg. emu, ostrich, rhea, elephant bird, etc, suggests that they all evolved from a large flightless bird which inhabited a super continent which once consisted of South America, Australia, India, New Zealand, Africa and the Antarctica. Adaptive radiation occurred when these continents became separated.

   (iii) Embryology: the study of embryos of the vertebrates shows that they have great similarities during their early development. They are very difficult to distinguish - they have tails, 'gill slits' and similar shapes. This supports the notion that they have a common ancestor and have evolved to suit a particular environment.

   (iv) DNA and Protein Analysis: the DNA and proteins which all living things possess suggest a common ancestry. The more closely two animal or plant species appear, the more DNA and protein they share as a general rule - which supports the idea that they have a recent common ancestor.

   (v) Palaeontology: the fossil record suggests that both the variety and the complexity of life on Earth has increased with time, since the first simple prokaryates appeared some 3½ - 4 billion years ago.

19. (i) The availability of food, water, shelter, places to reproduce, climatic conditions, eg. temperature range, wind strengths, humidity and rainfall.

   (ii) If the availability of water was to diminish, the organism may no longer be able to live in the area;

   or If suitable nesting sites, eg. hollows in old trees, were to disappear in the jarrah forest, cockatoos may not be able to reproduce there and they would disappear.

20. (i) An animal or plant is said to be extinct if no live sighting of the species is made for fifty years. The species is presumed to have disappeared from existence.

   (ii) The extinction of a species may occur because one (or more) of the factors which is a necessary condition for the species' survival changes. The species' requirements are no longer satisfied, reproduction and survival are no longer possible.

21. (i) Organisms require habitats which meet all their requirements. All the factors which determine where the organism lives must be satisfied. This means natural environments must be preserved in their natural state to provide a suitable habitat.

   (ii) The fencing off of swamps in the Swan Valley to provide a fox free habitat for the Western Swamp Tortoise, together with meticulous breeding programmes carried out at the Perth Zoo have helped to save this small reptile from extinction.

   and Baiting feral foxes and cats in selected areas of the S.W. has helped to reestablish populations of Chuditches, Numbats and other small marsupials in those areas.

Module 4– Ecosystems (Part 1)

SYLLABUS CHECKLIST

You should be able to:

✔ 4.1 Explain the concept of an ecosystem and how ecosystems are interlinked to form one biosphere.

✔ 4.2 Describe how energy entering ecosystems flows from autotrophs through heterotrophs in feeding relationships and is trapped as chemical energy or lost to the surroundings as heat.

✔ 4.3 Explain the roles of autotrophs/producers, hetertrophs/consumers and decomposers in maintaining energy flow and matter cycles in ecosystems.

✔ 4.4 Use the concept of food pyramids and biomass pyramids in explaining the transfer of energy and matter in ecosystems.

✔ 4.5 Analyse quantitative data concerning productivity and biomass in ecosystems.

REVIEW QUESTIONS

1. Use the diagram below to explain the concept of an **ecosystem** by discussing each of the arrows.

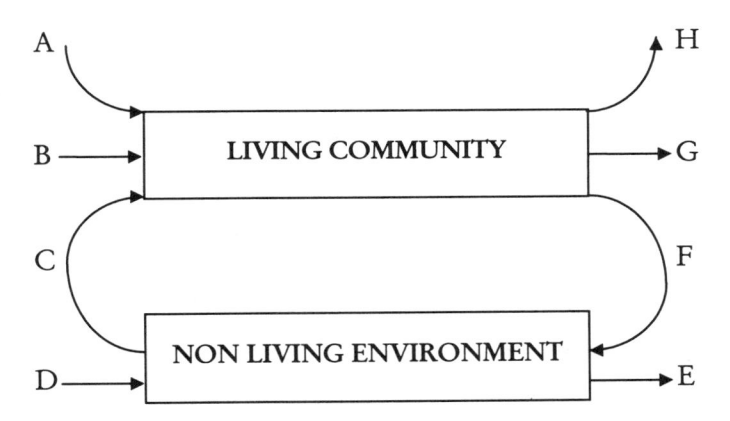

A _____

_____

_____

_____

_____

B _____

_____

_____

_____

_____

C _____

D _____

E _____

F _____

G _____

H _____

2. (i) Which of the arrows infer links with other ecosystems?

   (ii) Explain why. _____

3. What is meant by the biosphere?

4. Define the following terms and give two examples of each.
   (i) autotroph _____

(ii) heterotroph _____

_____

_____

_____

(iii) decomposer _____

_____

_____

_____

5. How is the energy absorbed as light by green plants used by the plants?

_____

_____

_____

_____

_____

6. From where do animals obtain their energy and what happens to the energy?

_____

_____

_____

_____

_____

7. (i) Referring to the diagram in question 1, which organisms bring about the process labelled arrow C? _____

(ii) Explain (i). _____

(iii) Which organisms bring about the process labelled arrow F? _____

(iv) Explain (iii). _____

(v) What would be the consequence to the following processes if the organisms involved disappeared?

C _____

_____

_____

_____

F _____

_____

_____

_____

(vi) If plants ceased to absorb light energy, what would be the consequences to the flow of energy through the system?
_____
_____

8. Explain what each of the "pyramids" below illustrate.

(i)
foxes — 0.1 kg
rabbits — 10 kg
grass — 100 kg
_____
_____
_____
_____

(ii)
willy wagtail — 2
beetles — 10,000
gum tree — 1
_____
_____
_____
_____

9. In question 8 (i), why is the mass of the grass greater than the mass of the rabbits?
_____
_____
_____
_____
_____

10. (i) Draw a food chain involving just three organisms.
_____

(ii) Now draw a possible "pyramid" of numbers for your food chain.

11. What is meant by:
(i) qualitative data _____
_____
_____
_____

(ii) quantitative data _____

_____

_____

_____

12. How might a change in the organic matter which makes up the leaf litter on a forest floor be measured annually to obtain, i) qualitative data, and ii) quantitative data?

(i) _____

_____

(ii) _____

_____

_____

_____

_____

_____

13. The diagram below shows a scheme which summarises the cycling of nitrogen compounds in nature. After studying it carefully, answer the questions below.

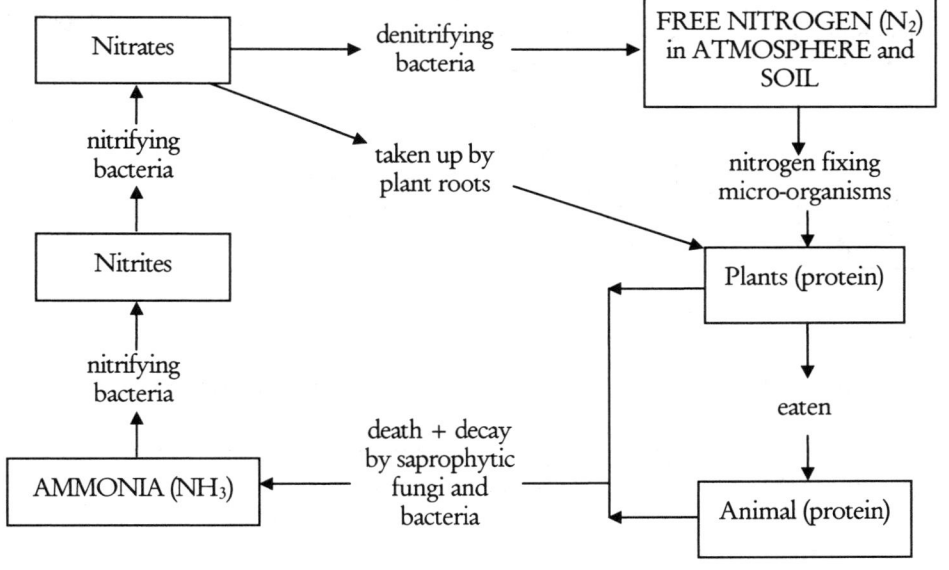

(i) Why is free nitrogen (N_2) not available to plants?

_____

(ii) Explain what nitrogen fixing micro-organisms do to free nitrogen.

_____

(iii) How do animals obtain their nitrogen?

_____

(iv) What do both plants and animals use nitrogen for?

___

(v) When plants and animals die, what becomes of the nitrogen in their bodies?

___

(vi) Nitrates which are formed by nitrifying bacteria may take at least two paths - what are they?

___

___

(vii) Lightening is not shown in this scheme. What role does it play in the cycle?

___

___

14. The carbon cycle illustrates the movement of carbon in an ecosystem. Study the diagram and answer the questions below.

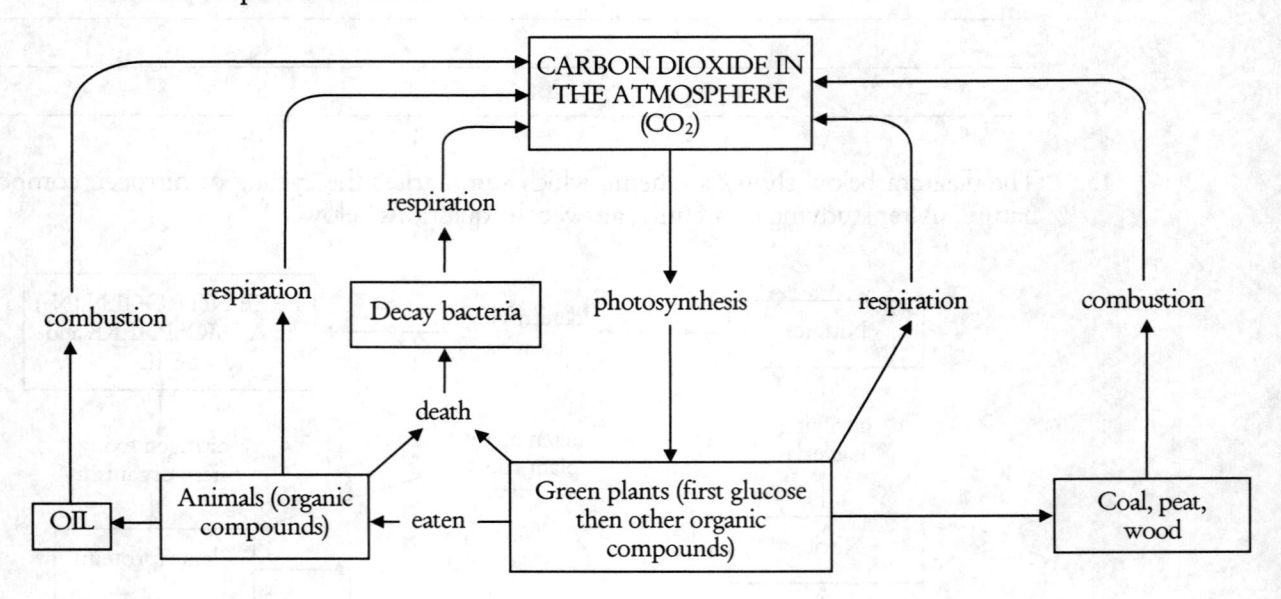

(i) How is carbon dioxide removed from the atmosphere?

___

(ii) How does it return to the atmosphere?

___ and ___

(iii) What other organic compounds does a plant produce (using glucose as a starting compound)?

___

___

(iv) In what compounds might carbon be present in an animal?

___

___

Module 4 - Ecosystems (Part 1)

15. The water cycle shown below illustrates how water may move in an ecosystem.

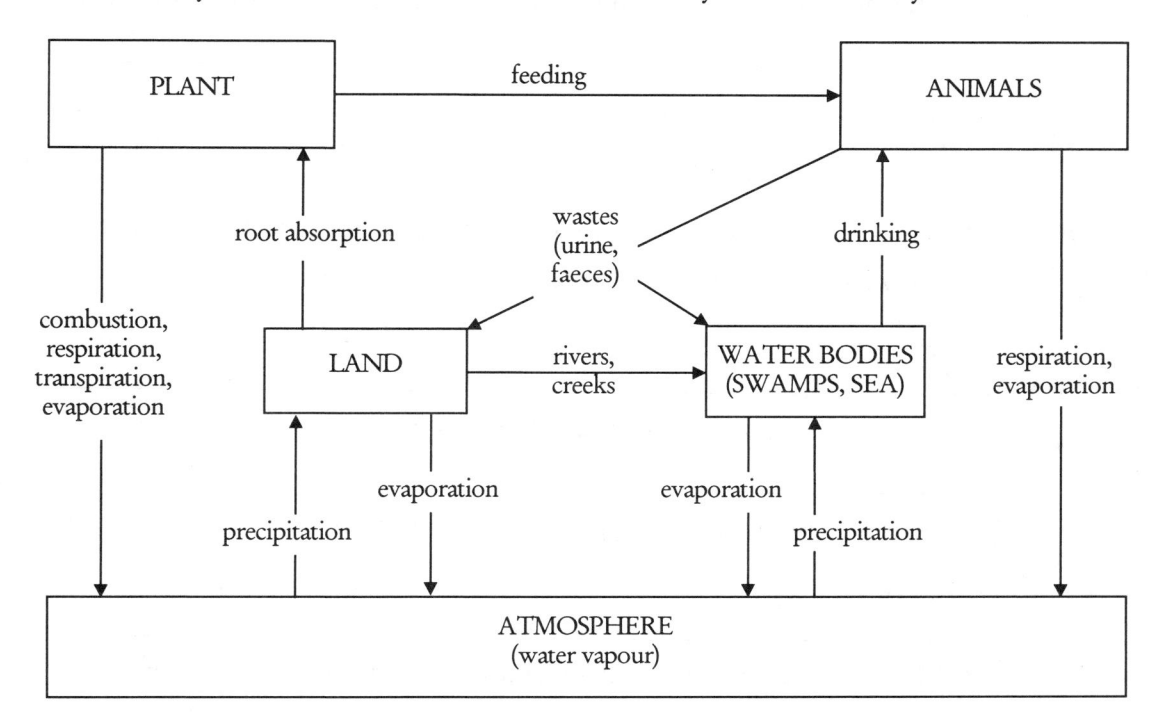

```
    ┌─────────┐       feeding        ┌─────────┐
    │  PLANT  │ ───────────────────▶ │ ANIMALS │
    └─────────┘                      └─────────┘
         │          wastes               ▲
         │     root   (urine,   drinking │
         │  absorption faeces)           │
  combustion,    │      │        │       │  respiration,
  respiration,   │      ▼        ▼       │  evaporation
  transpiration, │  ┌──────┐  ┌──────────────┐
  evaporation    │  │ LAND │  │ WATER BODIES │
         │       │  │      │──│(SWAMPS, SEA) │
         │       │  └──────┘  └──────────────┘
         │       │    │  ▲       │   ▲
         │       │    │  │       │   │
         │       │ precip. evap. evap. precip.
         ▼            ▼  │       ▼   │
    ┌──────────────────────────────────────┐
    │           ATMOSPHERE                 │
    │         (water vapour)               │
    └──────────────────────────────────────┘
```

(i) Define the following terms.

transpiration _____

_____

evaporation _____

_____

precipitation _____

_____

respiration _____

_____

(ii) From what parts does evaporation of water from an animal's body take place?

_____

(iii) a) How do plants obtain water?

_____

_____

b) How do animals obtain water?

_____

_____

(iv) How does water enter the atmosphere?

_____

_____

77

(v) A high proportion of the body weight of any animal or plant is water. Why is this?
_____
_____
_____

16. Answer the following general questions about the cycling of matter in ecosystems.

(i) In what compounds is **carbon** found in most organisms?
_____
_____

(ii) In what compounds is **nitrogen** found in most organisms?
_____

(iii) In what compounds is **oxygen** found in organisms?
_____
_____

(iv) How do animals obtain **carbon** and where may the carbon have been?
_____
_____

(v) From where do animals obtain their **oxygen**?
_____
_____

(vi) Where may the **oxygen** have been produced?
_____

(vii) Where does the **nitrogen** which animals obtain come from and in what form do animals ingest it?
_____
_____

(viii) In what forms do animals lose **nitrogen**?
_____

(ix) In what forms are **oxygen** and **carbon** lost from an animal?
_____
_____

(x) Why is it likely that much of the body of any organism has been used before?
_____
_____
_____

ANSWERS TO REVIEW QUESTIONS – Module 4– Part 1

1. A   represents light energy entering the ecosystem. A small proportion of the light is absorbed and converted to chemical energy by the autotrophic green plants.

    B   represents chemical energy from other ecosystems which may enter this system. Animals migrate, wind and water carry plant matter from one system to another.

    C   represents minerals, water and carbon dioxide which are taken up by the autotrophs in the living community and utilised using the light energy to make organic matter. Oxygen for respiration also makes up part of this intake.

    D   represents minerals, water and other inorganic substances which are carried by wind and water from other ecosystems into this ecosystem.

    E   represents the loss of part of the non-living environment. Minerals may be eroded, carbon dioxide may blow away from and water may flow in rivers out of this ecosystem to another.

    F   represents the return of mineral ions, CO_2, oxygen (from photosynthesis) and water largely through complete decomposition from the living community to the non-living environment. This is carried out by fungi and bacteria.

    G   represents the loss of some energy in the form of chemicals from the community. Emigration, dispersal of seeds by the wind, and loss of plants and animals either dead or alive in rivers contribute towards this removal.

    H   represents the loss of energy in the form of heat to the atmosphere. This process occurs at every trophic level from the autotrophs to the highest order consumers and decomposers. It results in all the chemical energy of an ecosystem being dissipated and none recycled.

2. (i) Arrows B, D, G and E.
    (ii) They indicate the inorganic and organic matter entering and leaving the natural ecosystem. However the gain matches the loss in a natural stable ecosystem and is often a fairly small exchange.

3. The biosphere is the sum of all the ecosystems on the earth's surface.

4. (i) Autotroph: an organism which converts simple inorganic compounds into more complex organic compounds by photosynthesis. egs. blue green alga, angiosperms.
    (ii) Heterotroph: an organism which relies on other organisms for its organic matter. It cannot synthesise its own food and relies either directly or indirectly on the organic compounds produced by autotrophs. egs. birds, fish.

4. (iii) Decomposer: an organism which breaks down organic compounds and returns the inorganic substances to the non-living environment, ie. the soil, atmosphere or the water. egs. bacteria, fungi.

5. The energy is first converted to chemical energy in A.T.P. This then is used as an energy source to synthesise glucose from carbon dioxide and water.

6. Animals obtain their energy by consuming the chemical energy in plants or by consuming other animals which have obtained their chemical energy from plants. Their chemical energy is either passed to the next trophic level as chemical energy or lost as heat energy to the atmosphere.

7. (i)   Autotrophic organisms ie. green plants.
    (ii) Green plants (terrestrial) absorb carbon dioxide through their leaves, mineral ions and water through their roots and when necessary oxygen through their roots and leaves. Oxygen is also absorbed by animals.
    (iii) Bacteria and fungi.
    (iv) Saprophytic fungi generally begin the decomposition of plants, animals and their wastes. The process is completed by the combined activities of bacteria.
    (v)   If the **autotrophic** organisms disappeared, no organic food would be available to the heterotrophs in the living community, so that the whole community would eventually disappear.
          If the **decomposers** were to disappear, matter would no longer be recycled in the ecosystem. The non-living environment would be unable to provide carbon dioxide and mineral ions to the autotrophs. The living ecosystem would not be sustained. The dead bodies of both plants and animals would accumulate as life in the ecosystem ceased.
    (vi) No light energy would be converted into chemical energy. No energy would flow through the system.

8. (i) This is a pyramid of biomass. It shows the total mass of organisms at each trophic level and illustrates the principle that the mass of producers usually exceeds the mass of first order consumers and so on up the food web. Sometimes a low biomass of autotrophs can sustain a higher mass of heterotrophs due to the autotrophs' high reproductive capacity.
    (ii) This is a 'pyramid' of numbers. It shows the numbers of organisms in a particular food chain and reflects the relative size of the individuals at each level.

9. Not all the chemical energy of the grass is transferred to the rabbits (even in the unlikely event that rabbits are the only animal feeding on the grass). This is because a large proportion of the chemical energy in the grass is lost as heat energy and is therefore not available to the rabbits. Also some of the mass of the grass must be conserved in order to enable reproduction to occur ie. the mass is passed on to the next generation. Not all of the chemicals entering the rabbits is used to build rabbit. Much is recycled into the environment as inorganic materials produced by the rabbits' respiration (eg. CO_2, H_2O).

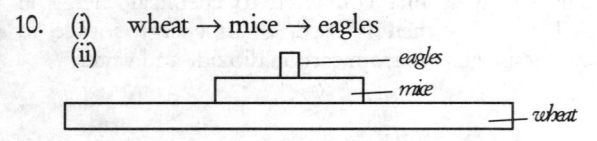

10. (i) wheat → mice → eagles
    (ii) [pyramid diagram: eagles (top), mice (middle), wheat (bottom)]

    (Note: Your answer to 10 (i) must start with an autotroph.)

11. (i) Qualitative data is information which has no numerical values associated with it. eg. a tree may be described as old, the rate of photosynthesis rapid or slow.
    (ii) Quantitative data is gathered information which is ascribed a numerical value eg. the tree is 455 years old (as determined by its number of annual growth rings), the rate of photosynthesis measured by collecting the oxygen produced is 45 mL/hour/gm of green plant.

12. (i) To obtain a qualitative measure we may describe the depth of litter as shallow, medium or deep.
    (ii) To obtain a quantitative measure we take an area (eg. m²) and collect the leaves and plant debris from it. Dry it to remove the water and weight it. More than one site is chosen and an average weight obtained. The data may be expressed as grams per m² per year.

13. (i) Nitrogen is chemically unreactive (therefore plants cannot absorb it through their leaves or roots).
    (ii) Nitrogen-fixing micro-organisms convert nitrogen into compounds which are soluble (eg. by combining nitrogen with oxygen) and can be absorbed by the roots of plants (eg. nitrates).
    (iii) Animals obtain their nitrogen by eating plants which contain compounds which contain nitrogen (eg. proteins).
    (iv) Both plants and animals use nitrogen in their proteins and nucleic acids.
    (v) It is released as ammonia (NH_3) from the nitrogen compounds (such as protein) by saprophytic microorganisms.
    (vi) The nitrates may be absorbed by the roots of plants or be broken down by denitrifying bacteria into nitrogen and released back into the environment (atmosphere/water).

13. (vii) Lightening causes the free nitrogen in the atmosphere to combine with oxygen and form nitrates and nitrites, which are carried by rain to the soil. These soluble compounds may then be absorbed by plant roots.

14. (i) CO_2 is absorbed by green plants in photosynthesis (some may also dissolve in water bodies).
    (ii) CO_2 returns via respiration **or** combustion.
    (iii) From glucose all the other compounds are formed eg. with the addition of nitrogen, amino acids are synthesised. Lipids, nucleic acids, vitamins and the more complex carbohydrates are all made from glucose with the addition of various other elements.
    (iv) Carbon is present in all the organic compounds in animals ie. carbohydrates, proteins, lipids, nucleic acids, hormones, vitamins and so on.

15. (i) **transpiration:** evaporation of water from a plant's leaves.
    evaporation: change of state from a liquid to a gas.
    condensation: change of state from a gas to a liquid.
    respiration: the breakdown in cells of organic matter (usually glucose) either with or without oxygen to release energy.
    (ii) Evaporation from the animal takes place from the skin and lung surfaces.
    (iii) a) Terrestrial plants absorb most water through their roots. A little may be absorbed through leaves.
    b) Terrestrial animals absorb water through the intestines from their food and drink.
    (iv) Water enters the atmosphere via transpiration, respiration, combustion and evaporation.
    (v) Water is the medium in which the organism's metabolism takes place. It also provides some support for the organism and may be used to help the organism remain cool, through its evaporation in hot weather. It is also important as a medium for transport (most of the blood plasma is water).

16. (i) All the organic compounds - proteins, carbohydrates, lipids and nucleic acids.
    (ii) Proteins and nucleic acids.
    (iii) Carbon dioxide, most organic compounds - carbohydrates, lipids, proteins, nucleic acids.
    (iv) Animals obtain carbon from the organic compounds they eat. It may have been part of another animal's organic matter and/or part of a plant.
    (v) Animals obtain oxygen largely from the atmosphere but also combined in organic compounds.
    (vi) Most of the oxygen is produced by plants in photosynthesis.

16. (vii) Nitrogen comes from proteins consumed in food.
    (viii) Animals lose nitrogen in their nitrogenous wastes (ie. as urea, uric acid creatinine).
    (ix) Oxygen is lost combined with carbon in both carbon dioxide and some organic wastes.
    (x) Because the elements in nature are continuously passed from plants to animals and are recycled via the non-living environment.

Module 4 – Ecosystems (Part 2)

SYLLABUS CHECKLIST

You should be able to:

- ✔ 4.6 Describe and illustrate with examples how changes in the living and non-living components of an ecosystem can influence how it functions.
- ✔ 4.7 Compare natural, agricultural (terrestrial and aquatic) and urban ecosystems in terms of their inputs, outputs, amount of recycling of matter and stability.
- ✔ 4.8 Predict possible direct and indirect effects of increasing human populations and their activities on the stability of existing ecosystems.
- ✔ 4.9 Discuss the biological consequences of large scale changes in the global ecosystem arising from human activity (deterioration of the ozone layer, the greenhouse effect and desertification).
- ✔ 4.10 Describe examples which illustrate how improved knowledge and understanding of the interactions in ecosystems are applied to manage and conserve them (biological control, development of new strains, conservation of wilderness areas and national parks, reafforestation).
- ✔ 4.11 Give a rationale for conserving natural ecosystems.

REVIEW QUESTIONS

1. How would the removal of each of the following affect the other organisms in an ecosystem?
   (i) the autotrophs _____

   (ii) the heterotrophs _____

   (iii) the decomposers _____

2. Provide an example of an instance in which (i) and (ii) have occurred.
   (i) _____

   (ii) _____

3. What factors of the non-living environment are likely to change **naturally** in the following?

   (i) a terrestrial environment _____

   _____

   _____

   (ii) a freshwater aquatic environment _____

   _____

   _____

   _____

   (iii) a marine environment _____

   _____

   _____

   _____

4. Choose one of the factors in each of the above and describe how the change could affect the way an ecosystem functions in -

   (i) _____

   _____

   _____

   _____

   (ii) _____

   _____

   _____

   _____

   (iii) _____

   _____

   _____

   _____

5. Complete the diagrams below to show the difference between a natural, an agricultural and urban ecosystem. (Use arrows to indicate relative inputs and outputs.)

LIVING COMMUNITY	LIVING COMMUNITY	LIVING COMMUNITY
(NATURAL)	(AGRICULTURAL)	(URBAN)
NON LIVING ENVIRONMENT	NON LIVING ENVIRONMENT	NON LIVING ENVIRONMENT

6. Complete the table below to show how the amount of chemical energy input and output compares in each ecosystem.

ECOSYSTEM	CHEMICAL ENERGY INPUT	CHEMICAL ENERGY OUTPUT
I) NATURAL		
II) AGRICULTURAL		
III) URBAN		

7. How does the amount of recycling in each compare?
   _____
   _____
   _____

8. Why is there only some recycling in the agricultural ecosystem?
   _____
   _____
   _____

9. As the population of a city grows, how might this growth affect nearby ecosystems both directly and indirectly?

   (i) directly _____
   _____

   (ii) indirectly _____
   _____
   _____

Module 4 - Ecosystems (Part 2)

10. (i) What is the "ozone layer"?

    (ii) How does it **benefit** life on earth?

    (iii) The ozone layer appears to be deteriorating. Why?

    (iv) What might be the consequences of this change?

    (v) What measures have been or might be taken to reduce or reverse the ozone layer's deterioration?

11. (i) What is the "greenhouse effect" or "accelerated global warming"?

    (ii) What are the major causes of the "greenhouse effect"?

    (iii) What might be the consequences of the "greenhouse effect"?

    (iv) How can mankind reduce the worsening greenhouse effect?

12. (i) What is meant by "desertification"? _____

    (ii) List the causes of "desertification". _____

    (iii) How might desertification be **reversed**? _____

13. (i) What is meant by "biological control"? _____

    (ii) When might this be used? _____

    (iii) What benefits does it have over pesticides? _____

    (iv) Give an example of a successful use of biological control.

14. (i) When might the development of new strains of plants or animals be beneficial?

    (ii) Give an example. _____

15. (i) What have been the major causes of natural ecosystem destruction?

   (ii) Why are national parks and conservation areas necessary for the survival of some species?

16. (i) Define "reafforestation".

   (ii) Why "reafforestate"?

   (iii) Describe instances of clearing when reafforestation did not take place.

17. What reasons are there for conserving natural ecosystems?

ANSWERS TO REVIEW QUESTIONS – Module 4 – Part 2

1. (i) Removing autotrophs would result in the food available normally to the heterotrophs disappearing. Light energy would no longer be converted to chemical energy. The heterotrophs would die out, followed by the decomposers.
   (ii) Removing heterotrophs would result in a decline in the diversity of decomposers. The rate of recycling would decrease. Autotrophs would become more dominant (especially those which do not rely on heterotrophs for pollination and dispersal).
   (iii) Removing decomposers would result in a breakdown in the recycling of matter. Scarce resources would become locked up in the bodies of dead plants and animals. The bio-diversity of life on earth would become diminished.

2. (i) Clearing of bushland for crops such as wheat has resulted in a decline in the populations and diversity of native animals in agricultural ecosystems.
   (ii) Many native animals have disappeared from S.W. forests. The populations of numbats and bandicoots have declined due largely to the introduction of feral cats and foxes and the destruction of their native habitat.

3. (i) A terrestrial environment: temperature, humidity, wind speed and direction, light intensity, water availability in soil.
   (ii) A freshwater aquatic environment: concentration of ions, water movement, temperature, light intensity, concentration of dissolved carbon dioxide and oxygen, turbidity, pH.
   (iii) A marine environment: (degree of change would be largely dependent on the depth; deep water being much more stable), temperature, light, turbulence, visibility, oxygen and carbon dioxide concentrations, salt concentration.

4. (i) An increase in temperature in a terrestrial environment, normally causes an increase in the rate of evaporation; living organisms therefore need to have adaptations to reduce water loss. Too great a rise in temperature will cause enzymes to denature so that organisms must also have means of increasing heat loss and decreasing internal heat production. Homeothermic animals become less active.
   The rate at which food is produced and matter cycled through the system will be reduced.

   (ii) A decrease in light intensity in a fresh water environment is likely to cause a slow down in the rate of photosynthesis. Therefore the rate of energy transfer from autotrophs to heterotrophs is likely to be reduced too. Decomposition is likely to proceed at a normal rate unless other factors (eg. temperature) also change.
   (iii) If the level of carbon dioxide rises in a marine environment, this may cause an increase in the rate of photosynthesis in this environment (where the CO_2 is a limiting factor). More chemical energy is made available to the heterotrophs and a greater amount of activity is likely overall.

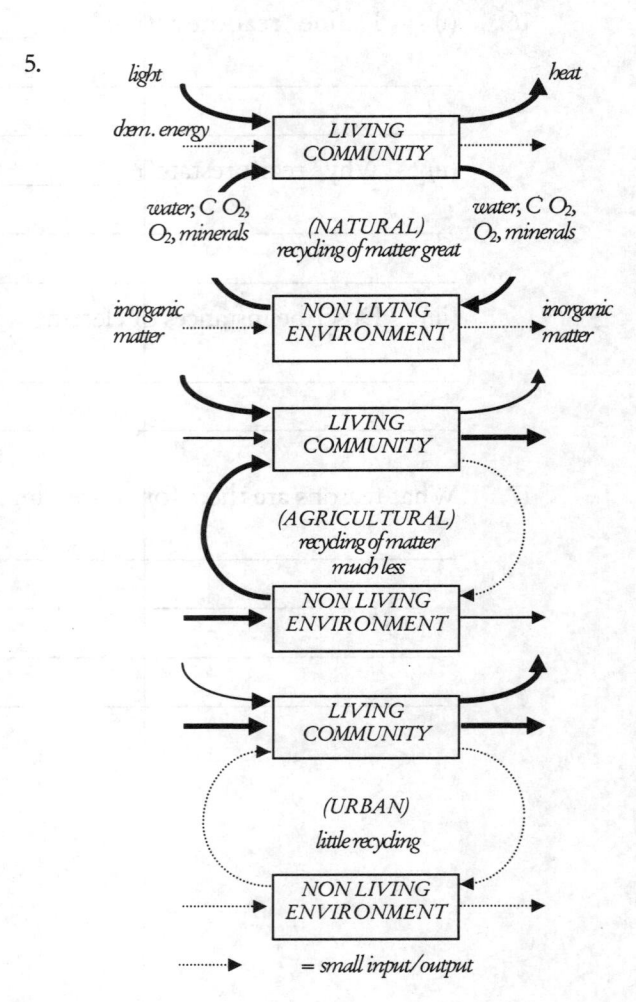

5. [Diagram: Three comparative systems showing energy and matter flow between LIVING COMMUNITY and NON LIVING ENVIRONMENT.
   - (NATURAL) recycling of matter great — inputs: light, chem. energy, water, CO_2, O_2, minerals, inorganic matter; outputs: heat, water, CO_2, O_2, minerals, inorganic matter.
   - (AGRICULTURAL) recycling of matter much less.
   - (URBAN) little recycling.
   - ┄┄► = small input/output]

6.

ECOSYSTEM	CHEMICAL ENERGY INPUT	CHEMICAL ENERGY OUTPUT
I) NATURAL	Small (little organic matter enters).	Small (little organic matter leaves).
II) AGRICULTURAL	Small (little organic matter enters).	Large (large quantities of organic matter are removed).
III) URBAN	Large (fuels and food make up a large input of organic matter).	Large (large amount of waste organic matter removed).

7. Natural ecosystems have a great deal of recycling, agricultural ecosystems have some and urban ecosystems have little.

8. Agricultural ecosystems have limited recycling as they export a great deal of matter to urban ecosystems. They therefore require a large input of matter to compensate for this loss.

9. (i) directly: nearby ecosystems are often destroyed to make room for housing, industry and agriculture.
   (ii) indirectly: nearby ecosystems are often the recipients of waste both household and industrial, they decay as a result of the increase in unwanted nutrients and pollution.

10. (i) The "ozone layer" is a layer of the gas in the upper atmosphere which contains a proportion of ozone. It continuously forms and is broken down by radiation from the sun.
    (ii) Ozone molecules absorb much of the ultra-violet (UV) radiation which reaches the earth's atmosphere from the sun. This blocking allows photosynthesis to occur especially in terrestrial ecosystems and also reduces the incidence of skin cancer in humans.
    (iii) The ozone layer has been deteriorating because it is being 'eroded' by the release of CFC's from refrigerators, air-conditioners, aerosols and industrial processes.
    (iv) A deterioration in the ozone layer may cause a drop in photosynthetic activity on the earth's surface, a decrease in food available to animals - a reduction in populations and biodiversity.
    (v) The banning of CFC's in aerosols with a replacement by more environmentally friendly hydrocarbon propellants. The replacement of CFC's in refrigeration and air-conditioning by other gases.

11. (i) The "greenhouse effect" - this is a rise in the average temperature of the earth's atmosphere together with a rise in the sea level and changing climatic conditions over the earth generally.
    (ii) The causes - rises in the levels of carbon dioxide and methane gases in the atmosphere. These trap the heat which is normally dissipated from the earth's surface up into space.
    (iii) A rise in the average temperature is likely to cause greater areas of desert and semi-desert areas over the earth's land surface, although it is predicted that these changes will not be uniform. Present climates are likely to change. Small islands which do not rise far beyond the present sea level are likely to disappear beneath the sea. Existing continents are likely to become smaller as low lying (often fertile) land becomes inundated with water. Areas currently suited for habitation may become uninhabitable. The world's total agricultural food production potential will become smaller.
    (iv) Reduce the burning of fossil fuels (ie. coal, oil, natural gas) and develop alternative sources of energy (eg. wind, solar, tidal, geothermal). Reduce the reliance on ruminant animals like cows and sheep which contribute to the level of methane released. Rice crops generate large quantities of methane - substitute rice for wheat and potatoes. Landfill sites which contain large quantities of plant matter which does not decompose fully also need to be modified to reduce the output of methane. More of this methane could be used as fuel.

12. (i) "Desertification" - the change of land from semi-desert to desert vegetation and climate. This is often evident on the margins of existing deserts as they expand in size.
    (ii) Desertification can be caused by overgrazing, overcropping, overclearing, rising salinity, removal of plants for fuel.
    (iii) Desertification can be reversed by reducing the population of grazing animals on land which is marginal, by eliminating feral animals like goats and rabbits, changing from annual to perennial crops which are more deep rooted, rehabilitating land by planting more trees, providing alternative fuels to wood burning in developing countries.

13. (i) Controlling pests by using biological means instead of chemical means. eg. sterilising large numbers of males then releasing these into the pest population so that large numbers of matings produce no offspring. The pest population is therefore reduced.
    (ii) Whenever a suitable biological means is available (and economical).
    (iii) Biological control is preferred to chemical control as fewer 'spectator' species are affected. The pest only is targetted, other parts of the ecosystem are not seriously disturbed. No residual poisons accumulate in higher order consumers. It is usually more long lasting in its effects though it rarely eradicates the pest altogether.

13. (iv) The introduction of the cactoblastis moth, a natural predator on the prickly pear, an introduced plant which had become a pest in rural parts of Queensland. The moth has successfully reduced the prickly pear population to small "pockets", where there is now a balance between the moth and the prickly pear populations.

14. (i) New strains of plants or animals which are resistant to disease may benefit human populations.
    (ii) Jarrah trees which are genetically resistant to the fungus which causes 'dieback' can be used to replant in areas of diseased forest.

15. (i) Natural ecosystems in Australia have been destroyed by clearing for agriculture (largely wheat) and grazing (largely sheep).
    (ii) They provide a habitat for species which cannot live and reproduce in agricultural ecosystems. These areas provide space, reduced competition, food and the necessary factors which enable successful reproduction to occur eg. suitable nesting sites.

16. (i) Reafforestation: the replanting of trees and their understorey in areas in which they have been cleared for mining, crops or grazing.
    (ii) Reafforestation is becoming necessary where land is increasingly degraded by erosion, rising salinity, overcropping and overgrazing, soil compaction and rising soil acidity.
    (iii) Mining sites have been cleared in the past, with a huge area around them also providing wood for the fuel and support structures. These sites were often not rehabilitated. However there are now legal requirements for mining companies to do so.
    Land cleared for grazing or crops has not been reafforestated, however many farmers now realise that the retention of some trees is essential and replanting is occurring. Some farmers are planting trees for timber.
    Urban clearing has rarely been reafforested.

17. Natural ecosystems -
    (i) provide a wealth of genetic information which has not yet been studied. The value of this is not known but is likely to be significant. There are likely to be animals and plants which could be of great benefit to man;
    (ii) the biodiversity should be retained for the safety of future generations and for people to enjoy;
    (iii) the organisms have a right to live;
    (iv) provide a large proportion of the earth's atmospheric oxygen and remove carbon dioxide - helping to maintain other life on earth;
    (v) provide a sustainable source of food and other resources for human populations.

Getting the most value from your
TRIAL TESTS

To gain maximum value from these tests you will need to:

- **PREPARE FIRST** - Don't attempt (or look through) the test until you are ready to do it under exam conditions. You may wish to prepare for the test through revision of important concepts in the appropriate section of the book.

- **SET A TIME** - When you attempt the test, ensure that you will not be interrupted. Work completely through the test under strict examination conditions and make use of all the time allocated. This will be valuable preparation for any school test or examination.

- **CHECK AND REVIEW** - After you have had a break, go through and **MARK** your test using the marking key provided. Hopefully it is good news. The most important part is to carefully go through the solutions to the questions with which you had difficulty. You should reattempt these questions at a later time under exam conditions. Finally, ensure that in your revision, you give special attention to those concepts that gave you particular problems.

Good luck!

TRIAL TEST 1 – MODULE O

Introduction to Scientific Method
- Time allowed: 60 minutes
- Total marks: 60

1. (i) Which of the following are areas of biological study? (Underline your choices.)

    histology , botany , meteorology , astrology , paleontology , cytology , geology , zoology , scientology , ecology

   (ii) List the studies you have underlined and briefly describe what each area involves.

   _____
   _____
   _____
   _____
   _____
   _____
   _____
   _____

   [6 marks]

2. What is meant by describing an experiment as controlled?

   _____
   _____
   _____
   _____

   [2 marks]

3. Into which category does each of the following statements fit? (a) an hypothesis (b) an observation (c) an inference (d) a prediction (e) a generalisation (f) a theory. Give a reason for each choice.

   (i) "I can smell a pleasant odour in the room."
   (ii) "If I open a door the pleasant odour will become less strong."
   (iii) "Someone must have used air freshener in this room before we arrived to leave it smelling so pleasant."
   (iv) "Most flowers are sweet smelling."
   (v) "The air freshener was made mainly from crushed sweet smelling flowers."
   (vi) "Flowers were probably the cause of the extinction of dinosaurs as they evolved to displace the green ferns which made up the diet of these huge animals."

(i) _____

(ii) _____

(iii) _____

(iv) _____

(v) _____

(vi) _____

[6 marks]

4. A student wanted to test her hypothesis that Blackbutt, a species of gum found in Western Australia, only grow in soils that have a high water content. She had limited time so she could not attempt to grow the plants in the required conditions.

   (i) Describe an experiment she could conduct in the field to test her hypothesis.

   _____

   [4 marks]

   (ii) If the student's hypothesis was correct, what results should she obtain?

   _____

   [1 mark]

   (iii) What results would refute her hypothesis?

   _____

   [2 marks]

5. What is -
   (i) a variable? _____
   (ii) data? _____
   [2 marks]

6. A biologist put forward the hypothesis that the temperature of wheat seeds alters the rate at which they use oxygen while germinating. To test this hypothesis he took samples of one hundred seeds, germinated them at different temperatures and obtained the following results.

Temperature (°C)	mm³ oxygen/hr
10	96
11	140
15	265
22	460
25	625
28	514
34	156
38	45
43	10

   (i) Name the independent variable and the dependent variable.
   _____
   [2 marks]

   (ii) List four other variables which would need to be controlled if his experiment was to be considered valid.
   _____
   _____
   [2 marks]

   (iii) Graph the results.

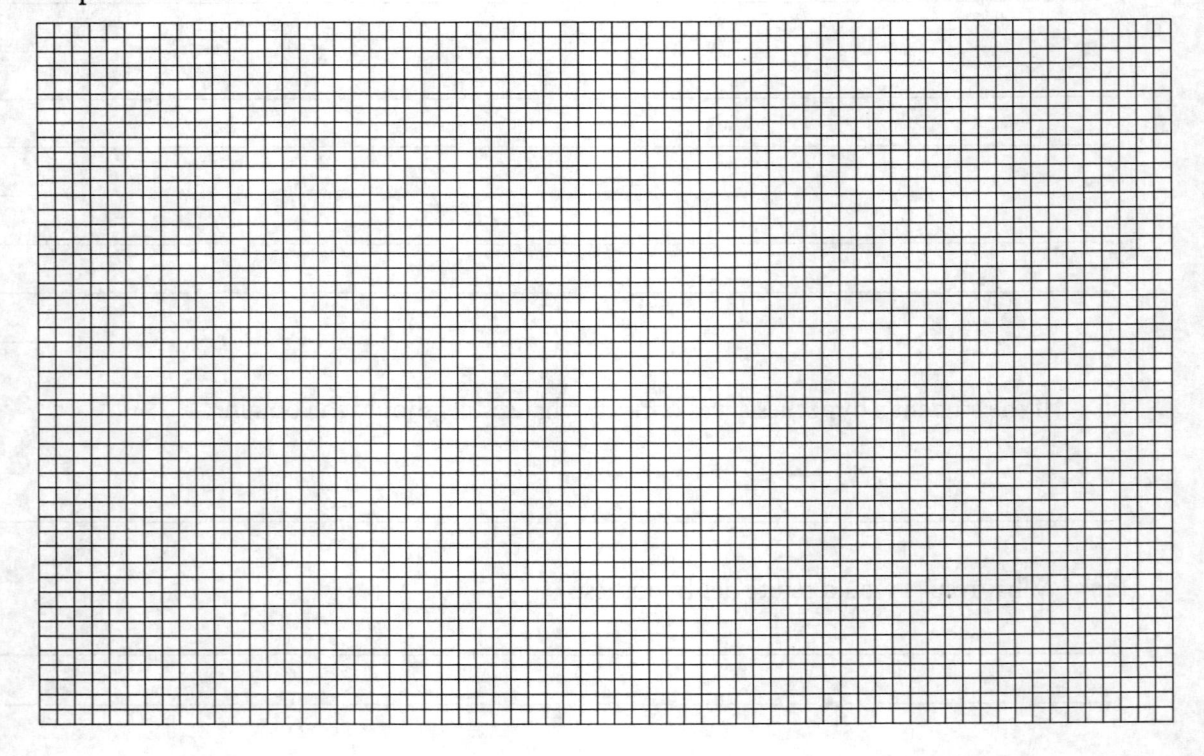

   [5 marks]

6. (iv) Was the biologist's hypothesis supported (or not) by these results? Justify your answer.

    _____

    _____
    [2 marks]

    (v) What appeared to be the optimum temperature for oxygen use by the seeds?

    _____
    [1 mark]

    (vi) How could he make his experiment more reliable? List two ways.

    _____

    _____
    [2 marks]

    (vii) Having completed this experiment he proceeded to test other types of seeds and obtained similar results in every case that he examined. What generalisation could he then make?

    _____

    _____
    [1 mark]

7. Suppose you were given the task of comparing the heights of two human populations of different ethnic origin. You randomly collected data but being a little disorganised jotted results down in the following way:

    Population 1: Heights (cm) - 160 , 115 , 145 , 180 , 190 , 134 , 156 , 134 , 176 , 154 , 189 , 108 , 165 , 145 , 165 , 184 , 134 , 123 , 143 , 154 , 123 , 157 , 154 , 132 , 146 , 65 , 87 , 178 , 149 , 137 , 128 , 167 , 145 , 180 , 190 , 134 , 156 , 134 , 176 , 154 , 75 , 156 , 134 , 176 , 154 , 89 , 108 , 165 , 145 , 165

    Population 2: Heights (cm) - 141 , 156 , 134 , 167 , 165 , 154 , 187 , 163 , 197 , 143 , 187 , 156 , 145 , 143 , 132 , 148 , 176 , 167 , 187 , 165 , 144 , 153 , 167 , 194 , 154 , 134 , 142 , 154 , 143 , 125 , 127 , 165 , 164 , 135 , 178 , 143 , 176 , 198 , 195 , 167 , 178 , 167 , 175 , 145 , 165 , 145 , 176 , 187 , 167 , 183

    Having collected this data, show how you might present it -

    (i) in a table so that the height distribution of the two populations could be easily compared and
    [5 marks]

    (ii) in a graph to make the comparison clearer still.
    [5 marks]

    (i) Table

    _____

    _____

    _____

    _____

    _____

    _____

    _____

    _____

7. (ii) Graph

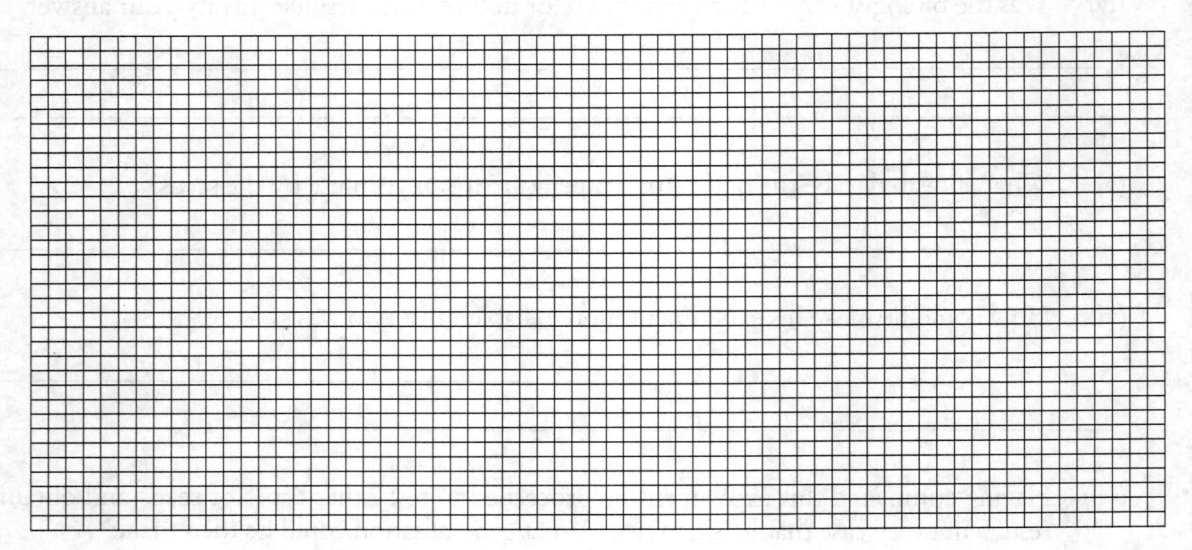

8. Convert (i) 10 mm to micrometres _____ , to centimetres _____
   (ii) 2500 sq metres to hectares _____
   (iii) 5 tonne to kilograms _____
   (iv) 7 megajoules to joules _____

   [5 marks]

9. Complete the table below to show the symbols for each of the units shown.

Quantity	Unit	Symbol
length	kilometre millimetre micrometre	_____ _____ _____
area	hectare	_____
volume	cubic metre	_____
volume (liquids)	litres millilitre	_____ _____
mass	tonne kilogram gram milligram	_____ _____ _____ _____
time	second	_____
temperature	degree Celsius	_____
energy	megajoule kilojoule joule	_____ _____ _____

[7 marks]

TOTAL 60 MARKS

TRIAL TEST 2 – MODULE 1

The Cell – Part 1
- Time allowed: 100 minutes
- Total marks: 105

1. What is the most significant difference between the structure of a prokaryotic cell and a eukaryotic cell?

   _____
   _____
   [1 mark]

2. (i) Describe what happens to an animal cell when it is placed in strong salt solution.

   _____
   _____
   [1 mark]

   Explain why this occurs. _____
   _____
   _____
   [2 marks]

   (ii) If a plant cell is placed in distilled water describe the changes which could be observed with the aid of a microscope.

   _____
   _____
   [2 marks]

   Explain why these changes would occur. _____
   _____
   _____
   [2 marks]

   (iii) How would the changes in a plant cell differ from those in an animal cell in distilled water if neither cell was adapted to life in distilled water.

   _____
   _____
   _____
   [2 marks]

   (iv) What structural feature produces these differences? _____
   [1 mark]

3. Study the diagram below. It is a diagram of a terrestrial plant cell normally found in a temperate environment. Draw a similar diagram to show how it would change if placed in a hot, dry environment. Under your diagram explain why the changes occur.

[Diagram of plant cell labelled: cell wall, cell membrane, nucleus, vacuole]

[3 marks]

_____
_____
_____
_____

[2 marks]

4. (i) What happens to the *surface area : volume* ratio of a particular cell as it grows?

_____
_____
_____

[1 mark]

(ii) Illustrate your answer using a cube of dimensions of one cm and a cube of two cm. Show their SA : Vol ratios below each cube.

[4 marks]

(iii) How might an increase in the size of an amoeba affect its survival in a typical freshwater lake? Explain your answer.

_____
_____
_____
_____
_____
_____
_____

[3 marks]

5. Complete the table below to describe and show the structure, functions and a small illustration of common cell organelles. Show details as seen with the aid of an electron microscope.

Organelle Name	Structure	Functions	Diagram
plasma/cell membrane			
chloroplast			
endoplasmic reticulum			
Golgi body			
mitochondrion			
centrioles			
nucleus			

[21 marks]

6. The diagram below shows the fluid mosaic model of membrane structure.

← EXTRA CELLULAR FLUID

← INTRA CELLULAR FLUID

(i) Why is this referred to as a 'model'? _____

_____

[1 mark]

(ii) If A and B are proteins, besides their shape, in what way are they apparently different?

_____
_____
[1 mark]

(iii) F represents one of the two lipid layers. Explain why on the outer layer, part D faces outwards and part E inwards but this is reversed on the inner layer.

_____
_____
_____
_____
[3 marks]

7. As they mature, red blood cells lose their nuclei and consequently room is made available in the cell cytoplasm for more haemoglobin. Explain why red blood cells have a limited life span. They only last on average 120 days.

_____
_____
_____
_____
[2 marks]

8. A cell appears in the field of view of a microscope as shown in figure 1. Using the same microscope a piece of mm graph paper looks like figure 2.

100 ×
(objective 10 ×
ocular 10 ×)

40 ×
(objective 4 ×
ocular 10 ×)

figure 1   figure 2

(i) What is the diameter of the field of view when using each of the two magnifications?

a) 40 × _____ mm or _____ μm

b) 100 × _____ mm or _____ μm

[2 marks]

(ii) What is the length and breadth of this cell?

a) length _____ μm

b) breadth _____ μm

[1 mark]

(iii) How many cells could fit side by side across the field of view with the 40 × magnification?

_____

_____

[1 mark]

9. Imagine a population of bacteria in a beaker of water with a single strand of filamentous alga all in a darkened room.

A light shines through the beaker and illuminates part of the alga. The bacteria shortly afterwards accumulate around the filament as shown.

(i) To what stimulus are the bacteria responding?

_____

[1 mark]

(ii) What is the bacteria's response?

_____

[1 mark]

(iii) How might the bacteria move toward the alga?

_____

[1 mark]

(iv) In their natural habitat, where are these bacteria likely to live?

_____

[2 marks]

10. Single-celled animals which are capable of movement to or from stimuli may do so by: (i) amoebic movement; (ii) the use of cilia; or (iii) the use of flagella. Briefly discuss each of these mechanisms giving an example of an organism which uses each method.

(i) _____

_____

(ii) _____

_____

(iii) _____

_____

[6 marks]

11. How could you test the hypothesis that a particular species of amoeba multiplies most rapidly in its aquatic environment when the water temperature is 28°C?

[8 marks]

12. When a wet mount of potato cells is irrigated with iodine, parts of the cytoplasm become a blue-black colour.

    (i) What might these structures be? Explain.

    [2 marks]

    (ii) If the same slide is first irrigated with strong hydrochloric acid, then iodine is added, which area/s will then turn blue-black? Explain.

    [2 marks]

13. A biology student has prepared a 'wet mount' of some leaf tissue which he now wishes to test with Benedict's solution for the presence of glucose. The slide appears as shown at right.

    (i) Describe how he might most efficiently "irrigate" the tissue with his reagent (Benedict's solution) without removing and disturbing the leaf tissue.

    [3 marks]

(ii) Having saturated the tissue with Benedict's solution, what must he do to complete the test?

_____

_____

[1 mark]

(iii) If glucose is present, what result will he obtain?

_____

_____

[1 mark]

14. Some plant cells have coloured pigment in their cytoplasm. What is likely to occur when such cells are immersed in -

   (i) a strong solution of alcohol;

   _____

   _____

   [1 mark]

   explanation;

   _____

   _____

   _____

   [2 marks]

   (ii) a strong solution of detergent;

   _____

   _____

   [1 mark]

   explanation;

   _____

   _____

   _____

   [2 marks]

   (iii) a strong salt solution;

   _____

   _____

   [1 mark]

   explanation.

   _____

   _____

   _____

   [2 marks]

15. The series of diagrams below illustrate the stages which occur when a white blood cell ingests a pathogenic bacterium. In the spaces provided describe what is occurring.

(i) _____
_____

(ii) _____
_____

(iii) _____
_____

(iv) _____
_____

(v) _____
_____

(vi) _____
_____

(vii) _____
_____

[7 marks]

16. (i) In which of the following processes does a cell need to expend energy? (Underline your choices.)

diffusion , osmosis , active transport , pinocytosis , phagocytosis , exocytosis

[2 marks]

(ii) For those which you have not underlined, explain why the cell does not have to provide energy.

_____
_____
_____
_____
_____
_____

[3 marks]

TOTAL 105 MARKS

TRIAL TEST 3 – MODULE 1

The Cell – Part 2
- Time allowed: 80 minutes
- Total marks: 80

1. A horse cell normally has sixty four chromosomes (diploid number). When a horse cell undergoes mitosis each of the two cells formed has sixty four chromosomes. Explain how this number of chromosomes is maintained.

   _____
   _____
   _____
   _____
   _____

   [2 marks]

2. The diagrams below show four different nucleotides.

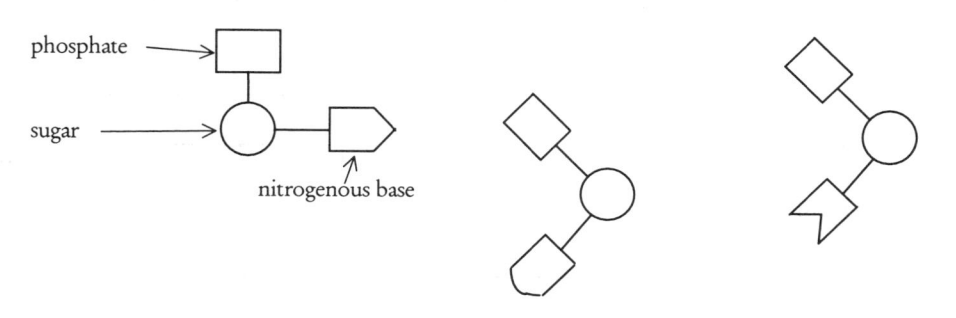

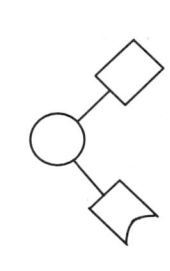

   (i) In what way is each nucleotide shown different?

   _____

   [1 mark]

   (ii) Draw a diagram below to show how these four nucleotides would be linked to form part of a DNA molecule.

   [2 marks]

(iii) A molecule of DNA contains thousands of nucleotides, not just four. Where in the DNA molecule is the cell's genetic information stored?

[1 mark]

(iv) Explain briefly **how** this information is stored and **how** it is translated.

[8 marks]

3. Cells which are undergoing mitosis can be 'fixed' and stained so that their chromosomes can be viewed with the aid of a microscope. Describe how you would distinguish between the following:

(i) cells in interphase and cells in prophase;

[2 marks]

(ii) cells in metaphase and cells in anaphase;

[2 marks]

(iii) telophase in plant cells and telophase in animal cells;

[2 marks]

4. Why does mitosis occur?

_____
_____
_____
_____
_____

[2 marks]

5. The first circle below represents a mouse cell which in the early prophase of mitotic division has 80 DNA units.

   (i) A number of mitotic divisions occur. Complete the diagram to illustrate how many DNA units are present at each stage shown (write the number in each circle).

   [3 marks]

   (ii) How many mitotic divisions are represented in this diagram? _____

   [1 mark]

   (iii) What is the total number of chromosomes in the final cells that have been formed?

   _____

   [1 mark]

   (iv) Where have the extra DNA molecules come from?

   _____
   _____

   [2 marks]

6. A freshwater amoeba may have as many as 600 chromosomes whereas a cat cell has only 38. Does this imply that the amoeba is a more complex animal than the cat?

   _____ Explain. _____
   _____

   [2 marks]

7. The following diagram illustrates the action of enzymes in a plant cell converting glucose into carbon dioxide and ethyl alcohol. This occurs when the cell is 'fed' glucose in the absence of oxygen.

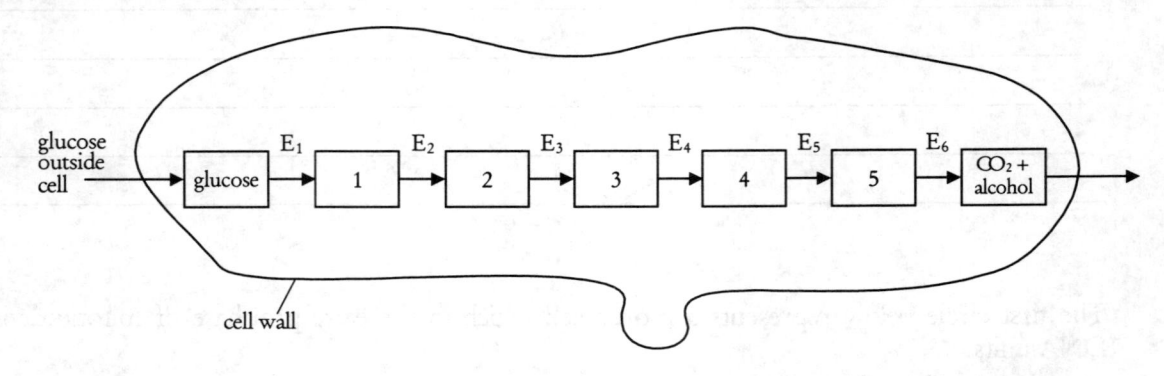

glucose outside cell → glucose →[E_1] 1 →[E_2] 2 →[E_3] 3 →[E_4] 4 →[E_5] 5 →[E_6] CO_2 + alcohol →

cell wall

The breakdown of glucose involves the intermediate compounds represented by the numbers 1 to 5 and each stage of the reaction is controlled by a different enzyme represented by the letters E_1 to E_6.

(i) What would happen if the enzyme E_6 was not present in the cell?

[1 mark]

(ii) Normally CO_2 and alcohol move out of the cell into the extracellular fluid. What might happen if alcohol accumulated in the cell while the CO_2 moved out?

[2 marks]

(iii) If the alcohol was allowed to diffuse from the cell's cytoplasm, but the carbon dioxide remained, how might this affect the breakdown of glucose?

[2 marks]

(iv) Suppose the cell was slowly heated to a temperature which well exceeded the normal temperature of the cell. How might this affect the process?

[2 marks]

(v) Explain your answer in terms of the 'lock and key' hypothesis.

[3 marks]

(vi) If glucose is broken down to CO₂ and alcohol and these products are lost to the cell, of what use to the cell is the breakdown process?

_____

_____
[2 marks]

(vii) If oxygen were introduced with the glucose, explain how the process would change.

_____

_____

_____
[2 marks]

(viii) What would be the difference in energy yield?

_____

_____

_____
[2 marks]

(ix) What are the a) general, and b) specific names for the two processes described above?

a) _____

b) _____ and _____
[3 marks]

(x) In which part of the cell does the sequence shown in the original diagram occur?

_____
[1 mark]

(xi) If this had been an amoeba supplied with glucose under the same anaerobic conditions, what changes would you make to the diagram? **Sketch** your answer below.

[2 marks]

(xii) If the end product was allowed to accumulate in the amoeba, how might this affect the cell?

_____

_____
[1 mark]

8. If the amoeba cell mentioned in question 7 is surrounded by an extracellular fluid containing very few calcium ions (as shown below), which it requires;

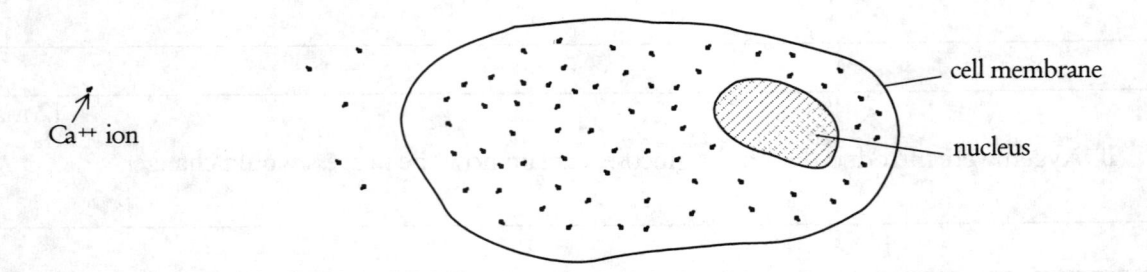

(i) How might the amoeba obtain calcium ions against the concentration gradient?
_____
[1 mark]

(ii) Since this is not a passive process, what compound supplies the energy needed?
_____
[1 mark]

(iii) Write a word equation to show how the energy is supplied by this compound.
_____
[1 mark]

(iv) Name three other processes for which the amoeba may need the compound as a source of energy.
_____ _____ and _____
[3 marks]

9. How could you use -

(i) a variegated plant to show that chlorophyll is needed for photosynthesis? (Use a diagram to illustrate your answer.)
_____
_____
_____
_____
_____
_____
[3 marks]

(ii) an aquatic plant to show that oxygen is produced during photosynthesis? (Use a diagram to illustrate your answer.)
_____
_____
_____
_____
_____
[3 marks]

10. A biologist painted clear latex (a harmless rubber compound) on the leaves of a plant which had been kept in the dark for 24 hours. On some he covered the upper surface with latex, on others only the lower surface, and on a third group he covered both surfaces. After he placed the plant in the light for several hours he removed all the treated leaves and tested them for the presence of starch. However he accidentally mixed all the leaves up. How could he tell which leaves were painted with latex on the upper surface?

    _____

    Explain. _____

    _____

    [2 marks]

11. Both aerobic and anaerobic respiration produce some **heat**.

    (i) Why?

    _____

    _____

    [2 marks]

    (ii) Which respiration releases the greatest **quantity** of heat? Explain.

    _____

    _____

    [2 marks]

    (iii) How might you demonstrate that heat is produced by a micro-organism when it respires?

    _____

    _____

    _____

    _____

    [4 marks]

12. The glucose which is produced during photosynthesis is not normally retained as glucose.

    (i) Why is it often converted to starch?

    _____

    _____

    [2 marks]

    (ii) What other carbohydrate is it commonly changed to for storage or movement?

    _____

    [1 mark]

    (iii) Other compounds are formed from glucose. Name three such groups.

    _____

    [1 mark]

    TOTAL 80 MARKS

TRIAL TEST 4 – MODULE 2

The Organism – Part 1
- Time allowed: 120 minutes
- Total marks: 120

1. Explain why a **heterotroph** requires each of the following.

    (i) organic compounds

    _____
    _____
    _____

    (ii) oxygen

    _____
    _____
    _____

    (iii) water

    _____
    _____
    _____

    (iv) mineral ions

    _____
    _____
    _____

    [4 marks]

2. Explain why an **autotroph** requires each of the following.

    (i) carbon dioxide

    _____
    _____
    _____

    (ii) water

    _____
    _____
    _____

(iii) light energy

(iv) mineral ions

[4 marks]

3. How do **vertebrates** generally respond to -
   (i) a rise in the level of CO_2 in their plasma;

   (ii) a fall in the level of **glucose** in their blood.

   (iii) a rise in the concentration of **nitrogenous wastes**, e.g. urea, in their blood;

   (iv) a fall in their normal body **temperature**;

   (v) a fall in the **osmotic pressure** of their blood plasma.

[10 marks]

Biology Study Guide

4. In each of the examples in question 3, outline the consequences for the animal if the mechanisms you have described did not occur.

   (i) _____

   (ii) _____

   (iii) _____

   (iv) _____

   (v) _____

   [5 marks]

5. When eutrophication of waterways occurs, often the increase in nutrient causes an algal bloom. The huge increase in algae may lead to an oxygen deficiency in still bodies of water at night.

   (i) Explain why the oxygen shortage occurs.

   _____

   [2 marks]

   (ii) How does this affect animals which share this aquatic environment?

   _____

   [1 mark]

6. (i) Although fish cells contain a high percentage of water, a human could not live on fish alone. Explain why such a diet is unsuitable.

   _____

   [4 marks]

   (ii) If the availability of water in an environment is limited, a mammal's diet may be restricted to carbohydrates and lipids. Why?

   _____

   [2 marks]

7. (i) Why is the excretion of ammonia the most efficient way to remove nitrogenous waste in most freshwater animals?

_____

_____

_____

[2 marks]

(ii) How and from what part of a fish is this waste removed?

_____

_____

_____

_____

[2 marks]

(iii) How is the life cycle of an amphibian likely to affect the type of nitrogenous waste it produces during its development?

_____

_____

_____

_____

[2 marks]

(iv) Reptiles and birds produce a nitrogenous waste called _____

The main advantages of this form of nitrogenous waste for these two animal groups are -

a) _____

and b) _____

_____

[3 marks]

(v) Mammals excrete most of their nitrogenous waste as urea. Explain why this is a more suitable waste than uric acid for most mammals.

_____

_____

_____

[2 marks]

(vi) Because mammals excrete nitrogen wastes as urea they must have a sufficient supply of water. Why is this necessary?

_____

_____

[2 marks]

(vii) This requirement has several consequences for mammals as a group.

a) Explain how it tends to restrict their distribution.

_____

_____

[1 mark]

b) Describe how those mammals which do live in arid climates must be adapted to do so. (List 5 adaptations.)

_____
_____
_____
_____
_____
[5 marks]

8. (i) The embryos of snakes, lizards and birds produce ammonia (NH_3) during their first few days of development. How might this toxic waste be removed from the animal?

_____
[1 mark]

(ii) Before these animals emerge from their eggs, they begin to produce uric acid instead of ammonia. What might happen to this waste? Explain.

_____
[1 mark]

9. Why is ammonia, dissolved in the cytoplasm of a cell, poisonous to that cell?

_____
_____
_____
[2 marks]

10. Complete the table below to compare the three most common nitrogenous wastes.

Nitrogen waste	Advantages	Disadvantages	Animal examples
ammonia NH_3			
urea CON_2H_4			
uric acid $C_5H_4O_3N_4$			

[9 marks]

11. (i) How does **temperature** affect the rate of metabolism in an animal?

_____
_____
_____
[2 marks]

(ii) What factor limits this change?

[1 mark]

(iii) A rise in the environmental temperature of 10°C may result in an increase in the activity of a reptile but a decrease in the activity of a mammal. Explain why there is this difference between the two animals.

[4 marks]

12. A mouse living in a Jarrah forest in the south-west of W.A. requires a greater intake of food energy than a reptile of a similar size living nearby.

(i) Why does the mouse require more energy?

[4 marks]

(ii) How does this reflect in their relative growth rates?

[2 marks]

(iii) What special problem might this cause for the mouse?

[1 mark]

(iv) What advantage does it give the mouse?

[1 mark]

Biology Study Guide

13. (i) Often the metabolic rate of an animal is expressed in terms of its rate of oxygen use. Clearly explain why this is both a reliable and convenient measure of metabolic rate.

   _____
   _____
   _____
   _____
   _____

   [4 marks]

   (ii) Calculate the metabolic rate in mL of oxygen used / kilogram of body mass / hour in the following cases. (Show all working out.)

   a) A man weighing 65 kilograms who uses 84 litres of oxygen while sitting watching T.V.

   _____
   _____
   _____
   _____
   _____

   [2 marks]

   b) A girl who weighs 50 kilograms who runs to school in 20 minutes and uses 30 litres of oxygen in the process.

   _____
   _____
   _____
   _____
   _____

   [2 marks]

14. Explain why an animal such as a mouse has a higher metabolic rate than a donkey when both animals live in a cool temperate environment.

   _____
   _____
   _____
   _____
   _____

   [4 marks]

15. Marsupials such as wombats which live on the Australian mainland are smaller in general than their counter-parts which live in Tasmania. What advantage would their greater size give to these animals that live in Tasmania?

_____
_____
_____
_____

[2 marks]

16. The hypothalamus, a small area of the brain just above the pituitary gland, detects changes in the internal temperature of mammals and birds.

    Discuss **two** responses which occur in mammals when the hypothalamus detects a -

    (i) rise in body temperature;

    _____
    _____
    _____

    [2 marks]

    (ii) fall in body temperature?

    _____
    _____
    _____

    [2 marks]

17. (i) To maintain a constant body temperature a numbat must balance heat gain and heat loss. Show this in a simple word equation.

    _____

    [1 mark]

    (ii) How does heat enter the numbat's body?

    _____
    _____
    _____

    [2 marks]

    (iii) Describe how heat is produced within the animal's body.

    _____

    [2 marks]

    (iv) How is heat lost from this animal's body?

    _____
    _____
    _____
    _____

    [4 marks]

18. The following diagram shows how the temperature varies along the length of an artery and a nearby vein which carry blood to and from the foot of an Antarctic bird which is standing on ice.

    (i) What is the exchange of heat between the artery and the vein called?

    _____
    _____
    [1 mark]

    (ii) Of what advantage to the bird is there in having the artery and the vein so close to one another in the animal's leg?

    _____
    _____
    _____
    [2 marks]

    (iii) What category of adaptation is this example: behavioural, structural or physiological? Explain.

    _____
    [1 mark]

19. When the hypothalamus of a mammal detects a rise in the body's blood temperature, it sends out nerve impulses which cause vasodilation of blood vessels close to the skin. This results in more blood flowing close to the surface of the skin and consequently a greater loss of heat from the body by radiation and conduction to the atmosphere (provided the atmosphere is cooler than the body).
    In the above, what is -

    (i) the stimulus? _____

    (ii) the receptor? _____

    (iii) the effector? _____

    (iv) the response? _____
    [4 marks]

    (v) Why is this called a negative feedback system?

    _____
    _____
    _____
    [1 mark]

20. Complete the following diagrams by writing in actual examples of each part for:

(i) TEMPERATURE REGULATION IN HOMEOTHERMIC ANIMALS

```
     STIMULUS
  Body's temp. rises
         ↓
     RECEPTOR
  _____
         ↓
    TRANSMISSION
  _____
         ↓
     EFFECTOR
  _____
         ↓
     RESPONSE
  _____
```
[2 marks]

(ii) PHOTOTROPISM IN AN ANGIOSPERM

```
     STIMULUS
        Light
         ↓
     RECEPTOR
  _____
         ↓
    TRANSMISSION
  _____
         ↓
     EFFECTOR
  _____
         ↓
     RESPONSE
  _____
```
[2 marks]

(iii) Which of the situations represents a **negative feedback system**?

_____ [1 mark]

(iv) Explain your answer to (iii).

_____
_____
_____
_____
_____ [1 mark]

TOTAL 120 MARKS

TRIAL TEST 5 – MODULE 2

The Organism – Part 2
- Time allowed: 120 minutes
- Total marks: 120

1. Using a cork borer, a student cut cylinders of tissue from a large potato. He then sliced these into uniform discs using a scalpel. Each disc was cut as close to 2 mm thick as he could get it. These discs were then grouped into seven batches of 100. The batches were then weighed (original weight) and placed into seven different salt solutions of varying concentration (see table below).
After one hour the discs were removed from their solutions, dried gently using paper towelling and reweighed (final weight). The table below shows the results obtained.

    (i) Complete the table to show the change in weight per batch and the change in weight per gram of potato tissue.

Concentration of salt solution (M)	Original weight of batch (g)	Final weight of batch (g)	Change in weight of batch (g)	Change in weight per g of potato tissue
0.2	83	87		
0.4	94	97		
0.6	91	93		
0.8	92	92		
1	101	99		
1.2	104	100		
1.4	81	77		

    [4 marks]

    (ii) Graph these results (plot the concentration of salt solution against the change in weight per gram). Use the grid below.

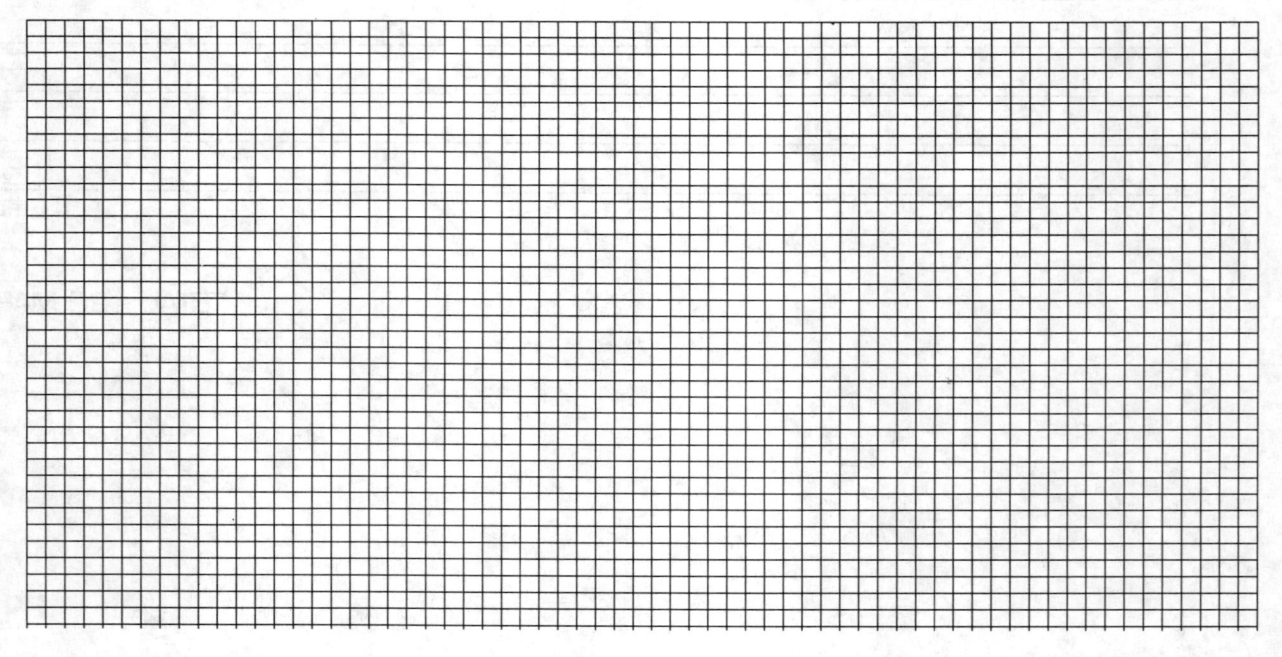

    [5 marks]

(iii) In the method used, why did the student use batches of 100 rather than single discs in each solution?

_____

_____

[1 mark]

(iv) Why was the change per gram of potato used (rather than the change in weight of the batches) in graphing this data?

_____

_____

[1 marks]

(v) Explain why the potato tissues lost weight in some solutions but gained weight in others.

_____

_____

_____

_____

_____

[4 marks]

(vi) At what concentration did the potato tissue neither gain nor lose weight? Explain why this occurred at this concentration.

_____

_____

_____

[3 marks]

(vii) Describe how animal cells would change if subjected to the same treatment as the potato in this experiment.

_____

_____

_____

_____

_____

[4 marks]

2. Active transport requires the use of energy. Sharks retain high levels of urea in their blood instead of excreting it in their urine. This retention of urea raises the osmotic pressure of their blood to the same level as that of the surrounding sea water. Of what value to the shark is this balancing of osmotic pressures?

_____

_____

_____

_____

[4 marks]

3. Study the diagrams of the fish types below before answering the questions which follow them.

Marine Fish — Water, Salts

Freshwater Fish — Salts, Water

What are the main problems, associated with osmotic pressure and concentration differences, faced by

(i) marine fish?

_____
_____
[1 mark]

(ii) freshwater fish?

_____
_____
[1 mark]

How does each type of fish solve its particular problems? What adaptation does each fish have to enable it to survive where it lives?

(iii) Marine fish.

_____
_____
_____
_____
[2 marks]

(iii) Freshwater fish.

_____
_____
_____
_____
[2 marks]

4. What is meant by saying that terrestrial animals have a "water problem"?

_____
_____
_____
[2 marks]

5. (i) Name the two tissues which are primarily concerned with transport in vascular plants.
_____
[1 mark]

   (ii) What does each tissue transport?
   a) _____
   b) _____
[2 marks]

6. A root hair cell has a long extension or "process" orientated horizontally as shown.

   (i) What is the function of this process (extension)?
   _____
   _____
[1 mark]

   As the root grows these cells die and are replaced by new root hair cells closer to the root cap.
   (ii) Why are they replaced?
   _____
   _____
[1 mark]

   (iii) Outline the path by which water reaches the photosynthetic cells of a leaf.
   _____
   _____
   _____
[2 marks]

   (iv) What may happen to water that is not used by the photosynthetic cells?
   _____
   _____
[1 mark]

7. The vascular tissue of angiosperms primarily provide a transport system in the plant, but its secondary function is to provide support.

   (i) Describe how xylem vessels assist in keeping terrestrial plants upright.
   _____
   _____
[1 mark]

(ii) Discuss what other features of the vascular tissue help support the plant.

_____
_____
_____

[2 marks]

8. The graph below shows the average width of the stomatal openings (see diagram) of a plant which is growing in a hot dry environment, measured over a period of 24 hours.

(i) At what time is the pore increasing in width most rapidly? _____

[1 mark]

(ii) At what time does the pore begin to close? _____

[1 mark]

(iii) Why does it begin opening in the morning?

_____
_____
_____

[3 marks]

(iv) Why does it begin to close later in the day?

_____
_____

[2 marks]

(v) Of what advantage to the plant is this change?

_____

[1 mark]

(vi) Does the closing have any disadvantage? Explain.

_____
_____

[2 marks]

9. (i)   On the axes below show how the same plant's CO_2 input and output is likely to vary over the same period of time.

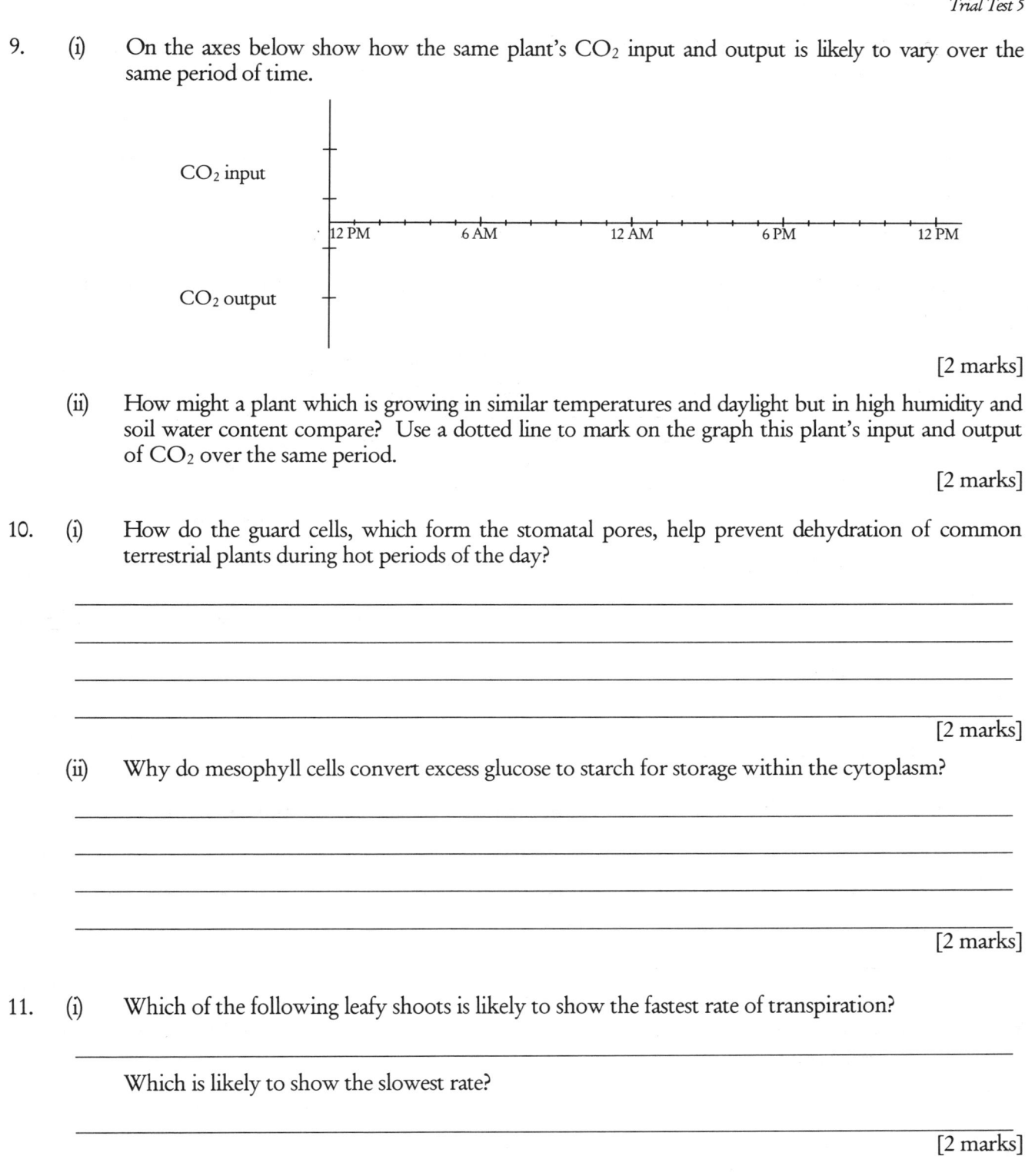

    CO₂ input

    12 PM   6 AM   12 AM   6 PM   12 PM

    CO₂ output

    [2 marks]

    (ii) How might a plant which is growing in similar temperatures and daylight but in high humidity and soil water content compare? Use a dotted line to mark on the graph this plant's input and output of CO_2 over the same period.

    [2 marks]

10. (i)   How do the guard cells, which form the stomatal pores, help prevent dehydration of common terrestrial plants during hot periods of the day?

    _____
    _____
    _____
    _____
    [2 marks]

    (ii) Why do mesophyll cells convert excess glucose to starch for storage within the cytoplasm?

    _____
    _____
    _____
    _____
    [2 marks]

11. (i)   Which of the following leafy shoots is likely to show the fastest rate of transpiration?

    _____

    Which is likely to show the slowest rate?

    _____
    [2 marks]

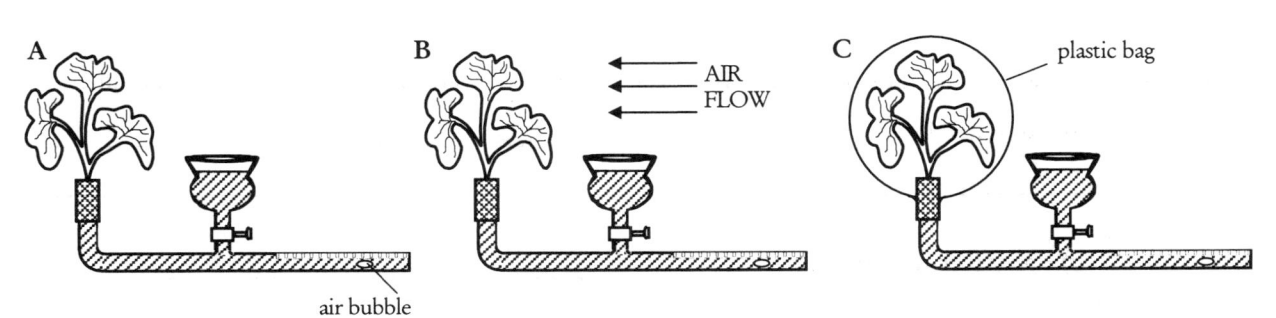

    A

    B — AIR FLOW

    C — plastic bag

    air bubble

11. (ii) What factors need to be controlled if valid comparisons between each experimental set up are to be made?

[2 marks]

The position of the air bubble in B was recorded over a period of 25 minutes from the time a fan was turned on near it and is shown in the table below.

Time (mins)	Air bubble's distance from original position (mm)
0	0
5	4
10	8
15	10
20	11
25	11

(iii) In which direction would the bubble have moved?

[1 mark]

(iv) Why does the bubble move?

[2 marks]

(v) Explain why the bubble movement begins to slow down then appears to stop at 20 minutes.

[3 marks]

12. (i) List three environmental conditions that may limit the soil water available to the roots of a terrestrial plant.

a)
b)
c)

[3 marks]

(ii) How does each of the following reduce the rate of water loss from a terrestrial plant?

a) small needle shaped leaves

[1 mark]

b) hairy (hirsute) leaves

[1 mark]

c) low number of stomata per square centimetre _____

_____
[1 mark]

d) shiny leaves _____

_____
[1 mark]

e) leaves which hang vertically _____

_____
[1 mark]

f) stomata which open only at night _____

_____
[1 mark]

g) leaves reduced to spines _____

_____
[1 mark]

13. How would each of the following experiments affect the subsequent growth of the plant shoots shown below? Complete the diagram to answer this question.

EXPERIMENT (AT THE START)	SUBSEQUENT GROWTH (AFTER 24 HOURS)	EXPLANATION
mica sheet inserted on light side of shoot, light from right		
mica sheet inserted below tip, light from right		
agar block below tip, light from right		
aluminium cap on tip, light from right		

[8 marks]

14. A plant growing normally in a pot is put on its side as shown below.

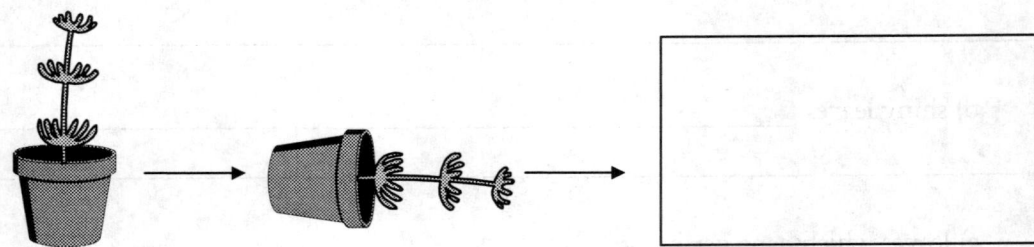

   (i) Draw a diagram in the box to show the likely responses that the plant will make (within days) to this change.

   [1 mark]

   (ii) It is believed that these responses are growth responses brought about by a change in the distribution of a hormone. Explain (using a diagram), how this hormone exerts its effects.

   _____
   _____
   _____
   _____

   [3 marks]

   (iii) In the above example, name -
   a) the stimulus; _____
   b) the effectors; _____
   c) the response. _____

   [3 marks]

   (iv) Is there an identifiable receptor in the above example? Explain.
   _____
   _____

   [2 marks]

15. A similar plant placed near a window for some days grows towards the window.

   (i) Discuss why this occurs.
   _____
   _____
   _____
   _____

   [3 marks]

   (ii) Of what advantage to the plant is this response?
   _____
   _____

   [2 marks]

(iii) How do hormones travel to their target in the plant?

_____

_____

[1 mark]

16. Freshwater amoeba have a contractile vacuole, an organelle to remove excess water. An experiment was carried out in which amoebae were placed in various salt concentrations and the average number of contractions per minute counted and tabulated.

Salt Conc. (%)	Average number of contractions per minute
0	6
0.1	4.5
0.2	4.1
0.3	4.0
0.4	3.8
0.5	3.7

(i) How does water enter the body of an amoeba?

_____

_____

[2 marks]

(ii) Draw a graph to show the effect of salt concentration on the activity of the contractile vacuoles.

[4 marks]

(iii) In this situation name the -

    a) stimulus _____

    b) response _____

[2 marks]

(iv) Does this example illustrate a negative feedback system? Explain.

_____

_____

[2 marks]

(v) In this experiment, name

    a) the independent variable _____

    b) the dependent variable _____

[2 marks]

(vi) Do you think that this species of amoeba would survive in salt water of higher concentrations than 0.5%? Explain.

_____

_____

_____

[2 marks]

TOTAL 120 MARKS

TRIAL TEST 6 – MODULE 3

The Species – Part 1
- Time allowed: 90 minutes
- Total marks: 90

1. (i) Monozygotic twins (or identical twins) are very similar. Explain why.

    _____

    _____

    _____
    [2 marks]

   (ii) In what respects (list two) are monozygotic twins likely to be significantly different, if they are separated at birth and brought up in very different families? Explain.

    _____

    _____

    _____
    [3 marks]

2. (i) What is a gene?

    _____

    _____
    [2 marks]

   (ii) What is the function of a gene?

    _____

    _____
    [2 marks]

   (iii) How is a genetic code translated into the synthesis of a protein?

    _____

    _____

    _____

    _____

    _____
    [4 marks]

3. (i) What is meant in describing two genes as **linked**?

    _____
    [1 mark]

   (ii) Are many genes in for example a dog, *Canis familiaris*, (a diploid number of 78), likely to be linked? Explain.

    _____

    _____
    [2 marks]

4. The diagram below shows the chromosomes of a grasshopper during the prophase of mitosis. Each chromosome has been numbered to its lower right hand side.

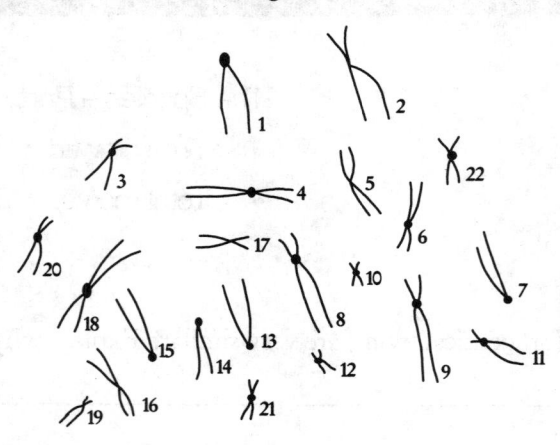

(i) What is the a) diploid number for this species; _____
[1 mark]

b) haploid number for this species? _____
[1 mark]

(ii) How many homologous pairs are evident in the diagram? _____
[1 mark]

(iii) Which chromosome is homologous to chromosome number 8 _____
and which is homologous to number 12? _____
[2 marks]

(iv) What is the origin of each homologous pair of chromosomes?
_____
_____
_____
[2 marks]

(v) Why does each chromosome, at this stage of mitosis (ie. prophase), appear as two "strands"?
_____
_____
_____
[1 mark]

(vi) What is the point of attachment of these "strands" called? _____
[1 mark]

5. (i) Albinism in humans is a recessive trait. What function would its allele have?
_____
_____
[1 mark]

(ii) Where would its allele be located?
_____
_____
[2 marks]

6. (i)   When would the genotypes of both parent and offspring be identical?
    _____
    [1 mark]

    (ii) When are the genotypes of both parents and offspring different? Explain.
    _____
    _____
    [3 marks]

7. The highly simplified diagram below illustrates a cell undergoing **meiosis**.

    (i)   When is each chromosome copied to become a double-stranded chromosome?
    _____
    [1 mark]

    (ii) When do the chromosomes pair?
    _____
    [1 mark]

    (iii) How many chromosomes does this parent cell contain? _____
    [1 mark]

    (iv) How many chromosomes does each gamete contain? _____
    [1 mark]

    (v)   How many types of gametes are possible in this "organism"? _____
    [1 mark]

    (vi) If the parent cell had a diploid number of six, how many different gametes could it produce?
    _____
    [1 mark]

    (vii) If the parent's diploid number was eight, how many different gametes could it produce?
    _____
    [1 mark]

    (viii) At which stages would the spindles attach to the centromeres in the division shown above?
    _____
    [1 mark]

(ix) Why is the diploid number halved during meiosis in this organism?

_____
_____
_____
[2 marks]

(x) Where does this type of cell division occur?

_____
[1 mark]

8. (i) Asexually reproducing organisms are less likely to adapt to changing environments than sexually reproducing organisms. Why?

_____
_____
_____
_____
[2 marks]

(ii) Explain how each of the following contributes to variation in sexually reproducing organisms.

a) "Crossing Over" during meiosis.

_____
_____
_____
[2 marks]

b) Independent sorting of homologous chromosomes during a meiosis.

_____
_____
_____
[2 marks]

c) The random fusion of gametes.

_____
_____
_____
[2 marks]

9. Under what conditions is asexual reproduction likely to be more efficient than sexual reproduction?

_____
_____
_____
_____
[2 marks]

10. In the grasshopper species, *Melanoplus differentialis*, males have 23 chromosomes in each somatic cell, while females have 24. Describe how the sex of their offspring is determined.

_____
_____
_____
_____
_____
_____

[4 marks]

11. The pedigree below shows the incidence of a disease in rats which causes total baldness.

Key:
- ▨ bald male
- ☐ hairy male
- ◍ bald female
- ○ hairy female

(i) a) How is this disease inherited, ie. what is its mode of inheritance?

_____

[2 marks]

b) Explain how you arrived at your answer.

_____
_____
_____
_____

[4 marks]

(ii) Write down the possible genotypes of each individual in the pedigree. Use a key.

I 1_____   I 2_____

II 1_____   II 2_____   II 3_____   II 4_____   II 5_____

III 1_____   III 2_____   III 3_____

IV 1_____   IV 2_____   IV 3_____

V 1_____   V 2_____   V 3_____

[8 marks]

(iii) Which individuals are twins in this pedigree?

[2 marks]

(iv) Which twins are monozygotic and which are dizygotic? Explain.

[3 marks]

(v) Where did the genes which gave rise to rat V 2's baldness come from?

[1 mark]

12. A rare inherited form of human rickets is shown on the pedigree below.

This disease is unusual because it is caused by a gene carried on the X chromosome (sex linked).

(i) How is this defective gene different from the usual sex-linked defective gene?

[1 mark]

(ii) Which parent did individual II 2 inherit the defective gene from?

[1 mark]

(iii) Under each individual in the spaces provided write possible genotypes. (Use a key to indicate what your letters stand for.)

[5 marks]

(iv) Would you expect more males or more females to inherit this disease? Explain.

[2 marks]

13. A girl who breeds guinea pigs was unsure as to whether her normal coloured guinea pig was homozygous (NN) or heterozygous (Nn) for coat colour. Albino guinea pigs are homozygous recessive (nn). Which of the following crosses would give her the best information regarding her normal coloured guinea pig?

   (i)   Cross it with a homozygote for normal colour.

   (ii) Cross it with an albino.

   (iii) Cross it with a heterozygote for normal colour.

   Explain your answer.

   [5 marks]

   TOTAL 90 MARKS

TRIAL TEST 7 – MODULE 3

The Species – Part 2
- Time allowed: 60 minutes
- Total marks: 60

1. Explain what is meant by each of the following statements.

    (i) "Mutations arise spontaneously, they are undirected by the environment."

    _____
    _____
    _____
    [2 marks]

    (ii) "Mutations are relatively persistent."

    _____
    _____
    _____
    [2 marks]

    (iii) "Mutations, the vast majority, confer disadvantages on the organisms that inherit them."

    _____
    _____
    [2 marks]

2. (i) What kind of mutations are likely to be most important in evolution? Explain.

    _____
    [2 marks]

    (ii) What happens to unfavourable mutations?

    _____
    _____
    [2 marks]

3. (i) In the peppered moth population in England, which came first, the gene controlling dark colour or the darkening of the environment through pollution? Explain.

    _____
    _____
    _____
    _____
    [2 marks]

(ii) How did the Industrial Revolution affect gene frequencies in the peppered moth population?

[2 marks]

4. How does the majority of a population of bacteria become resistant to an antibiotic such as streptomycin? List the steps in sequence.

[3 marks]

5. Sexual reproduction tends to create variation within a population. How does natural selection affect this variation? Illustrate your answer with an example.

[4 marks]

6. The mechanism of natural selection involves four basic steps. These can be summarised by completing the following -
    (i) Inherited variation exists due to _____

[2 marks]

(ii) A small proportion of offspring reaches sexual maturity. This high mortality rate is due to -

_____

_____
[1 mark]

(iii) Certain members of a species survive better in particular environments because -

_____

_____
[1 mark]

(iv) The characteristics of the whole population change to suit the environment because -

_____

_____
[1 mark]

7. (i) What kinds of forces or pressures might act upon the native frog populations of the SW of Western Australia? List two biotic and two abiotic forces.

_____

_____
[2 marks]

(ii) Give an example of how each of the forces you have mentioned above might affect the frequency of particular genes in the frog population.

_____

_____

_____

_____

_____

_____

_____

_____

_____
[4 marks]

(iii) How might any one of the forces you have described lead to the extinction of frog species in the SW?

_____

_____
[2 marks]

(iv) On what does the ability of any population to survive environmental changes depend?

_____

_____
[2 marks]

8. (i)   Rottnest was once part of the W.A. mainland. How has it become separated?

    _____
    _____
    [1 mark]

    (ii) Animals, like the quokka, which are genetically isolated from similar animals on the mainland may in time become a separate species. How?

    _____
    _____
    _____
    [2 marks]

    (iii) Removal of the barrier may result in three possible outcomes. What are they?

    a) _____
       _____

    b) _____
       _____

    c) _____
       _____
    [6 marks]

9. Scientists sometimes study the proteins possessed by isolated populations. How can these studies provide an index of genetic similarity?

    _____
    _____
    _____
    [2 marks]

10. A small disc containing an antibiotic is placed on a petri dish containing a bacterial culture as below. (Diagram A.)

    DIAGRAM A

    (bacterial colony, disc containing antibiotic, petri dish)

    Soon afterwards many colonies have been wiped out. (Diagram B.)

    DIAGRAM B

    However some remain. If these remaining colonies are cultured on new nutrient agar -

(i) How will the same antibiotic affect the new cultured bacteria?

_____
_____
[1 mark]

(ii) What is the significance of this to the control of pathogenic bacteria?

_____
_____
[1 mark]

11. How does each of the following support the theory of evolution?
    (i) The pentadactyl limb of most mammals.

    _____
    _____
    [1 mark]

    (ii) The finches of the Galapagos islands.

    _____
    _____
    [1 mark]

    (iii) The embryos of common vertebrates.

    _____
    _____
    [1 mark]

    (iv) The chemical structures of organisms generally.

    _____
    _____
    [1 mark]

    (v) The fossil record.

    _____
    _____
    [1 mark]

12. (i) The black cockatoos of the SW of WA have a particular requirement for reproduction. They need large holes in tree trunks. These holes occur when a large branch falls off a tree and may take many years to form. How might the removal of old trees from the jarrah forest, affect the black cockatoo population of the SW?

    _____
    _____
    [2 marks]

    (ii) What conservation strategies could be used to reduce this selection pressure which could cause these species to become extinct?

    _____
    _____
    [1 mark]

TOTAL 60 MARKS

TRIAL TEST 8 – MODULE 4

Ecosystems – Part 1
- Time allowed: 60 minutes
- Total marks: 60

1. (i) Define the term "ECOSYSTEM".

   _____

   _____
   [2 marks]

   (ii) What is meant by referring to an ecosystem as "stable"?

   _____

   _____
   [2 marks]

2. (i) By writing a single word in each of the three boxes complete the diagram which shows the energy and matter movements in an ecosystem.

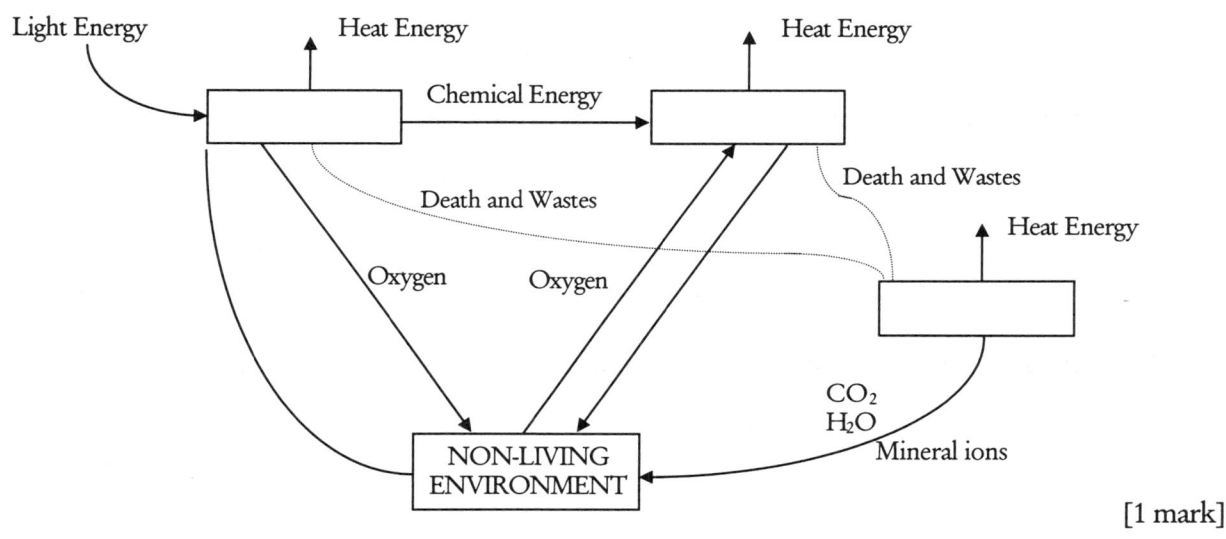

   [1 mark]

   (ii) Where does the heat energy go?

   _____
   [1 mark]

   (iii) Is energy recycled in the ecosystem? Explain.

   _____
   [1 mark]

   (iv) From where do the decomposers obtain their energy and in what form is this energy?

   _____
   [1 mark]

   (v) What is taken up by producers from their non-living environment?

   _____
   [2 marks]

(vi) What is returned to the non-living environment by both animals and plants?
_____
_____
[2 marks]

(vii) How are decomposers different from other consumers?
_____
_____
[1 mark]

3. (i) If only ten percent of the energy absorbed at each level is passed on to a successive trophic level, how many units of energy are available to the lizards in the following food chain?
_____
[1 mark]

100 Energy Units Absorbed (sunlight) → Eucalypts → saw fly larvae → ants → lizards

(ii) If the Eucalypts are eaten by several other first order consumers as shown below.

100 Energy Units Absorbed (sunlight) → Eucalypts → saw fly larvae → ants → lizards
Eucalypts → possums (3), moths (3), wasp larvae (1) Energy units

How much energy is available to the lizards in this case? _____
[1 mark]

(iii) Which of the above is closest to what might exist in nature? Explain.
_____
_____
[2 marks]

(iv) Is it likely that the lizards will have the amount of energy predicted in (ii)? Explain.
_____
_____
[3 marks]

4. What is meant by -
(i) "biomass"
_____
_____
[2 marks]

(ii) "productivity".
_____
_____
[2 marks]

5. (i) Describe the method by which the productivity of the plants in one ecosystem can be compared to those of another?

[6 marks]

(ii) Describe how you might determine what percentage of energy is transferred from one trophic level to the next highest trophic level in the simple food chain below.

grass ⟶ grasshoppers ⟶ birds

[4 marks]

6. Suppose that in two equal sized fields of 4 hectares a farmer's yield of wheat was 100 kg and 120 kg in one year.
(i) List what factors might account for the difference?

[2 marks]

(ii) How might he raise the productivity of his poorer yielding field?

[1 mark]

(iii) What is the productivity of each field, measured in g per m² per week?

[6 marks]

7. The table below shows the mean net primary productivity for a number of different ecosystems.

	Productivity (g/m²/yr)
Tropical rain forest	2200
Temperate evergreen forest	1300
Woodland	700
Desert and semidesert scrub	90
Cultivated land	650

(i) Why is the productivity of a tropical rain forest greater than that of a temperate evergreen forest?

_____

_____

[2 marks]

(ii) By how much on average is the productivity of a tropical rain forest greater than that of desert scrub?

_____

_____

[1 mark]

(iii) What effect is the difference in (ii) likely to have on the biomass of first order consumers in each ecosystem type?

_____

_____

[2 marks]

(iv) If the productivity of a tropical rain forest is so high, how would its absorption of CO_2 compare with that of other ecosystems?

_____

_____

[2 marks]

(v) The biomass of the tropical rain forests of the world represent about 41% of the earth's biomass. However the area occupied by tropical rain forest is 3% of the earth's total area. How is this reflected in the density of the biomass in tropical rain forests?

_____

_____

[2 marks]

8. Study the diagram of the Nitrogen Cycle below before answering the questions which follow it.

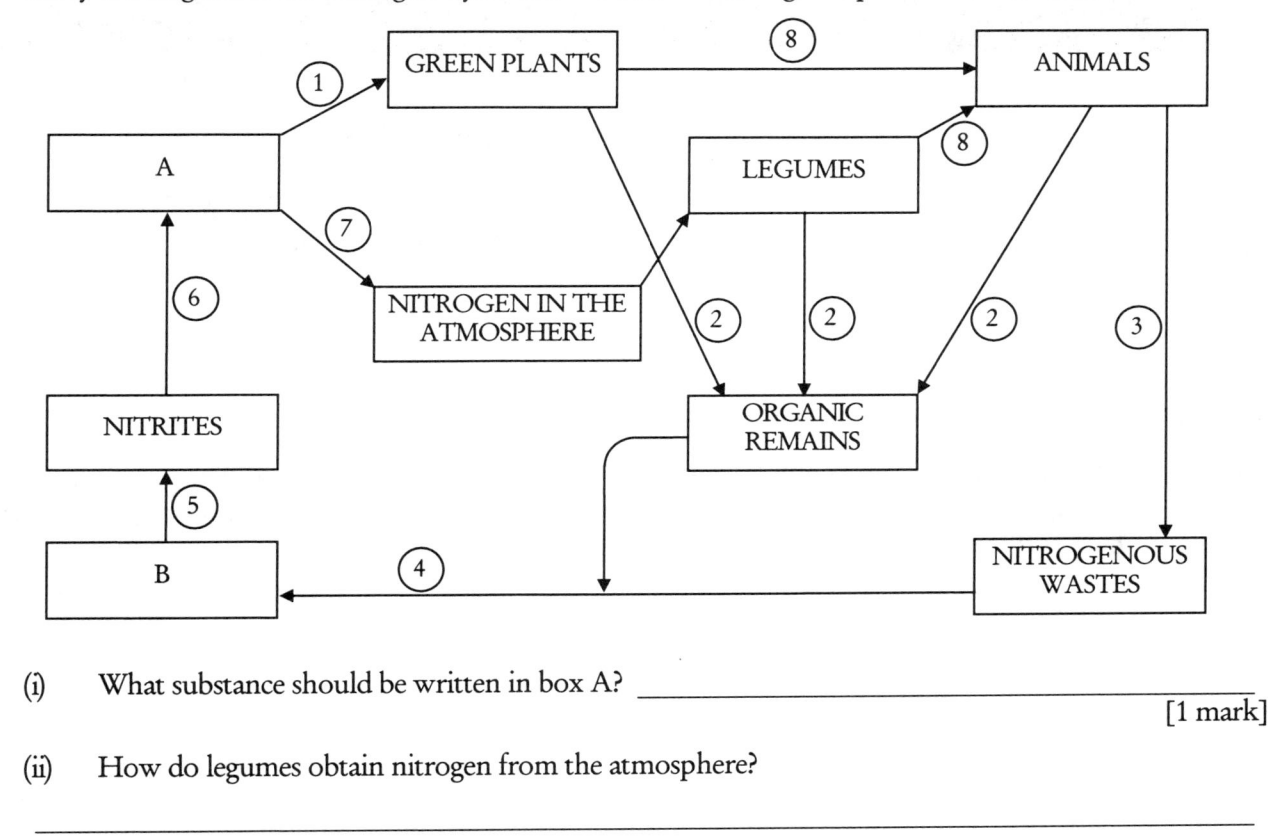

```
                        ⑧
    ┌─────────┐  GREEN PLANTS ──────────→ ANIMALS
    │    A    │ ① ↗                    ⑧ ↗   │
    └─────────┘                 LEGUMES       │
         ↑ ⑥    ⑦ ↘           ↗              │
         │      NITROGEN IN THE  ② ② ②       ③
    NITRITES    ATMOSPHERE                    │
         ↑ ⑤                  ↓              ↓
    ┌─────────┐           ORGANIC       NITROGENOUS
    │    B    │ ←──④──    REMAINS  ←──   WASTES
    └─────────┘
```

(i) What substance should be written in box A? _____ [1 mark]

(ii) How do legumes obtain nitrogen from the atmosphere?

_____

_____ [1 mark]

(iii) What gas should be written in box B? _____ [1 mark]

(iv) If each of the numbered arrows represents a process, write down what that process is.

1. _____   5. _____
2. _____   6. _____
3. _____   7. _____
4. _____   8. _____

[4 marks]

TOTAL 60 MARKS

TRIAL TEST 9 – MODULE 4

Ecosystems – Part 2
- Time allowed: 100 minutes
- Total marks: 100

1. (i) Draw the food web described below:

    "Spinifex and mulga are eaten by beetles. The beetles are in turn eaten by spiders, lizards and assassin bugs. Lizards are eaten by goannas and dunnarts. Dunnarts also eat beetles and assassin bugs and are themselves eaten by goannas."

    [5 marks]

   (ii) Name two producers in this food web.
   _____
   [1 mark]

   (iii) Name a first order consumer. _____
   [1 mark]

   (iv) Name two second order consumers.
   _____
   [1 mark]

   (v) Which animal is the highest order consumer? _____
   [1 mark]

   (vi) If goats entered this food web and ate a large proportion of the mulga, describe how this might affect the other organisms.
   _____
   _____
   _____
   [2 marks]

(vii) If an introduced pest, the cane toad, removed the beetles from the food web, how might this affect other organisms?

_____

_____

[2 marks]

2. (i) If in the food web described in question 1 the feral goats were to remove most of the vegetation, how might this affect the **non-living** environment?

_____

_____

[2 marks]

(ii) What effect might this have on the ecosystem in the long term?

_____

_____

[2 marks]

(iii) If the cane toad eliminates the beetles from this ecosystem but continues to feed on other insects, what effect might this have on plants in the ecosystem?

_____

_____

_____

[2 marks]

3. (i) It has been shown that crops grown with fertilisers have a much greater productivity than those grown without them. Explain why.

_____

_____

[2 marks]

(ii) The harvesting of jarrah trees removes nutrients from the jarrah forest. Why?

_____

_____

[2 marks]

(iii) Why will the productivity of the forest gradually decline unless nutrients are returned to the forest?

_____

_____

[2 marks]

4. Complete the table below to compare Natural, Agricultural and Urban Ecosystems.

CHARACTERISTIC	ECOSYSTEM		
	NATURAL	AGRICULTURAL	URBAN
Matter recycling	most matter recycled		
Energy use		respiration slow heat release photosynthesis	
Energy input			fossil fuels, chemical energy (food)
Stability		unstable - single crop dominates	
Biodiversity	great, many different species		

[5 marks]

5. (i) Why are agricultural ecosystems less **stable** than natural ecosystems?

_____
_____

[2 marks]

(ii) Why is there little recycling of matter in urban ecosystems?

_____
_____

[2 marks]

(iii) Name the two types of organisms which are most involved in recycling matter.

_____

[1 mark]

(iv) Explain why an agricultural ecosystem must have a large input of matter.

_____

[1 mark]

(v) Where does the heat energy, which is released from each ecosystem, go to?

_____
_____

[1 mark]

6. Describe how each of the following factors may affect human population growth. Give an example in each case.
(i) food

_____
_____
_____

(ii) space

(iii) waste products

(iv) climate

(v) natural disasters

(vi) other organisms

[12 marks]

7. What impact does the increasing urban population of Perth have on:
   (i) the surrounding bush ecosystems;

   [2 marks]

   (ii) Swan/Canning river ecosystems;

   [2 marks]

   (iii) the nearby marine ecosystem.

   [2 marks]

8. Which gases are the main contributors to -
   (i) the Greenhouse Effect;
   _____
   [1 mark]

   (ii) the Ozone layer depletion?
   _____
   [1 mark]

9. Name two processes which contribute towards each of the following:
   (i) accelerated Greenhouse Effect;
   _____
   _____

   (ii) ozone layer depletion;
   _____
   _____

   (iii) desertification.
   _____
   _____
   [6 marks]

10. (i) Name two native animals which have a greatly reduced distribution as a result of European settlement.
    _____
    [1 mark]

    (ii) Describe where their distribution has changed.
    _____
    _____
    [2 marks]

    (iii) Name two feral animals which have become widely dispersed in Australia.
    _____
    [1 mark]

    (iv) Describe these feral animals' present distribution.
    _____
    _____
    [2 marks]

    (v) How might populations of threatened native animals be secured so that they do not become extinct?
    _____
    _____
    _____
    [2 marks]

(vi) Give three methods by which feral animal populations might be reduced.

[3 marks]

(vii) Which of the above methods are biological?

[1 mark]

(viii) Name two introduced plant species which have become pests in Australia.

[1 mark]

(ix) Eliminating these plant pests by using herbicides has some benefits and some disadvantages.
   a) Describe two benefits.

[2 marks]

   b) Describe two disadvantages.

[2 marks]

(x) How might an introduced plant species be controlled using biological techniques? Discuss two such examples.

[3 marks]

11. (i) How does clearing land of trees affect the depth of the water table?

[1 mark]

(ii) Explain why this occurs.

[2 marks]

(iii) Why does this affect salt levels in the soil near the surface?

[1 mark]

(iv) How are water courses affected by this change?

[1 mark]

(v) Discuss two ways in which this problem might be reduced.

_____

_____

[2 marks]

(vi) What would be the likely consequence of ignoring the salt problem in Australia?

_____

_____

[1 mark]

(vii) How might people who live in urban areas help to reduce this problem?

_____

_____

[1 mark]

12. Swamps in and around the metropolitan area have often, in the past, been filled with household and industrial wastes. They were then covered with sand and used for building developments or playing fields.

(i) How does filling the swamps with waste, affect the ground water in the vicinity of the swamps?

_____

_____

[1 mark]

(ii) How does this "reclaiming" of swampland affect native swamp communities?

_____

_____

[2 marks]

(iii) What effects does this have on migrating and resident birds?

_____

_____

[2 marks]

(iv) What are three benefits of retaining the lakes and swamp that remain?

_____

_____

_____

[3 marks]

TOTAL 100 MARKS

SOLUTIONS - TRIAL TEST 1

1. (i) histology, botany, paleontology, cytology, zoology, ecology
   (ii) histology: the study of tissues and their arrangement in organs.
   botany: study of plants
   paleontology: study of fossil remains
   cytology: study of cells
   zoology: study of animals
   ecology: study of biotic and abiotic environments and the interactions between them

2. A **controlled** experiment is one in which **only** the variable which is being deliberately manipulated, ie. the independent variable, is changed. The effect of this change on the dependent variable is observed and recorded. Experiments are controlled for validity of conclusions.

3. (i) Observation: a statement about something that is sensed.
   (ii) Prediction: a guess about something which is likely to happen in the future.
   (iii) Inference: an explanation of an observation.
   (iv) Generalisation: a comment about a shared characteristic.
   (v) Hypothesis: a testable statement.
   (vi) Theory: there may be some evidence to support this idea but not enough to call it a law.

4. (i) The student could -
   - identify areas of the forest where Blackbutt are found and areas where they may be expected but are not present;
   - collect soil samples from both areas, making sure that they are randomly selected and are from a good range of matched depths;
   - the % of water in each sample can then be measured (by dehydrating each sample);
   - compare the % of water in soil from both areas.
   (ii) If correct, the results should show a greater % of water in soil samples taken from the area in which the Blackbutt trees were growing.
   (iii) If there was no difference in the % of water in the two areas **or** if the % soil water in areas where no Blackbutt were found was greater than in those areas where the trees were found.

5. (i) A variable is a factor which can change eg. wind speed, humidity.
   (ii) Data refers to information, either qualitative or quantitative, that is gained through observation or experiment.

6. (i) independent variable: temperature of wheat seeds
   dependent variable: rate of oxygen use
   (ii) light, moisture, seed type, seed age or seed size
   (iii) Title: Oxygen intake by 100 wheat seeds versus temperature.

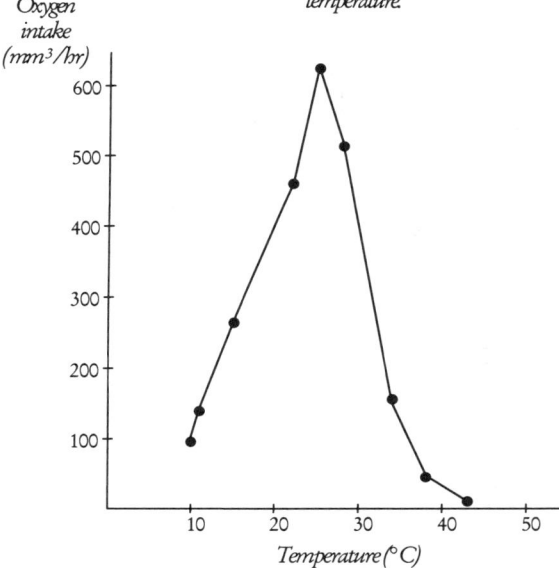

   (iv) Yes: the oxygen intake reached a maximum at about 25°C. At temperatures lower or higher than this, the rate of oxygen use declined rapidly.
   (v) The optimum temperature was about 25°C.
   (vi) The experiment could be made more reliable by:
   - increasing the range of temperatures used, particularly on either side of the optimum temperature (ie. include 23°C, 24°C, 26°C, 27°C);
   - increasing the number of wheat seeds in each sample;
   - repeat the experiment several times;
   - use different varieties of wheat seed.
   (vii) Germinating seeds take up oxygen at a rate which is dependent on temperature.

7. (i)

	HEIGHT RANGE IN TWO POPULATIONS (cm)				
Popn	60 - 89	90 - 119	120 - 149	150 - 179	180 - 209
1	1111 (4)	111 (3)	1111 1111 1111 111 (18)	1111 1111 1111 1111 (19)	1111 1 (6)
2			1111 1111 1111 11 (17)	1111 1111 1111 1111 1111 (24)	1111 1111 1111 1111 (9)

(Note: The choice of ranges is up to the student. They could be narrower. However the data given fits these ranges reasonably well.)

7. (ii) (Since the data is not continuous, the best choice of graph is a bar graph or histogram.)

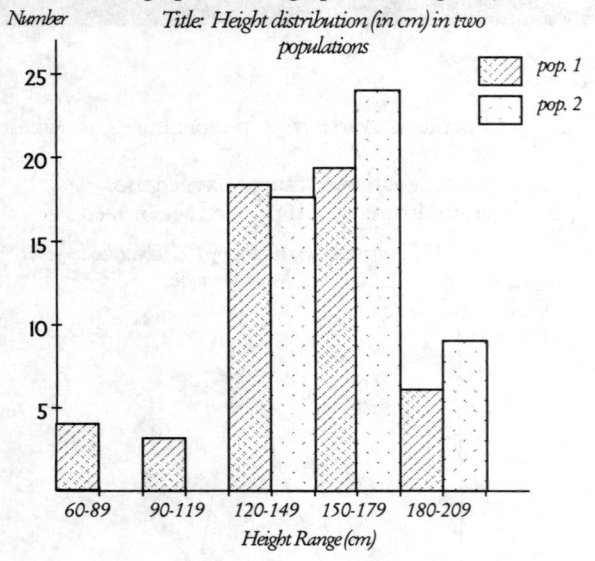

Title: *Height distribution (in cm) in two populations*

[Bar graph showing Number vs Height Range (cm) with bars for pop. 1 (hatched) and pop. 2 (dotted) across ranges 60-89, 90-119, 120-149, 150-179, 180-209]

[Marking guide: Deduct -
1 mark for missing title;
1 mark for each missing axis label;
1 mark for each incorrect height of column (max. −5);
1 mark for any untidy lines.
Total loss cannot exceed 5 marks.]

8. (i) 10,000 µm, 1 cm
   (ii) 2,500/10,000 ha = 0.25 ha
   (iii) 5,000 kg
   (iv) 7×10^6 J

9.

Quantity	Unit	Symbol
length	kilometre	km
	metre	m
	centimetre	cm
	millimetre	mm
	micrometre	µm
area	hectare	ha
volume	cubic metre	m³
volume (liquid)	litre	L
	millilitre	mL
mass	tonne	t
	kilogram	kg
	gram	g
	milligram	mg
time	second	s
temperature	degree Celsius	°C
energy	megajoule	MJ
	kilojoule	kJ
	joule	J

SOLUTIONS - TRIAL TEST 2

1. Prokaryotic cells have **no** membrane bounded organelles, eg. no nuclear membrane. Eukaryotic cells do have membrane bounded organelles, eg. nucleus, mitochondria, chloroplasts.

2. (i) The cell shrivels.
    Explanation: water will leave the cell by osmosis. Some salt will enter the cell. But the net water movement will be greater, therefore the cell will shrivel.
   (ii) The cell will appear to enlarge slightly, its walls will bulge outwards and its large vacuole will expand.
    Explanation: water will enter the cell by osmosis and move into the vacuole. The pressure of the water inside the cell will force the cell membrane out and push out on the cell wall.
   (iii) The plant cell will become distended, the cell wall will bulge out. The animal cell is likely to distend to the point of bursting, because it has no cell wall to prevent this. It may lyse.
   (iv) The cell wall in plants prevents plant cells from lysing.

3.

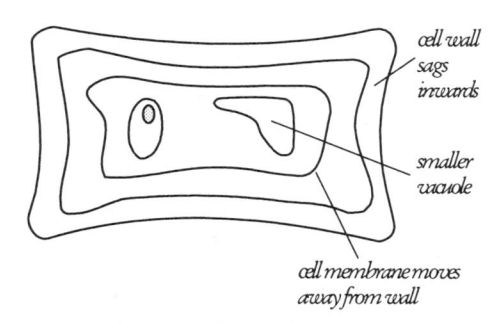

   The cell is losing water rapidly. Water is lost from both the cytoplasm and the large vacuole. The cell membrane shrinks away from the cell wall. The pressure (hydrostatic) inside the cell becomes smaller. Therefore the cell wall sags inwards. The cell loses its turgidity.

4. (i) The SA : Vol ratio becomes smaller (both the s.a. and vol increase, but the s.a. increases less than the volume).
   (ii)

   1 cm cube: SA = 6 cm², Vol = 1 cm³, SA : Vol = 6 : 1 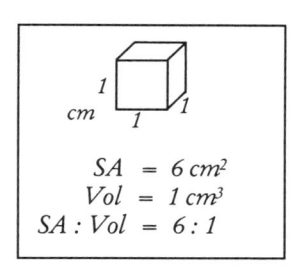

   2 cm cube: SA = 24 cm², Vol = 8 cm³, SA : Vol = 24 : 8 = 3 : 1 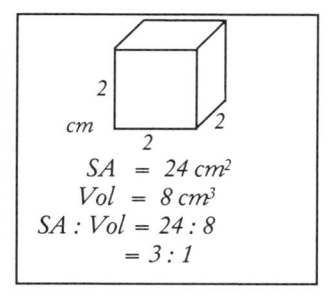

   (iii) Provided its shape remains the same, as it becomes larger its efficiency decreases. A larger body results in a smaller s.a. : vol ratio. Oxygen and food will diffuse more slowly to the centre of the cell. Wastes will diffuse more slowly from the cell. Its survival will therefore become less likely.

5. See page 161.

6. (i) It is referred to as a 'model' because it is a theoretical picture of what the membrane **might** look like (since it is only just visible with an electron microscope). A 'model' allows predictions to be made and tested.
   (ii) "A" does not penetrate right through the two lipid layers. It is 'floating' on the outer lipid layer. "B" penetrates right through the two lipid layers.
   (iii) Part "D" is referred to as the hydrophilic region of the lipid molecule. It is attracted to water (water is a major component of the extra-cellular fluid and the intra-cellular fluid).
   Part "E" is referred to as the hydrophobic region of the lipid molecule. It is repelled by water (both in the extra- and intra- cellular fluids).

7. The nucleus is essential for the repair of damaged parts of the cell because it controls protein synthesis. As the r.b.c. has no nucleus it is unable to repair any damaged parts (including the cell membrane). Therefore it does not live long.

8. (i) a) 4 mm or 4000 μm (± 0.1 mm, ie. answers in the region 3.9 - 4.1 mm accepted)
      b) $4 \times \frac{40}{100}$ = 1.6 mm or 1600 μm (± 0.1 mm)
   (ii) a) $\frac{1}{2} \times 1.6$ mm = 0.8 mm or 800 μm (± 0.05 mm)
      b) $\frac{5}{32} \times 1.6$ mm = 0.25 mm or 250 μm (± 0.05 mm)
   (iii) no. of cells = $\frac{4000}{250}$ = 16 (± 1)

9. (i) oxygen (produced during photosynthesis)
   (ii) bacteria move towards the oxygen (chemotaxis)
   (iii) they may have flagella to propel them through the water
   (iv) close to the surface where the oxygen concentration is greatest or near photosynthetic algae

10. (i) Amoebic movement: the organism 'grows' outwards in the direction of movement by pushing its cytoplasm forward. eg. amoeba, some white blood cells.
   (ii) Cilia (singular: cilium): short hair-like structures which beat rhythmically to move the cell. eg. paramecium.
   (iii) Flagella (singular: flagellum): long thin projections from the cell, used like a whip to propel organism forward. eg. protozoa - flagellates, some algae.

11. ① Set up cultures of the amoeba of equal size and population density at various temperatures, ranging from well below 28°C to well above 28°C. eg. 10°C, 15°C, 20°C, 25°C, 28°C, 30°C, 35°C, 40°C.
   ② Maintain the same conditions within each culture (except for the temperature) to replicate their normal aquatic environment (eg. similar oxygen levels, nutrients, pH, and plant species).
   ③ Periodically take water samples from each culture and count the numbers of amoeba present in each sample.
   (The hypothesis would be supported if the number in the culture at 28°C was consistently higher than in the other cultures.)

12. (i) Starch granules, because starch turns iodine blue-black.
   (ii) The cell wall will turn blue-black as this is a test for cellulose and the cell wall contains cellulose.

13. (i) Place a drop of Benedict's solution on one edge of the cover slip as shown below.

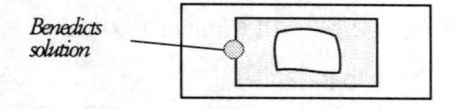

   Benedict's solution

   Then place absorbent paper on the other side (see diagram below), to draw fluid through the tissue. The Benedict's solution will move through the tissue also.

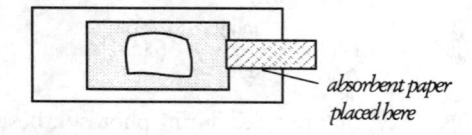

   absorbent paper placed here

   (Note: diagrams are not essential to your answer, but they would make the answer easier for you to do.)
   (ii) Warm the slide **gently** over a burner flame.
   (iii) The Benedict's solution will turn from a blue to an orange colour (or green if there is only a little glucose present).

14. (i) The cells are likely to lose some of their pigment to the surrounding alcohol solution.
   explanation: alcohol dissolves lipids, it therefore dissolves the cell membranes allowing the pigment to diffuse from the cell into the surrounding liquid.

14. (ii) Again pigment is lost to surrounding detergent solution.
   explanation: detergent emulsifies lipids (ie. it breaks lipids into small droplets forming a suspension). The membrane is partly emulsified. The pigment then diffuses from the cell.
   (iii) The cells will soften, losing their turgidity, they become flaccid. Colour will appear to darken in some areas.
   explanation: water will leave the cytoplasm by osmosis. The cell membrane will move away from the cell wall. The coloured pigment will therefore move to occupy a smaller area within the cell.

15. (i) The bacterium gives off some chemicals, antigens, which are 'detected' by the cell membrane of the white blood cell.
   (ii) In response a small 'growth' appears from the cell, an extension of its cytoplasm called a pseudopod.
   (iii) The pseudopod grows around and encloses the bacterium.
   (iv) The bacterium is enclosed within part of the cell membrane which forms a vacuole around the bacterium.
   (v) A lysosome containing digestive enzymes approaches the vacuole and touches it.
   (vi) The lysosome empties its contents (enzymes) into the vacuole containing the bacterium.
   (vii) The bacterium is digested by the enzymes and the products move by diffusion into the cytoplasm of the white blood cell.

16. (i) Active transport, pinocytosis, phago-cytosis and exocytosis: - need energy.
   (ii) Diffusion occurs due to the kinetic energy of the particles. Their random movements result in the particles moving away from where they are in greatest concentration to where they are least concentrated. ie. down a concentration gradient. Osmosis is a special case of diffusion, where a solvent (usually water in living organisms) moves through a membrane from where there is proportionally more solvent to where there is less solvent (ie. usually from areas of lower salt concentration to areas of higher salt concentration).

5.

Organelle Name	Structure	Functions	Diagram
plasma/cell membrane	Two layers of lipid with proteins floating in the layers.	Controls exchange between cell and its environment.	
chloroplast	Double membrane. Large plastid containing chlorophyll arranged on stacked sheets of membranes called lamellae.	Carries out photosynthesis producing sugar. May store starch.	
endoplasmic reticulum	Flattened, membrane-bounded sacs forming tubes and sheets. Continuous with outer membrane of nuclear envelope.	Transports proteins made by ribosomes. Smooth E.R. is site for lipid synthesis.	
Golgi body	A stack of flattened membrane-bounded disc shaped sacs. Vesicles bud off at edges.	Collecting and packaging centre for substances manufactured by the cell.	
mitochondrion	Rod shaped organelle. Double membrane. Inner membrane folded forming cristae.	Site for aerobic respiration. Production of ATP.	
centrioles	Small cylindrical bodies.	Forms a spindle during cell division (not found in higher plants).	
nucleus	Double membrane bounded large organelle containing DNA and RNA. Membrane has large pores.	Controls other organelles by controlling protein synthesis (contains hereditrary code).	

SOLUTIONS - TRIAL TEST 3

1. Each of the sixty four chromosomes replicates during the interphase. This results in a total of one hundred and twenty eight chromosomes. Each daughter cell receives one copy of each pair of chromosomes. Therefore each daughter cell receives sixty four chromosomes.

2. (i) Each nucleotide shown has a different nitrogenous base.

   (ii) [diagram of nucleotides]

   (iii) The genetic information is in the sequence of nucleotides.

   (iv) The information is stored in the number and order of the nucleotides. These form a code. The code is translated in the following way:

   a) A section of the molecule unzips along part of its length (a gene).
   b) Free nucleotides in the nucleoplasm move in to fit on to the exposed nitrogenous bases.
   c) These nucleotides join to form mRNA.
   d) The mRNA moves out of the nucleus through the nuclear pores and onto ribosomes in the cytoplasm.
   e) The mRNA forms a 'template' on the ribosomes. The ribosome "reads" its three bases at a time.
   f) Molecules of tRNA combine temporarily to specific amino acids in the cytoplasm and deliver each to matching parts of the mRNA. Each tRNA molecule will only fit on to a particular section of the mRNA.
   g) The order and number of amino acids which are assembled at the ribosome is therefore determined by the type of mRNA which is there. The type of mRNA is determined by the type of DNA which is in the nucleus. Therefore the DNA determines the type of proteins which are synthesised at the ribosomes.

3. (i) Cells in the interphase have a nucleus with a grainy like appearance. The DNA is not organised as chromosomes but exists as long thin molecules and is called chromatin. In the early prophase, the DNA coils into chromosomes which therefore become visible (with the aid of a light microscope).
   In the prophase the nuclear membrane begins to disappear and the centrioles replicate and move to opposite poles of the cell. In late prophase spindles form and attach to the centromere of each chromosome.

   (ii) Cells in the metaphase have their chromosomes arranged across the equator of the cell. In the anaphase the spindles appear to pull the centromere apart so that each chromatid is separated from its replicate and moves to opposite sides of the cell.

   (iii) Telophase in plant cells is characterised by the development of a cell 'plate' which becomes a common cell wall which separates the two daughter cells. Telophase in animals results in two daughter cells which form through cytoplasmic constriction.

4. Mitosis occurs because cells cannot work efficiently if they become too large (their SA : Vol ratio becomes too small for efficient uptake of food and oxygen). Therefore if an organism is to grow, its cells must divide (and increase in number).

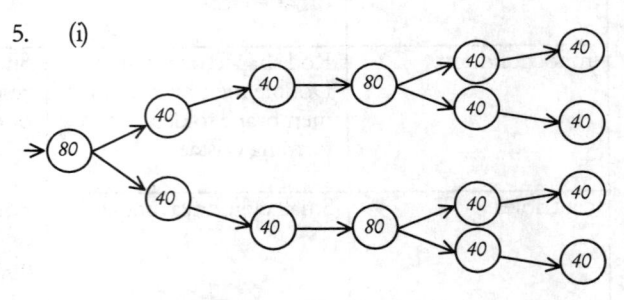

5. (i) [branching diagram showing 80 → 40, 40 → 40, 40, 80, 80 → 40, 40, 40, 40 → 40, 40, 40, 40, 40, 40, 40, 40]

   (ii) three in total
   (iii) 160
   (iv) The original DNA molecules have replicated before each cell division.

6. No. Each amoeba chromosome has a smaller length of DNA and much less genetic information on it than the cat's chromosome.

7. (i) Substance 5 would form but the final products of CO_2 and alcohol would not.

   (ii) The accumulation of alcohol is likely to inhibit the action of the enzymes, resulting in less glucose being broken down.

   (iii) Carbon dioxide dissolves to form a weak acid (carbonic acid). This will lower the pH of the cytoplasm and inhibit the enzyme activity. Less glucose will be respired.

   (iv) The heat will denature the enzymes and the breakdown of glucose will cease.

   (v) Enzymes fit on to their substrates because they have an appropriate shape. Part of their three dimensional shape is called an 'active site' or 'catalytic site'. This is where the substrate locks on to the enzyme. Heat can change the overall shape of an enzyme, and when it is extreme heat, the change is permanent. The enzymes are 'denatured' and no longer fit with the substrate.

   (vi) The breakdown releases energy. This energy is stored as chemical energy in ATP which can be used where and when it is needed by the cell.

7. (vii) With oxygen the glucose would be broken down completely to carbon dioxide and water. No alcohol would be formed, but more carbon dioxide.
   (viii) The energy yield with oxygen (aerobic) will be up to 19 times as much as without oxygen. One molecule of glucose respired aerobically will produce up to thirty eight (38) molecules of ATP, whereas one molecule of glucose respired anaerobically will produce only two (2) ATP molecules.
   (ix) a) Respiration.
        b) Aerobic and anaerobic respiration.
   (x) Anaerobic respiration occurs in the cytoplasm.
   (xi)

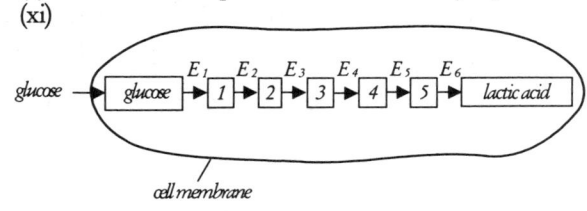

   glucose → [glucose → E_1 1 → E_2 2 → E_3 3 → E_4 4 → E_5 5 → E_6 lactic acid]
   cell membrane

   (Note: some of the enzymes involved would be different from those of the plant cell.)
   (xii) The accumulation of lactic acid would lower the pH inhibiting enzyme action in the cell.

8. (i) The calcium ions may be absorbed by active transport. Carrier molecules in the membrane will 'push' calcium into the cell, a process which requires energy.
   (ii) ATP (adenosine triphosphate)
   (iii) ATP → ADP + P + ENERGY

   adenosine triphosphate → adenosine diphosphate + inorganic phosphate + energy
   (iv) movement (of whole cell), cell division and synthesis of proteins.

9. (i) a) Place destarched leaf in light.
       b) Remove chlorophyll from leaf using warm alcohol.
       c) Flood whole leaf with iodine. (Only the area which had chlorophyll should show blue-black areas due to starch.)

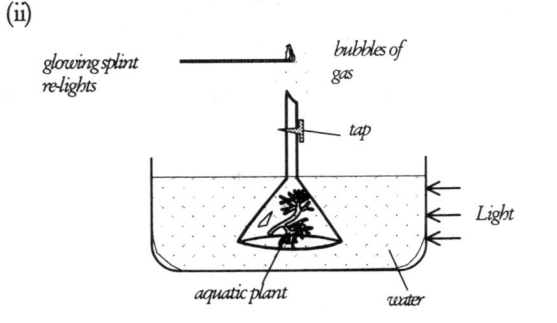

   (ii)
   a) Place an inverted filter funnel over the plant.
   b) Expose the aquatic plant to light.

9. (ii) c) Collect the gas which bubbles from the plant.
        d) Test this gas with a glowing splint. (The gas should re-light a glowing splint, as it is oxygen which is produced during photosynthesis.)

10. Those painted on the upper surface would show the most positive reaction with iodine, ie. they contain most starch.
    Explanation: Carbon dioxide enters the leaf through its stomates. Most stomates are on the underside of the leaf (in most plants). If these are blocked less carbon dioxide enters the plant, less starch is synthesised.

11. (i) Not all the chemical energy released by the glucose which is broken down in respiration is transferred to the ATP molecules. As much as 50% is lost as heat.
    (ii) Aerobic respiration, as aerobic respiration involves more energy transformations and produces more energy. Therefore more energy is lost.
    (iii) Place the organism in water in a vacuum flask. Provide sufficient nutrient for growth, a suitable temperature and glucose. Measure the temperature periodically over the following twenty four hours. Test for the presence of glucose at the end of this period.
    Repeat the experiment without the glucose.

12. (i) Its accumulation as glucose increases the osmotic pressure within the cell. The glucose is therefore converted to starch which is far less soluble and therefore does not cause the increase in osmotic pressure.
    (ii) Sucrose (a disaccharide is often formed). This is the form in which the sugar moves in the phloem.
    (iii) Proteins, nucleic acid, lipids.

SOLUTIONS - TRIAL TEST 4

1. (i) organic compounds are needed for -
   a) growth and repair e.g. proteins
   b) energy e.g. carbohydrates and fats
   c) as co-enzymes e.g. vitamin B
   d) as co-factors e.g. vitamin C
   (ii) Oxygen: essential for aerobic respiration, heterotrophs (unlike autotrophs) cannot make oxygen but rely on oxygen from their surroundings.
   (iii) Water: medium in which all the metabolic processes in cells occurs. The amount of water present determines the concentration of both reactants and products.
   (iv) Mineral ions: required as co-factors in enzyme controlled reactions e.g. calcium. Also as constituents in the synthesis of organic compounds, e.g. iron needed in haemoglobin. Minerals are needed in bone e.g. calcium, phosphorus. For nerve impulses egs. sodium, potassium.

2. (i) Carbon dioxide: necessary reactant for photosynthesis. The carbon is used in the synthesis of all the organic compounds derived from the glucose produced.
   (ii) Water: also necessary for photosynthesis. It is split such that the oxygen is released while the hydrogen ions produced take part in synthesising the glucose. Water is also a medium for all the metabolism which occurs in the cell's cytoplasm and nucleoplasm.
   (iii) Light energy: required as a source of energy for the chemical bonds which must be formed in photosynthesis and the subsequent synthesis of other compounds. Light energy is converted into chemical energy.
   (iv) Mineral ions: needed for the synthesis of many organic chemicals, e.g. chlorophyll contains magnesium, proteins contain nitrogen (from nitrates). Also used as co-factors e.g. calcium.

3. (i) Most vertebrates generally breathe more rapidly and more deeply. Fish will force more water over their gills. These activities eliminate CO_2 from their bodies.
   (ii) This may cause a decrease in activity, as less energy becomes available from respiration. If stored glucose is available (e.g. glycogen) it will be converted to glucose (in the liver and muscles) and released into the blood stream. Other sources of energy will be utilised e.g. fats.
   (iii) Nitrogenous wastes are poisonous, therefore the organism will excrete more wastes e.g. urea and/or uric acid.
   (iv) Mammals and birds will tend to **increase heat production** (e.g. increased levels of thyroxine from the thyroid glands causes an increased level of metabolism) and **reduce heat loss** by vasoconstriction of surface blood vessels and hair/feather erection. Many vertebrates will seek a warmer part of their environment - that is use behaviour to reduce heat loss.

3. (v) A fall in osmotic pressure, may be due to either an increased level of water concentration in the blood or a loss of dissolved solutes e.g. minerals. The organism may excrete more dilute urine thus reducing the water concentration and/or reabsorb more solutes from the kidney filtrate in order to increase solute concentration in the blood plasma.

4. (i) If CO_2 accumulated in the vertebrates body it would decrease the pH of the blood plasma and the cells' cytoplasms. Intracellular and extracellular enzyme activity would decrease. Cells may begin to die.
   (ii) If the fall in glucose continued unchecked cells would begin to stop respiring and they would die.
   (iii) Nitrogenous wastes such as ammonia, urea and uric acid are toxic. Their high concentration is harmful to cells. If they are not removed the animal will become sick and eventually die.
   (iv) Enzyme activity is sensitive to temperature. If the temperature continues to fall, enzymes will cease to function. The body's metabolism will slow down and eventually stop.
   (v) If the level of water in the blood plasma continued to rise, too much water would begin to enter the body cells by osmosis. Because of the dilution factor, chemical reactions, both anabolic and catabolic would slow down. The cells themselves may begin to lyse. The animal may die.

5. (i) Oxygen is not highly soluble. Therefore not all of the oxygen produced by photosynthesis during the day stays in the water. At night the algae need oxygen from the water to continue to respire. All the available oxygen will be used up and little will be available for other organisms and the algae itself.
   (ii) Aquatic animals which share this water will suffer a shortage of oxygen, particularly at night and in warm weather (when oxygen solubility is lowest). Many are likely to die through oxygen starvation.

6. (i) Fish cells are rich in protein. Therefore a diet consisting of fish alone would result in a high production of nitrogenous waste (in humans this would be urea). The excretion of urea requires the loss of water. Therefore any water consumed would be lost in voiding the urea. The human would therefore dehydrate.
   (ii) Protein intake would be restricted because of the necessity to excrete too much urea and therefore too much water. Such an environment may therefore support herbivorous mammals but few carnivorous mammals.

7. (i) Ammonia is very soluble. Its toxicity is reduced by dissolving it in copious quantities of water. The loss of water (especially in fresh water animals) is not a problem for many aquatic animals. Also the formation of ammonia as a nitrogenous waste requires less energy than other nitrogenous wastes.
    (ii) Fresh water fishes lose large quantities of dilute urine via their kidneys. Marine fishes lose small quantities of urine via their kidneys. The latter also actively excrete salts from special gill cells.
    (iii) During the tadpole stage in fresh water, water loss is not a problem, ammonia is the preferred nitrogenous waste. When the frog leaves the water at least for part of its life, urea which requires less water is the preferred waste.
    (iv) Uric acid.
    a) Its excretion does not require much water.
    b) Less water requirement results in less weight to be carried by the animal. This is particularly important for birds.
    (v) While it has the disadvantage of requiring more water to excrete, it requires less energy to synthesise than uric acid.
    (vi) Urea is very soluble in water and less toxic to body cells when diluted.
    (vii) a) Mammals are generally restricted to areas where water is readily available all year round, unless they have special adaptations like those of the Australian Hopping Mouse (*Notomys alexis*).
    b) Mammals which live in arid climates must have special means to conserve water and obtain whatever water is available. These adaptations include -
    - nocturnal behaviour
    - storing dry seeds in burrows which absorb moisture before being consumed
    - reduced water loss from skin
    - greater efficiency in absorbing moisture from the digestive wastes
    - greater water reabsorption from urine
    - greater use of water produced by respiration
    - burrowing
    - storing urea until water is available
    - use of water in food
    - seeking shade during the day.

8. (i) The ammonia diffuses through the egg shell and into the atmosphere.
    (ii) The uric acid is stored in a membrane bag within the egg. As it is confined to the bag and is not very toxic it is no longer a problem to the developing foetus.

9. Much of the cytoplasm is water. Ammonia dissolves very readily in water forming an alkaline solution which destroys most enzymes. (In humans 0.001 mg NH_3/litre of blood is lethal.)

10.

Nitrogen waste	Advantages	Disadvantages	Animal examples
Ammonia (NH_3)	- Easily transported because it dissolves readily in water. - Requires little energy to produce.	- Highly toxic. - Must be removed rapidly. - Requires copious amount of water to remove.	- Amoeba - Tadpoles - Fish
Urea (CON_2H_4)	- Easily transported because it dissolves readily in water. - Less toxic than NH_3.	- Requires water to remove. - Cannot accumulate as is toxic. - More energy is needed to synthesise than NH_3.	- Mammals - Adult frogs - Sharks
Uric acid ($C_5H_4O_3N_4$)	- Little or no water needed for removal. - Less toxic than both urea and ammonia.	- More difficult to transport in body. - More energy is needed to synthesise than urea.	- Reptiles - Birds - Insects

11. (i) Temperature increases the rate of chemical reactions in general. Therefore as the temperature of an animal increases its rate of metabolism increases. However, as enzymes are involved and enzymes are very dependent on temperature, as the temperature becomes high enzymes begin to denature and the rate of metabolism will slow down.
    (ii) The presence of enzymes which control metabolic reactions.
    (iii) The body temperature of a reptile tends to follow the temperature of their surroundings (as they are ectothermic). A rise in temperature will cause an increase in the reptile's metabolic rate and therefore an increase in its level of activity.
    The body temperature of a mammal tends to remain fairly constant regardless of the environmental temperature (within limits). Therefore a rise of 10°C should not affect the metabolic rate of this endothermic animal. In order to maintain a constant temperature this animal may become less active.

12. (i) The mouse is endothermic. In order to maintain its temperature at a constant level, when it is cold, it requires more food energy.
    The reptile is ectothermic. Its body temperature may drop with the environmental temperature. It does not need extra food energy to raise its body temperature in these circumstances.
    (ii) The growth (and activity) of the mouse is less dependent on the weather than that of the reptile. Its growth rate on average will be greater than that of the reptile.

12. (iii) The mouse will need a constant supply of food. Its need for food is likely to be greater during cold weather when less food is available.
    (iv) The mouse remains active throughout the year. Its activity is not dependent on the weather. Its population will increase more rapidly than that of the reptile.

13. (i) Respiration is an important metabolic process. The rate of respiration determines the rate at which energy is made available for other chemical processes. It is therefore a reliable indicator of the rate at which many other chemical reactions are taking place.
    It is convenient as a measure of metabolic rate because the oxygen input (inhaled) and the oxygen output (exhaled) can both be measured under experimental conditions. From these the rate of oxygen consumption can be calculated.
    (ii) a) M.R.
    $= 84$ L of oxygen / 4 hours / 65 kg
    $= \dfrac{84}{4 \times 65}$ L / hour / kg
    $= \dfrac{84 \times 1000}{4 \times 65}$ mL / hour / kg
    $= 323$ mL / hour / kg
    b) M.R.
    $= 30$ L of oxygen / 20 mins / 50 kg
    $= \dfrac{30 \times 3}{50}$ L of oxygen / hour / kg
    $= \dfrac{30 \times 3 \times 1000}{50}$ mL / hour / kg
    $= 1800$ mL / hour / kg

14. Both animals are endothermic. If the environmental temperature is lower than their body temperature, both will lose heat to the environment. The rate at which each loses heat is dependent on their surface area to volume ratio. The surface area to volume ratio of the mouse is greater than the surface area to volume ratio of the donkey. The mouse will lose heat more rapidly per unit volume than the donkey. Its metabolic rate will therefore need to be greater than the donkey's to produce the heat necessary to compensate for the greater heat loss per unit volume.

15. The increased size of the wombats on Tasmania result in a reduced surface area to volume ratio. The Tasmanian wombat will therefore lose less heat to its colder environment than would its mainland counterpart should the counterpart be transported to Tasmania.

16. (i) Vasodilation: blood vessels close to the skin dilate, allowing more blood to pass close to the atmosphere. This increases heat loss.
    Hair/feathers lay flat: reduces the blanket of air that insulates the animal and keeps in heat, more heat is lost.
    Sweat production increases: (only in mammals) which increases heat loss due to evaporation of water from the skin. Thyroids release less thyroxine which reduces cell metabolism (therefore less body heat is produced).

16. (ii) Vasoconstriction: reduces heat loss.
    Hair follicle/feather erection: increases insulation and reduces heat loss.

17. (i) HEAT PRODUCED + HEAT GAINED = HEAT LOST
    (ii) Heat enters body by conduction and radiation from hot surroundings (when environmental temperature is greater than the animal's body temperature).
    Heat may also be absorbed by intake of warm food/drink.
    Heat enters body as radiation from the sun.
    (iii) Heat energy is released when respiration occurs in body tissue.
    (iv) Heat may be lost by conduction and radiation from the animal's body where the animal's body temperature is higher than its surroundings.
    Heat is lost in the wastes the animal produces (e.g. urine, faeces).
    Heat is lost as water evaporates from the respiratory surfaces and the skin.
    Heat is lost as sweat/saliva evaporates from the skin/mouth.
    Heat is lost in warming cool air in the lungs.

18. (i) Counter-current heat exchange.
    (ii) Where the two vessels are close, heat is exchanged from the blood in the artery to the blood in the vein before the blood reaches the extremity of the foot. The temperature difference between the ice and the blood in the foot is therefore reduced and the rate of heat loss is reduced.
    (iii) The arrangement of vessels in the leg is a structural adaptation. The shape and position of the vessels provide an advantage.

19. (i) rise in body temperature
    (ii) hypothalamus
    (iii) blood vessels near the skin's surface
    (iv) dilation of the blood vessels near the skin's surface
    (v) This is a negative feedback because the response causes a drop in the body's temperature, that is, it reduces the stimulus.

20. (i) *TEMPERATURE REGULATION IN HOMEOTHERMIC ANIMALS*

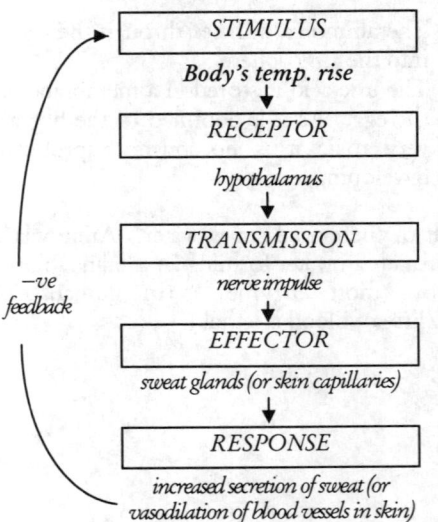

    STIMULUS
    Body's temp. rise
    ↓
    RECEPTOR
    hypothalamus
    ↓
    TRANSMISSION
    nerve impulse
    ↓
    EFFECTOR
    sweat glands (or skin capillaries)
    ↓
    RESPONSE
    increased secretion of sweat (or vasodilation of blood vessels in skin)

    −ve feedback (loops back to STIMULUS)

20. (ii)

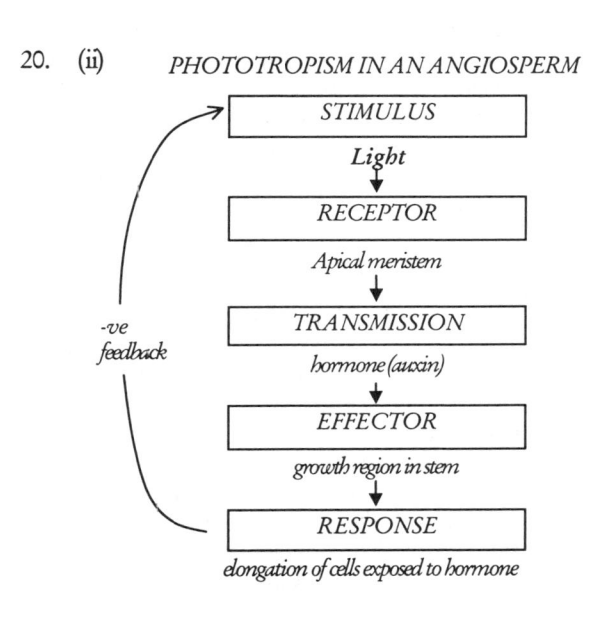

PHOTOTROPISM IN AN ANGIOSPERM

```
        STIMULUS
           |
         Light
           ↓
        RECEPTOR
           |
      Apical meristem
           ↓
       TRANSMISSION
           |
      hormone (auxin)
           ↓
        EFFECTOR
           |
     growth region in stem
           ↓
        RESPONSE
```
elongation of cells exposed to hormone

-ve feedback (loops from RESPONSE back to STIMULUS)

(iii) Both, see diagrams above.
(iv) The response reduces the stimulus. In (i) increased sweating and vasodilation result in an increase in heat loss. This lowers the body's temperature. In (ii) the plant's bending alters the distribution of light (ie. stimulus) falling on the apical meristem.

SOLUTIONS - TRIAL TEST 5

1. (i)

Conc. of salt solution (M)	Change in weight of batch (g)	Change in weight per g of potato tissue
0.2	+4	0.05
0.4	+3	0.03
0.6	+2	0.02
0.8	0	0.00
1	−2	−0.02
1.2	−4	−0.04
1.4	−4	−0.05

(ii) *Graph: Conc. of Salt vs Change in wt of Potato Tissue*

(graph showing Change in wt (per g of potato tissue) on y-axis from -0.05 to 0.05, vs Conc. of salt soln (M) on x-axis from 0.2 to 1.4; linear decreasing trend crossing x-axis at 0.8)

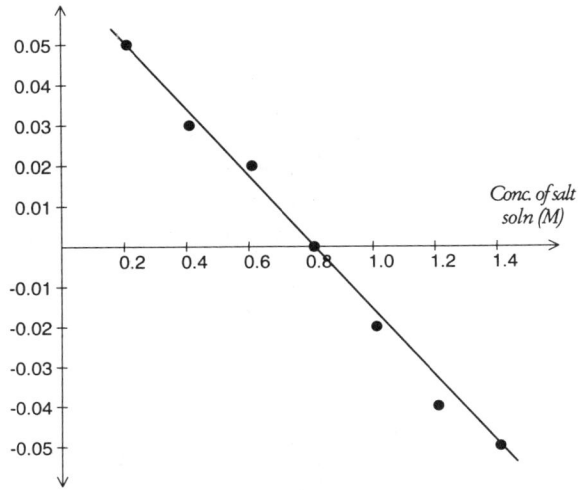

(iii) Using batches of 100 makes the experimental results more reliable. One disc may be abnormal. (Using a large number reduces error likely to occur when atypical discs are selected).

1. (iv) Using the change per gram enables comparisons to be made. (Where the original weights of the batches were different no comparisons could be made of the effects of each different salt solution. Converting each result to a change per gram, standardises each treatment.)

(v) Where the salt concentration of the solution outside of the potato cells was higher than the salt concentration in the cytoplasm of the cells, water diffuses from the cytoplasm to the surrounding salt solution. This causes a loss in weight.
Where the salt concentration of the solution outside was lower than the salt concentration in the cytoplasm water diffuses from the surrounding solution into the cytoplasm. This causes a gain in weight.

(vi) This occurs at a concentration of 0.8 M (i.e. where the line passes through the horizontal axis).
It occurred here because the concentration of solutes inside the potato cells must have been equal to the concentration of the surrounding salt solution.

(vii) The animal cells are likely to lose weight if placed in a solution of higher concentration (ie. a hypertonic solution), as water would again leave the cells by osmosis. They may shrivel if the difference between salt concentrations is great.
If the animal cells are placed into a hypotonic solution i.e. where the salt concentration is less than the cytoplasm's, they will gain water by osmosis to the point of bursting if the difference is great i.e. if the surrounding solution is very dilute.

2. Sharks tend to lose water by osmosis from their bodies to the strong salt water around them (largely through their gills). An increased level of urea in their blood reduces the osmotic difference between the blood and the salt water surroundings. Less water is therefore lost from their bodies.
(Sharks have enzymes which tolerate higher urea concentrations than most other animals.)
Less energy is therefore needed to maintain the water level within their bodies.

3. (i) Marine fish tend to lose too much water from their gills and gut and gain too much salt.
   (ii) Fresh water fish tend to gain too much water through their gills and gut and lose too much salt.
   (iii) Marine fish may have special glands on their gills that excrete excess salts. e.g. mackerel and other bony fish.
   Cartilaginous fish like the shark retain urea (see answer to question 2 above).
   (iv) Fresh water fish drink little water, absorb salts across their gills by active transport and excrete copious amounts of dilute urine.

4. Terrestrial animals are generally surrounded by a dry atmosphere which results in a high rate of water evaporation from their body, especially from their respiratory surfaces. However their body cells must retain a level of water which permits their metabolic processes to continue. (To compensate for loss of water they must have efficient means of obtaining water and adaptations which minimise the rate at which water loss occurs.

5. (i) xylem and phloem
   (ii) a) Xylem transports water and minerals (from roots to leaves).
   b) Phloem transports sugar and proteins (from leaves to stem and roots, and then from stem or roots to growing regions).

6. (i) Absorbs water and minerals from the soil; it increases the absorptive surface area of the root, increasing its efficiency.
   (ii) They cannot move down through the soil because soil is abrasive. The region of elongation is below them, just behind the root cap.
   (iii) Water enters root hair cell, moves through adjacent cortex cells into root xylem, passes up xylem in stem into leaf, enters leaf mesophyll where photosynthesis may occur.
   (iv) Water not used in photosynthesis may evaporate from mesophyll cell walls into leaf's intercellular spaces then pass out through stomatal pores into the atmosphere. As water evaporates more is pulled through the xylem.

7. (i) Xylem vessels are made up of dead cells arranged end to end with their common walls decomposed so that a 'straw' is formed. The remaining cellulose walls are impregnated with a tough fibrous material called lignin, which makes them strong. The lignified xylem adds strength to the stem.

7. (ii) Often the xylem is arranged in a concentric circle around the stem. This pattern provides structural strength. The ends of xylem cells are offset so that no cleavage planes are formed. Fibre cells, which are elongated cells aligned vertically, parallel to xylem, are also lignified and add strength.

8. (i) 9.30 - 11 am
   (ii) 11 am
   (iii) The guard cells chloroplasts begin to make sugar. The osmotic pressure in the cells increases. Water moves by osmosis into the cells. They become turgid and open the stomatal pore between them.
   (iv) As the temperature increases, the rate of water loss exceeds the rate of water intake through the roots. Cells in the plant, including the guard cells, begin to wilt. The stomatal pore closes.
   (v) Closure of the stomatal pores reduces water loss. If the plant loses too much water it will die.
   (vi) Yes. Once closed, carbon dioxide can no longer enter the leaf from the outside atmosphere. Therefore photosynthesis ceases and the plant must rely on stored starch/sugar to respire.

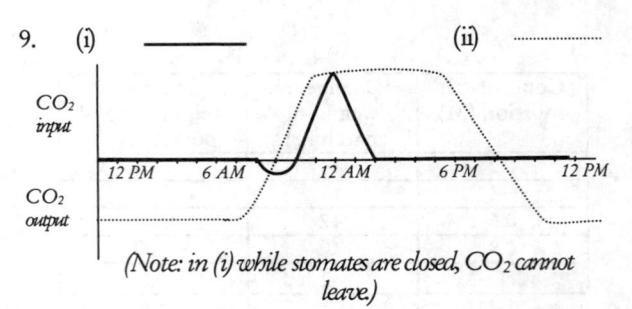

9. (i)   (ii)

CO_2 input

CO_2 output

12 PM   6 AM   12 AM   6 PM   12 PM

(Note: in (i) while stomates are closed, CO_2 cannot leave.)

10. (i) During hot periods the guard cells will lose their turgidity ie. become flaccid. This reduces the size of their stomatal pores. Thus less water can be lost through the pores.
    (ii) Starch is only sparingly soluble. Therefore in the cytoplasm it does not increase the osmotic pressure and does not draw water into the cell.

11. (i) Experiment B - fastest
       Experiment C - slowest
    (ii) Each experimental set up should have a leafy shoot of the same plant species, with the same total area of leaf (e.g. with the same number of similarly sized leaves), leaves of each should be of similar age, the ambient temperature in each should be the same, the starting air humidity the same and intensity of light on each should be the same.
    (iii) In the diagram, from right to left i.e. towards the shoot.
    (iv) The bubble moves as the water is drawn along the glass tubing and up into the shoot's xylem tissue in the transpiration stream.
    (v) It is likely that the rate of loss of water exceeds the rate at which it is being taken up. Therefore the plant cells have begun to wilt. The guard cells have lost their turgidity and the stomata are closed after 20 minutes.

12. (i) a) Freezing temperatures may cause soil water to freeze.
    b) Saline soil may exert an osmotic pressure which prevents water entering the root cells.
    c) Dry soil, due to low rainfall.
    (ii) a) Reduce surface area and number of stomata - slower transpiration.
    b) Reflect heat radiation and trap layer of humid air around the leaf - slower transpiration.
    c) Less openings/pores from which water can escape.
    d) Reflect heat radiation - lower leaf temperature therefore less evaporation.
    e) Less direct sunlight and therefore heat radiation from sun in absorbed by leaf - therefore less evaporation.
    f) CO_2 for photosynthesis is stored within leaf for use during the day. Stomata are closed when evaporation rate would cause excessive water loss.
    g) Stems have lower density of stomata - slower transpiration.

13. See following page.

14. (i)

    (ii) A hormone called Auxin accumulates on the lower (shaded in diagram) part of the horizontal stem. This is due to gravity. Auxin causes elongation of stem cells in this region. Therefore the plant stem bends upwards.

    auxin accumulates here (on the lower side)

    (iii) a) Gravity.
    b) Stem cells on the lower side.
    c) Growth (elongation in this case, not cell division).
    (iv) There is no identifiable receptor for gravity. (However light stimulates the production of auxin from near the apex of the shoot.)

15. (i) Less auxin travels down that side of the stem facing the light. More auxin appears on the shaded side. Therefore cell elongation occurs more on the shaded side.
    (ii) The plant's leaves are better presented to the light for photosynthesis.
    (iii) Most travel in the phloem (though auxin is believed to travel by diffusion from cell to cell down the stem and is therefore an exception).

16. (i) Water enters the cell by osmosis. It moves from the outside, where the water has a lower osmotic pressure (lower concentration) through the semi-permeable cell membrane, into the cell, to the cytoplasm which has a higher osmotic pressure (higher concentration).
    (ii) *Title: Salt conc. vs Average number of contractions of contractile vacuole per minute.*

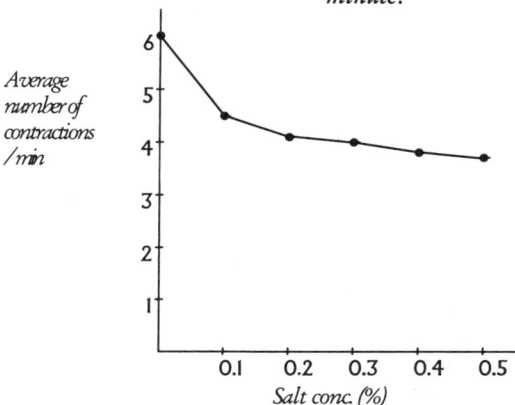

    (iii) a) Osmotic pressure in cytoplasm.
    b) Change in the rate of contractions.
    (iv) Yes, as the osmotic pressure in the cell decreases, the no. of contractions per minute increases to eliminate excess water. The osmotic pressure in the cell therefore would tend to increase.
    (v) a) Salt concentration.
    b) No. of contractions/minute (or rate of contractions).
    (vi) Unlikely as the cell would begin to lose water by osmosis and dehydrate. This cell is adapted to live in a fresh water habitat. It has no apparent means of reducing water loss.

13.

EXPERIMENT (AT THE START)	SUBSEQUENT GROWTH (AFTER 24 HOURS)	EXPLANATION
shoot with mica sheet, light from right	*straight shoot*	Little growth as growth hormone (auxin) cannot pass through mica.
shoot with mica sheet on lit side, light from left	*shoot bent with region X on shaded side*	Auxin travels down shaded side of shoot – cells in region marked X elongate.
shoot with agar block, light from left	*shoot bent, light from left*	Growth slow but not prevented as auxin passes through agar on shaded side.
shoot with aluminium cap, light from left	*straight shoot with cap*	Cap prevents apical meristem from receiving light and producing auxin.

SOLUTIONS - TRIAL TEST 6

1. (i) Monozygotic twins originate from the same zygote. The zygote begins to divide by mitosis but the clump of cells formed splits into two separate clusters. Each cluster gives rise to a separate individual. Differences between monozygotic twins are caused mainly by the environment in which each develops. They are genetically the same, therefore differences are generally small.
    (ii) Different IQ's and weights. IQ's appear to be at least significantly influenced by environmental stimulation particularly in the first few years of life. Weight is partly determined by diet.

2. (i) A gene is a small segment of DNA which controls a particular trait or characteristic of the organism by determining the synthesis of a protein.
    (ii) Genes control characteristics by controlling the type of proteins which the cell synthesises.
    (iii) A part of the DNA in the nucleus (called a gene) is copied into Messenger RNA (mRNA). It moves out to a ribosome in the cytoplasm (often on endoplasmic reticula) and forms a 'template' on which amino acids are assembled. The order in which the amino acids are assembled is determined by the sequence of nucleotides on the mRNA. Therefore the type of protein formed is determined by the DNA.

3. (i) Linked genes are genes which occur on the same DNA molecule, ie. the same chromosome.
    (ii) Yes. Thousands of genes are present in the cells of a mammal, as thousands of different proteins are manufactured by them. Therefore the limited number of chromosomes contain thousands of genes. Many genes must therefore be linked.

4. (i) a) 22 (twenty two)
        b) 11 (eleven)
    (ii) 11 (eleven) pairs
    (iii) 8 pairs with 9, 12 pairs with 10
    (iv) One of each pair comes from the male gamete and one from the female gamete (ie. one is paternal, one is maternal).
    (v) Each DNA molecule has replicated prior to becoming visible as a chromosome (ie. made a copy of itself) and consists of two identical strands of DNA called chromatids.
    (vi) centromere

5. (i) Its allele would cause pigmentation of skin (ie. it would produce melanin).
    (ii) At the same locus on the homologous chromosome.

6. (i) Only in cases of asexual reproduction.
    (ii) In sexual reproduction. Offspring are a combination of two gametes. They receive half of their genes from one parent and half from the other. The zygote is therefore different from both parents.

7. (i) Between stage A and stage B, prior to chromosomes becoming visible in the interphase.
    (ii) They pair up in the late prophase.
    (iii) four
    (iv) two
    (v) four (2^2) (provided no 'crossing over' occurs)
    (vi) eight (2^3) (provided no 'crossing over' occurs)
    (vii) sixteen (2^4) (provided no 'crossing over' occurs)
    (viii) stage B
    (ix) So that when gametes fuse to produce a zygote it has the same diploid number of chromosomes as both its parents.
    (x) The gonads (ie. ovaries, testes, stamens).

8. (i) Asexually produced offspring have little variation. Therefore although they may be well suited to their parents' present environment, a change in conditions may not suit any. Therefore all may die if a change occurs.
    (ii) a) Crossing over - forms combinations of genes which are not on parental chromosomes. This gives rise to combinations of characteristics which are new combinations, unlike their parents and other siblings.
        b) Chromosomes may align on either side of the cell at metaphase I. There are two possibilities. Each pair of homologous chromosomes can arrange itself in two ways, either with the maternal chromo-some of the left and the paternal chromosome on the right or vice versa. Therefore the combinations are numerous resulting in numer-ous gamete types and again many different combinations in the zygote.
        c) The random fusion of gametes means that any two gametes can come together at fertilisation, with an equal probability. This creates a greater variety than would be the case if only certain gametes combined.

9. In a stable environment. Asexual reproduction results in offspring that are well adapted to the parents' environment. A large proportion of such offspring are likely to survive to maturity in stable conditions.

10. Males produce sperm of two types. Half have 12 chromosomes and half have 11 chromosomes. The females produce ova all of which have 12 chromosomes. If a sperm with 12 chromosomes fertilises an ovum with 12 chromosomes the resulting zygote has 24 chromosomes and is a female. If a sperm with 11 chromosomes fertilises an ovum with 12 chromosomes, the resulting zygote will have 23 chromosomes and be a male.

11. (i) a) Recessive and autosomal.
   b) It appears to be recessive as individuals II 4 and II 5 are not bald but have offspring, some of which are bald (IV 1 and 2 confirm this). It appears to be autosomal as individuals IV 1 and IV 2 are normal but have a **female** offspring V 2 who is bald. If this was a sex-linked trait, male individual IV 2 would have to be bald too.

   (ii) Key: Let B ≡ normal hair gene
              b ≡ bald gene
   I 1 Bb , I 2 bb
   II 1 Bb , II 2 bb , II 3 Bb , II 4 Bb , II 5 Bb
   III 1 bb , III 2 bb , III 3 BB/Bb
   IV 1 Bb , IV 2 Bb , IV 3 Bb
   V 1 BB/Bb , V2 bb , V 3 BB/Bb

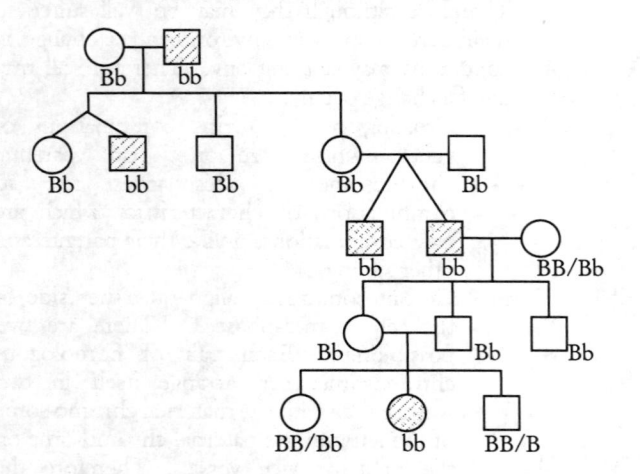

   (iii) twins II 1 and II 2
        and III 1 and III 2
   (iv) monozygotic III 1 and III 2
        dizygotic II 1 and II 2
        This is indicated by the symbols used -

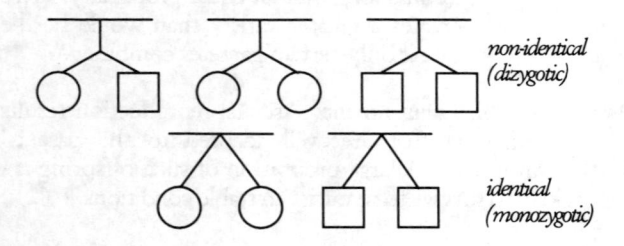

        non-identical (dizygotic)

        identical (monozygotic)

   (v) From V 2's parent, but they received the genes from individual III 2 since they were siblings.

12. (i) This gene is dominant.
    (ii) I 2
    (iii) Key: Let X^R ≡ gene for rickets
               X^r ≡ gene for normal development

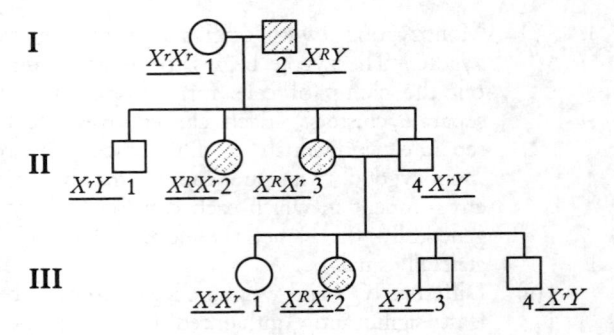

    I: X^rX^r 1 — 2 X^RY
    II: X^rY 1 , X^RX^r 2 , X^RX^r 3 , 4 X^rY
    III: X^rX^r 1 , X^RX^r 2 , X^rY 3 , 4 X^rY

    (iv) More females would be expected to inherit this dominant disease, as they have two X chromosomes (and therefore two chances to inherit the rare disease) whereas males only have one X chromosome (and therefore only one chance to inherit it).

13. The best information would come from (ii):
    If the unknown is NN then none of the offspring will be albino. They will all be Nn and have normal coat colour.

	n	n
N	Nn	Nn
N	Nn	Nn

    If the unknown is Nn then half the offspring will be normal and half will be albino.

	n	n
N	Nn	Nn
n	nn	nn

    Using the homozygous recessive to determine an unknown genotype is called a "test-cross".

# SOLUTIONS - TRIAL TEST 7

1. (i) Environmental influences can affect the rate of mutations in a population. However the environment cannot cause a particular mutation to occur.
    (ii) A mutant gene may be transmitted through many generations unchanged. It may mutate again producing another unusual feature or it may revert back to the original gene. Because it may persist for many generations it is possible for natural selection to "work" on it.
    (iii) Useful mutations are very rare. Random change to a gene which is functioning well is more likely to lead to its dysfunction rather than improvement.

2. (i) Advantageous mutations are most important. They offer increased chances of survival and are selected by the environment. They are responsible for the wide variety of well adapted organisms which have appeared on the earth.
    (ii) Unfavourable mutations are selected against. They are not likely to persist in a population for long. Natural selection works against them and eventually removes them from the population.

3. (i) The gene controlling dark colour probably came first. This is a mutation which under normal conditions is unfavourable and selected out. However, it is likely to have arisen spontaneously from time to time but not persisted for long (before the countryside became polluted).
    (ii) The Industrial Revolution resulted in an outpouring of soot into the environments near industrial centres. This provided moths of a dark colouring with camouflage. The gene controlling dark colouring offered improved advantage in the change of environment. Genes controlling light colours were selected 'against'. Thus the frequency of the gene for dark colour increased while the frequency of the gene for light colouring decreased.

4. - Some bacteria have a natural resistance to streptomycin.
    - The population of the bacteria are exposed to streptomycin.
    - Most bacteria die.
    - The few resistant bacteria live and reproduce.
    - Their offspring inherit a resistance to streptomycin.
    - The majority of the population of bacteria in a few generations have an inherited resistance to streptomycin.

5. Natural selection results in better adapted varieties surviving, while less well adapted varieties disappear. Therefore natural selection tends to reduce the variety.
    In the example of the bacteria - before the introduction of the antibiotic streptomycin, bacteria may have had genes for a resistance to the antibiotic or genes which offer no resistance. There would appear to be no advantage or disadvantage involved, so the genes controlling these varieties would persist from generation to generation. The frequency of these genes would remain unchanged.
    With the use of the antibiotic in the environment, one variety ie. the non-resistant strain, would tend to disappear leaving only the resistant strain ie. variation would be reduced.

6. (i) - crossing-overs during meiosis
        - random segregation of chromosomes during meiosis
        - random fertilisation by gametes
        - mutations
    (ii) - scarce resources - leading to competition
        - disease
        - predation
    (iii) they have inherited more favourable genes
    (iv) those with favourable genes are more likely to survive and reproduce offspring which inherit their favourable genes

7. (i) **Biotic** - predators eg. snakes, eagles
        - competition for food eg. interspecific and intraspecific
        Abiotic - increase in water turbidity caused by erosion
        - increase in salinity caused by excessive clearing of plants in the catchment area.
    (ii) Predation - selects variety and colour in each environment, reduces the variety of colour and patterns on frog's skin. Those frogs that are best camouflaged are more likely to survive and reproduce. Competition for food - when food is scarce selects those that mature most rapidly and are larger and better equipped to obtain food.
        Water turbidity - as the water becomes less clear, frogs with enhanced senses - smell and sight may be selected.
        Salinity - if salinity increases those frogs and their tadpoles capable of retaining water have an advantage, as they are less likely to dehydrate in the water.
    (iii) Rising salt levels may reach a concentration which neither the tadpole nor adult cannot tolerate. If any part of the life cycle becomes threatened the species may disappear.
    (iv) Its ability depends on the variety of its genes and the presence of genes which are suited to a change in the environment. If no such genes are present, the organism may disappear from an area.

8. (i)   As the sea level has risen the 'land bridge' which once connected Rottnest Island to the mainland has become flooded.
    (ii) As the isolated population evolves independently of the mainland population, through mutations and natural selection it may become more and more genetically different, until a point is reached when it is so different that its chromosomes are incompatible with those of the mainland animals.
    (iii) a) The two populations may interbreed (likely if their separation has been relatively short).
          b) Breeding may take place on the boundaries of their distributions which produces hybrids which form a third population.
          c) No interbreeding occurs, since the populations have become genetically too different. Two separate species have arisen during their long isolation from one another.

9. If two populations have similar proteins, this indicates that their DNA is similar. If their DNA is similar then they are likely to be closely related ie. probably share a fairly recent common ancestor.

10. (i) It is unlikely to kill many of the bacteria colonies as they are derived from a resistant strain.
    (ii) New antibiotics are required to treat the new strain. This means that the pharmaceutical industry must continue to develop new antibiotics (at an alarming rate).

11. (i)   This suggests that mammals have a common ancestor.
    (ii) These suggest that the islands were originally colonised by one species of finch from the mainland of South America. They have evolved to suit their particular island niche. This demonstrates adaptive radiation (or speciation).
    (iii) Embryos of common vertebrates have a tail and 'gill' slits. They are difficult to distinguish between, this suggests shared DNA which is active during their embryonic development. Shared DNA implies common ancestry.
    (iv) DNA and many proteins are common to all organisms. This suggests that they are derived from common ancestry.
    (v)   The fossil record shows that life on earth has become more and more diverse and some animals and plants have become more and more complex. This supports the idea of adaptive radiation as organisms evolved to fill the available niches in almost every environment.

12. (i) Removing old trees with suitable sized holes reduces the number of breeding places for the black cockatoo. Unable to reproduce the species will disappear.
    (ii) Older trees with holes and with the potential to form holes should be left in the forest. This strategy may help these birds to survive.
    In areas which have already been logged, nest boxes may help such birds survive until older trees grow.

SOLUTIONS - TRIAL TEST 8

1. (i) Ecosystem: the living and non-living parts of an environment which interact such that there is a cycling of matter between them.
   (ii) A stable ecosystem does not change greatly from one year to the next. There is a constant recycling of matter and an uninterrupted flow of energy through the system.

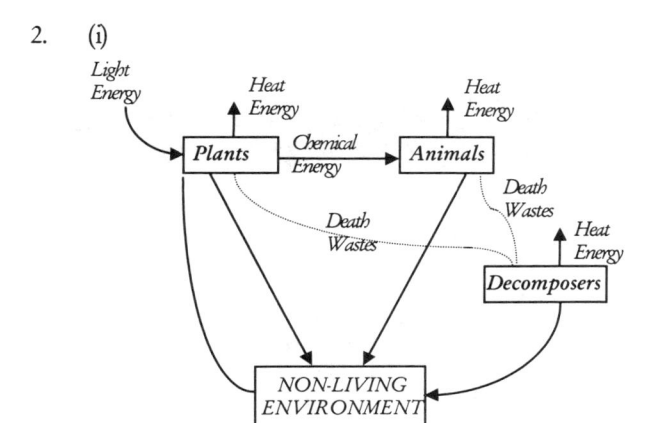

2. (i) [Diagram: Light Energy → Plants (Chemical Energy) → Animals; Heat Energy lost from Plants, Animals, and Decomposers; Death/Wastes from Plants and Animals feed Decomposers; arrows to NON-LIVING ENVIRONMENT]
   (ii) Lost into space.
   (iii) Energy is not recycled, it flows through.
   (iv) Decomposers obtain their energy as chemical energy in the form of organic matter which they break down.
   (v) Producers take up carbon dioxide, water, minerals and light energy.
   (vi) Animals and plants return carbon dioxide water and minerals and heat to the non-living environment.
   (vii) Decomposers return nutrients to the soil (or water).

3. (i) 0.1 energy units
   (ii) 0.03 energy units
   (iii) Example (ii) - it is a food web (although the feeding relationships in a community are likely to be more complex than this!).
   (iv) No. There are probably other animals which eat sawfly larvae and others that eat ants. The lizards are likely to get far less energy than 0.03 energy units.

4. (i) Biomass: total mass of living matter in a population or a community. It is often expressed as the dry weight/unit area.
   (ii) Productivity: rate at which energy is fixed in photosynthesis. This is measured by the rate at which organic matter is stored in producers and therefore available as food for consumers. It can be expressed as the change in dry weight/unit area/unit time.

5. (i) - Random areas are sampled in both ecosystems.
   - The biomass of the photosynthetic organisms is measured in each area.
   - Some time later, further random areas are sampled.
   - Photosynthetic biomass again is measured.
   - Changes for each ecosystem can be calculated (expressed for example in kg/m²/yr).
   - Comparisons between these figures indicate relative productivity.
   (ii) - Estimate the biomass of the grass (X kg/m²).
   - Estimate the biomass of the grasshoppers (Y kg/m²).
   - % transferred = $\dfrac{Y}{X} \times \dfrac{100}{1}$
   ie. = $\dfrac{\text{biomass of grasshoppers}}{\text{biomass of grass}} \times \dfrac{100}{1}$

6. (i) - soil type
   - soil drainage
   - aspect (ie. south facing or north facing slope)
   - fertilisers used
   - diseases present
   - water received
   (ii) He might add fertiliser, irrigate it, reduce insect pests and reduce plant competitors, improve the soil drainage.
   (iii) Poorer field - 100 kg/4 hectares/year
   = 100 × 1000 g/4 hectares/year
   = $\dfrac{100 \times 1{,}000}{40{,}000}$ g/m²/year
   = $\dfrac{100 \times 1{,}000}{40{,}000 \times 52}$ g/m²/week
   = 0.048 g/m²/week
   Better field = $\dfrac{120 \times 1{,}000}{40{,}000 \times 52}$ g/m²/week
   = 0.058 g/m²/week

7. (i) A tropical rain forest is generally warmer and has a greater amount of light and water available for photosynthesis than does a temperate evergreen forest where the growth is more dependent on seasons.
   (ii) Tropical rain forest 2200 g/m²/yr
   Desert scrub 90 g/m²/yr
   Difference 2110 g/m²/yr
   (iii) The biomass of the first order consumers in the rain forest is likely to be of the order of 24 times that of the biomass of first order consumers in the desert - as there is approximately 24 times the chemical energy available to them.
   $\left(\dfrac{2200}{90} \approx 24\right)$

7. (iv) Carbon dioxide absorption is directly related to the rate of photosynthesis. Therefore CO_2 is likely to be absorbed at an average rate 24 times higher in the tropical rain forest than that of the desert scrub.
   (v) The density of the organisms is much greater in the tropical rain forests. Consequently they have a much greater carrying capacity for the animals which live in them.

8. (i) NITRATES.
   (ii) They have nitrogen fixing bacteria which live in nodules in their roots.
   (iii) Ammonia (NH_3)
   (iv) 1) absorption (in roots)
        2) death
        3) excretion
        4) decomposition
        5) nitrification
        6) nitrification
        7) denitrification
        8) feeding (ingestion)

SOLUTIONS - TRIAL TEST 9

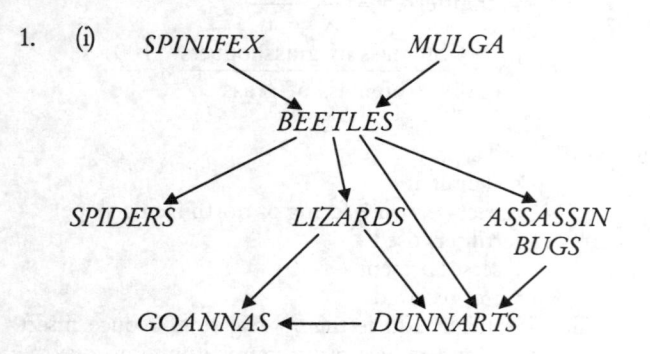

1. (i)
   ```
   SPINIFEX          MULGA
        ↘           ↙
          BEETLES
        ↙    ↓    ↘
   SPIDERS LIZARDS ASSASSIN
                    BUGS
        ↓     ↓    ↙
   GOANNAS ← DUNNARTS
   ```

   (ii) spinifex and mulga
   (iii) beetles
   (iv) spiders, lizards, assassin bugs, dunnarts
   (v) goannas
   (vi) Less food would be available to beetles - their numbers may decrease. Less food would be available for other higher order consumers. Goannas and dunnarts may not have sufficient food to survive.
   (vii) Spinifex and mulga may increase in density whereas higher order consumers (spiders, lizards, dunnarts, assassin bugs, etc) may disappear from the environment.

2. (i) With less vegetation there is likely to be greater wind erosion which may cause dust storms and water erosion in the wet season. Both would result in loss of the topsoil, a loss of fertility.
   (ii) Even if the feral animals were removed, the damage caused to the land may be permanent. Revegetation of the environment may occur only very slowly. The capacity of the land to support grazing animals may be permanently lost.
   (iii) If the cane toad removes insect populations, this may result in less pollination occurring and a subsequent decline in the flowering plant species. However, it could reduce insect grazing pressure and cause some plant populations to increase.

3. (i) Often soils, particularly in Australia, have deficiencies in nitrogen and phosphorus compounds. These deficiencies limit the rate of growth of introduced crop species.

3. (ii) When a tree is removed from the forest, minerals which make up compounds in the tree are removed.
   (iii) If minerals are continuously removed from an ecosystem and not replaced then the soil gradually loses its fertility.
   It becomes less capable of supporting plant growth, therefore productivity declines.

4.

	Ecosystem		
Characteristic	Natural	Agricultural	Urban
Matter recycling	Most matter recycled.	Some recycling.	Little recycling.
Energy use	Respiration - slow heat release. Photosynthesis.	Respiration. Slow heat release. Photosynthesis.	Fossil fuels burned - rapid heat release.
Energy input	Light energy.	Light energy and some fossil fuel.	Fossil fuels and food (chem. energy).
Stability	Very stable.	Unstable - single crop dominates.	Unstable - few plants.
Bio-diversity	Great, many different species.	Little diversity - often monocultures.	Little diversity - one dominant (human) species.

5. (i) Agricultural ecosystems often have just a few different species of plants and animals often with little genetic variability. A disease or small change to the environment may lead to the destruction of whole crops and whole animal populations. A disease in a natural ecosystem is likely to affect some species but not all. The ecosystem is therefore not changed greatly. A small change to the environment is not likely to affect all of the organisms in a natural ecosystem.

5. (ii) In urban ecosystems much of the waste produced is not decomposed rapidly, nor is it dispersed to parts of the environment where it may be useful. Much of the waste is buried in the ground in landfill sites and not returned to any ecosystem for recycling.
   (iii) bacteria and fungi
   (iv) Agricultural ecosystems have a large output of matter in the form of food (wheat, oats, barley, mutton, beef and pork, etc). This matter consists of organic molecules made up of carbon, hydrogen, oxygen and numerous elements such as nitrogen, calcium, phosphorus, copper, iron, magnesium, etc. These substances must be put back into the agricultural ecosystem if it is to continue to produce. Therefore it must have a large input of matter.
   (v) The heat is dissipated into the Earth's atmosphere then to space.

6. (i) Food - where food is readily available the death rate due to starvation and malnutrition is low. eg. thousands of people have starved in eastern Africa (Ethiopia, Sudan, Chad) in the last decade due to crop failures.
   (ii) Space - not normally a limiting factor. However, where populations have become too great attempts have been made to 'persuade' people not to migrate to those areas eg. it is difficult for the peasants to move from rural China into the cities.
   (iii) Waste products - where the disposal of human waste is not hygienic and efficient, disease may cause a reduction in human population growth due to diseases like cholera and typhoid.
   (iv) Climate - the distribution of people over the earth's surface is very much determined by the earth's capacity to produce food in various places. eg. few people live in the deserts and polar regions.
   (v) Natural disasters - where flooding, fires, earthquakes, mudslides and droughts occur population growth is reduced eg. the intermittent flooding in Bangladesh reduces the rate of growth of that population.
   (vi) Other organisms - human populations are reduced by disease caused by pathogenic organisms (bacteria, viruses, fungi and parasitic animals). eg. the death rate in developing countries is significantly increased by pathogenic organisms.

7. (i) Surrounding bush ecosystems are continuously being cleared for further housing/industrial development. If they are not destroyed in this way - often they are used as repositories for waste. Also destruction of vegetation by various motorised transport, dune buggies, off-road four wheel drive vehicles, and motor bikes causes erosion and general degradation of bush ecosystems.

7. (ii) Swan/Canning Rivers - the level of use by the urban population increases as the population rises. There is a potential for further pollution if the septic tanks are not replaced by deep sewage in suburbs which flank the rivers. Much of the damage to these rivers is caused by fertiliser run off and rising salt levels in their tributaries.
   (iii) Marine ecosystems - pollution by industry and human effluent will further degrade the marine ecosystems eg. Cockburn Sound, unless steps are taken to reduce the waste load put upon them.

8. (i) carbon dioxide and methane
   (ii) chlorofluorocarbons (CFC's)

9. (i) Burning fossil fuels, clearing forests.
   (ii) Release of CFC's from old refrigerators and airconditioners.
   (iii) Overgrazing in marginal farming areas (ie. allowing too many sheep or cattle to populate areas of low rainfall).
   Overclearing in marginal farming areas (ie. clearing too much land in low rainfall areas - these often quickly lose productivity and become arid wastelands).

10. (i) Numbat, Noisy Scrub Bird.
    (ii) Numbat was once common throughout most of southern Australia especially in Wandoo open forest ecosystems. Its distribution is now confined to a small area of Eucalyptus woodland in the S.W. of W.A.
    Noisy Scrub Bird was once common along the South coast of W.A. The species is now reduced to a small area east of Albany called Two Peoples Bay.
    (iii) fox and cat
    (iv) The fox is dispersed over the entire country apart from the far north. The cat is dispersed over entire continent.
    (v) Their natural habitats need to be protected, so that they have sufficient food and breeding places and freedom from predation by feral animals.
    (vi) Feral animals may be reduced by hunting, poisoning or introduced diseases.
    (vii) introduced disease
    (viii) Prickly pear cactus
    Pattersons Curse
    (Skeleton weed, Blackberry)
    (ix) Herbicides - benefits - usually rapid, usually affects only selected plants (may be economical).
    - disadvantages - often needs continual application, sometimes affects other plant (and animal) species, often has harmful effects on user. May be concentrated in food chains.
    (x) Introduced plant species may be controlled by the introduction of a natural predator eg. cactoblastus moth used to reduce prickly pear populations.
    Lantana is an introduced plant which has become a pest in Queensland and NSW. The lantana beetle which feeds on lantana has been introduced and has been successful in warmer Queensland in reducing the spread of lantana there.

11. (i) The water table rises closer to the surface of the soil.
   (ii) Because the roots of the trees no longer draw water from the soil and pass it to the leaves, where it is then transpired into the atmosphere, the water table rises.
   (iii) As the water moves up through the soil, it dissolves salt which has accumulated there and carries it to the surface. When the water evaporates salt is left behind, often forming a visible white film of salt over the surface of the land.
   (iv) The water which flows into creeks and rivers has much of this dissolved salt in it. The water courses often become too salty for even stock to drink and naturally occurring animals and plants disappear from these rivers and are replaced by halophytes.
   (v) - The rising salt levels may be reduced by replanting deep rooted trees and shrubs in cleared areas to lower the water table.
   - Land should not be cleared before the effects of soil salinity are determined.
   - Salt tolerant plants may be introduced in areas most severely affected to help lower the water table.
   (vi) There would be a continuing loss of useful farming land. Much of rural Western Australia would become totally unproductive.
   (vii) Urban dwellers may volunteer to help raise and plant tree seedlings on farming properties **or** be prepared to pay higher taxes to pay contractors to do this or pay more for food.

12. (i) Often pollutants from the waste leach into the ground water contaminating it.
   (ii) Swamp communities disappear. There is a loss of birds, fish, lizards, snakes, small marsupials etc from the area.
   (iii) Migratory birds lose important feeding areas. Birds entering Australia to feed or reproduce during the northern hemisphere's winter are unable to do so. Their numbers decline.
   (iii) Resident birds, those that live here all year have their only habitat destroyed. Their numbers decline.
   (iv) - They provide an alternative recreational area.
   - The biodiversity of the area is maintained.
   - The quality of ground water is maintained.
   - Helps maintain bird populations in other parts of the world because migration is still possible.

GLOSSARY

ABIOTIC Factors in the environment which are not living, eg. temperature, humidity, are described as abiotic. (cf biotic)

ABSORPTION The uptake of substances into an organism or cell.

ABUNDANCE The density of organisms in a particular part of their range, eg. number per hectare of Jarrah forest near Dwellingup.

ACID A substance which produces hydrogen ions in water. Acids have a pH of less than 7.

ACQUIRED CHARACTERISTIC / TRAIT A feature which is not inherited. It is caused by the environment or by use, eg. enlarged biceps through weight lifting.

ACTIVE SITE / CATALYTIC SITE see page 25

ACTIVE TRANSPORT see page 18

ADAPTATION A trait which enables an organism to survive and reproduce better in its environment.

ADAPTIVE RADIATION / SPECIATION The evolution of two or more species from one original species.

ADENOSINE TRIPHOSPHATE ATP An important source of energy in many cells. It releases energy when it breaks down to adenosine diphosphate and inorganic phosphate.

ANTIDIURETIC HORMONE ADH A hormone released from the pituitary gland which targets the kidneys and increases their reabsorption of water from the urine.

AEROBIC A biological process which requires oxygen. (cf anaerobic)

AESTIVATION When an animal becomes inactive during the summer.

ALCOHOL A class of chemical compounds to which the colourless liquid called ethanol or ethyl alcohol (C_2H_5OH) belongs.

ALKALI A substance which has a pH of more than 7 and which produces hydroxide ions (OH^-) when mixed with water.

ALLELE Alternative forms of a gene which occur at the same locus on homologous chromosomes.

ALLOPATRIC Populations of the same species which are separated and are unable to interbreed because of their isolation.

AMBIENT TEMPERATURE The temperature of the surroundings.

AMINO ACID The basic organic molecular unit which when linked in a chain forms a protein molecule. Amino acids contain nitrogen (attached to two hydrogen atoms, $-NH_2$). see protein

AMMONIA A gas (NH_3) which dissolves readily in water. It is toxic to cells and if not immediately excreted when formed in the body, must be converted to urea or uric acid, less toxic compounds.

ANABOLISM The production of more complex molecules from simpler ones. (cf catabolism)

ANAEROBIC A biological process which occurs in the absence of oxygen, eg. fermentation. (cf aerobic)

ANALOGOUS Parts of different organisms that have a similar function but which have a different structure, eg. wings of bats and wasps.

ANAPHASE A phase in both mitosis and meiosis in which the chromatids move from the equator to opposite poles of the cell. Once separated, the chromatids are called chromosomes.

ANATOMY The structure of an animal or plant. (Also used to refer to the study of animal and plant structure.)

ANIMAL An organism which is heterotrophic, able to move and has body cells which do not have a cell wall. (cf plants)

ANTIBIOTIC A substance which destroys or inhibits the growth of microorganisms like bacteria.

ANTICODON Three nitrogenous bases along-side each other on a tRNA molecule. These pair with a matching codon of three nitrogenous bases on a mRNA molecule.

APICAL MERISTEM The area of growth near the tip of the stem or root of vascular plants. Mitosis occurs in these areas.

APPENDIX A vestigial organ attached to the first part of large intestine.

AQUATIC ENVIRONMENT A water environment, marine or fresh water.

ARTERIOLE A small branch of an artery which branches further into capillaries.

ARTERY A blood vessel which carries blood away from the heart to other body tissue.

ARTIFICIAL SELECTION The selection by humans of animals or plants, which have useful features, for breeding programmes. (cf natural selection)

ASEXUAL REPRODUCTION Reproduction which does not involve the fusion of gametes, eg. binary fission, budding, spore formation.

ASSIMILATION Process whereby food is changed into living material in cells.

AUTOSOME A chromosome which is not a sex chromosome.

AUTOTROPH An organism capable of making its own food, by photosynthesis in most cases, or by chemosynthesis in some bacteria.

AUXIN A plant hormone produced by roots or shoots which causes cell elongation. Synthetic auxins include 2,4,5-T and 2-4D which are used as herbicides.

BACKCROSS A cross between an F_1 hybrid and a homozygous parent.

BACTERIA (singular bacterium) Microscopic organisms which have no membrane bounded organelles. Bacteria are therefore prokaryotes. Saprophitic bacteria are very important in decomposition of dead organisms.

BANDING When chromosomes are treated with stains during cell division they exhibit characteristic stripes or bands.

BASAL METABOLISM The rate of metabolism which is just sufficient to provide the energy for life while an organism is awake and resting.

BEHAVIOUR The way or pattern in which an animal acts.

BENEDICT'S TEST A chemical test for glucose (and other reducing sugars). Benedict's solution normally blue, when added to glucose and warmed, changes to green (in low glucose concentrations) and to brick-red (in high glucose concentrations).

BENTHOS Organisms which live on the bottom of the ocean and lakes.

BINARY FISSION Cell division which results in two similar organisms.

BIOCHEMICAL OXYGEN DEMAND (B.O.D.) The oxygen needed by microorganisms as they decompose organic matter in water bodies.

BIOCIDE A chemical which is used to kill living organisms.

BIODEGRADABLE A substance which is broken down by bacteria or other decomposers.

BIOGENESIS The theory that states that all living organisms came from pre-existing organisms.

BIOLOGICAL AMPLIFICATION Where the tissue concentration of insecticides, heavy metals, etc increases up the food chain so that it is highest in highest order consumers.

BIOLOGICAL CONTROL Pest control using biological means, eg. an introduced natural predator, release of sterilised males.

BIOLOGY The scientific study of life. Biology includes botany, zoology, ecology.

BIOMASS The total mass of living matter in a given area, normally expressed as dry weight per unit area, eg. kg/m^2.

BIOME An important and distinct community which has particular abiotic and biotic features, eg. temperate forest, grassland.

BIOSPHERE That part of the earth where living things live.

BIOTA The plants and animals in an area.

BIOTECHNOLOGY Industrial use of biological processes, eg. fermentation, genetic engineering.

BIOTIC Environmental factors which are living, eg. predators, competitors. (cf abiotic)

BIURET'S TEST Test for proteins. A blue alkaline solution with copper sulphate. It turns purple if protein is present.

BIVALENT Paired homologous chromosomes during the prophase 1 and metaphase 1 of meiosis.

BLOOD SUGAR The glucose which is dissolved in blood plasma.

BLUE-GREEN ALGAE A Division of bacteria which contains chlorophyll. They are prokaryotes. (cf bacteria)

BOTANY The scientific study of plant life.

CALIBRATION The adjusting of an instrument to ensure that its readings are accurate.

CAMOUFLAGE An organism's use of colour and shape to blend in with its background. Often for protection from predators.

CANCER The uncontrolled growth of cells, often able to spread via the circulatory or lymphatic system to invade other tissue.

CARBON DATING A method of dating organic matter which uses the percentage of undecayed carbon-14 as a measure of the age of a fossil. The older the fossil is, the smaller the proportion of carbon-14 that will be left.

CARBON DIOXIDE A colourless, odourless gas present in the atmosphere in small amounts (approx. 0.03% by volume). CO_2 is essential for photosynthesis.

CARNIVORE A flesh eating animal.

CATABOLISM A chemical breakdown of complex molecules into simple substances. (cf anabolism)

CATALASE An enzyme which speeds up the decomposition of toxic hydrogen peroxide (a common metabolic waste) into water and oxygen.

CATALYST A chemical which speeds up chemical reactions but is itself not used up. (cf enzyme)

CELL The basic "building block" of living things (except viruses). Consists of a membrane bounded protoplasm.

CELL DIFFERENTIATION The development of specialised cells in multicellular organisms from unspecialised cells in the early stages of the organism's growth.

CELL DIVISION This occurs when a cell's nucleus divides followed by its cytoplasm. Each time division occurs two cells are formed. (cf meiosis and mitosis) see cytokinesis

CELL MEMBRANE The protective layer of lipids and proteins which encloses a cell's protoplasm. see page 17

CELL PLATE The disc-shaped structure which forms between the daughter cells, produced when a plant cell divides. It later becomes the common cell wall between the two new cells.

CENTRIFUGE A machine which spins about a central axis, used to separate substances of different densities, eg. proteins from sugar and to separate various organelles.

CENTRIOLE Two small organelles which lie just outside the nucleus of animal cells. They form the spindles during cell division.

CENTROMERE The point of attachment of two chromatids. The spindles attach to the centromere during cell division.

CHEMORECEPTOR A special receptor which is sensitive to specific chemicals, eg. taste receptors, aortic body receptors (sensitive to CO_2 in the blood).

CHEMOSYNTHESIS The synthesis of more complex organic chemicals where the energy is not provided by the sun but by chemical decomposition.

CHEMOTAXIS The response by an animal in moving towards a chemical stimulus.

CHEMOTROPISM A plant's response in growing towards or away from a chemical stimulus.

CHIASMA Where two homologous chromosomes cross over they from an X shape, called a chiasma.

CHITIN A polysaccharide that forms the exoskeleton of arthropods and the cell walls of fungi.

CHLOROPHYLL A green pigment which absorbs light energy during photosynthesis.

CHLOROPLAST A membrane bounded organelle which contains chlorophyll. The site of photosynthesis in eukaryotic cells.

CHROMATID Each chromosome replicate held together by the centromere after replication.

CHROMATIN Thin uncoiled strands of DNA as it exists during the interphase.

CHROMOPLAST A membrane bounded organelle which contains a pigment which often gives a leaf or fruit its characteristic colour.

CHROMOSOME Chromatin which has short-ened and thickened ("condensed") to become visible (with the aid of a microscope) as a separate body during cell division.

CHROMOSOME MAPPING Scientific determination of the location of genes on a chromosome.

CILIA (singular cilium) Short hair-like structures protruding from specialised cells which beat rhythmically to move the cell or move substances over the cell (eg. in the trachea ciliated epithelial cells help clear the lungs of mucus and dust, etc).

CLIMAX COMMUNITY A community which has reached its final stage in ecological succession. It is stable while the environment remains unchanged, eg. Rain Forest.

CLINE A gradual change in a trait over a particular species' range, eg. size of a tree species may range from tall near the base of a mountain through to short near the summit.

CLONES Asexually reproduced organisms which have arisen from the same parent.

CO-DOMINANCE (OR INCOMPLETE DOMINANCE) When two different alleles are present in an organism but neither is dominant. Both genes are expressed, eg. group AB in the ABO blood grouping results from the genotype $I^A I^B$ where both the gene for A, I^A and gene for B, I^B are expressed.

COENZYME An organic compound (eg. a vitamin) which assists enzymes by carrying chemical groups or atoms from one enzyme to another.

COFACTOR Some enzymes only work in the presence of a particular cofactor. The cofactor may bind the enzyme and the substrate together or it may serve as the active site of the enzyme itself. Some cofactors are metal ions (eg. Zn^{++}, Fe^{++}), others are vitamins.

COHESION The attraction that particles of the same kind have for each other, eg. water molecules are attracted to other water molecules by cohesive forces.

COLLENCHYMA see page 46

COMMUNITY The plants, animals and microorganisms which live together in a particular place at a particular time.

COMPANION CELL A cell which is in close association with a phloem cell. It contains a nucleus which may control the phloem cell.

COMPETITION An association between two organisms where both strive to obtain the same resource (eg. food, shelter, mates). May be interspecific (between two species) or intraspecific (within the one species).

COMPLEMENTARY BASES The nitrogenous bases which fit together in nucleic acids, eg. guanine and cytosine; thymine and adenine.

CONGENITAL A trait which is possessed from birth.

CONSERVATION The preservation of plants and animals and their environments for future generations.

CONSUMER/HETEROTROPH An organism which feeds on other organisms. First order consumers (herbivores) feed on plants, second order consumers (carnivores) feed on first order consumers (and so on).

CONTINUOUS VARIATION A feature which is controlled by many genes. Shows a graduated range, eg. height in the population.

CONVERGENT EVOLUTION The evolution of features which are similar in different organisms, eg. wings in insects and birds, due to similar habitats.

CO-ORDINATION The working together of organs or organ systems in order that the organism functions as a whole, eg. nervous and endocrine systems work together to maintain stability within a mammal.

CROSS The mating of two organisms in a genetics experiment.

CROSS BREED The offspring which results from mating two different breeds or races.

CROSS FERTILISATION The fusion of gametes from two different individuals. (cf self-fertilisation)

CROSS OVER The exchange of genes which occurs between two homologous chromatids during the metaphase I of meiosis. It results in greater variation in the offspring.

CROSS POLLINATION When pollen from a different plant settles on the stigma of a particular flower.

CULL The removal of some animals from a given population.

CULTIVAR A variety of a plant species bred to promote a desirable trait that does not occur in nature.

CYTOKINESIS The splitting of a cell's cytoplasm during cell division.

CYTOKININS Plant hormones that stimulate mitosis.

CYTOLOGY The scientific study of cells.

CYTOPLASM The fluid part of the cell containing the organelles (other than the nucleus) and including the cell membrane. (cf protoplasm)

CYTOPLASMIC STREAMING The flowing mass movement of cytoplasm within some cells.

DAUGHTER CELL One of the cells resulting from cell division. (cf 'parent' cell)

DEAMINATION The breakdown of excess amino acids in the liver. This involves the removal of the amino group of atoms (NH_2) from the amino acid. Ammonia (NH_3) is formed. This is excreted by many aquatic animals, which have no 'water problem'. It is converted to urea (CON_2H_4), by mammals and uric acid ($C_5H_4O_3N_4$) by birds and reptiles for excretion.

DECAY To breakdown, rot or decompose. This is carried out by bacteria and fungi.

DECIDUOUS Describes a tree or shrub which annually sheds its leaves. Usually this occurs during autumn, although in arid climates it may occur in early summer.

DECOMPOSE see decay

DECOMPOSER A heterotrophic organism which breaks down the remains and wastes of other organisms, returning nutrients to the soil or water.

DENATURATION see page 25 (question 8 (v))

DENDOCHRONOLOGY Using the annual rings in tree trunks to determine their age and the age of associated fossils.

DENITRIFICATION The process whereby some soil bacteria break down nitrates to return nitrogen to the atmosphere.

DEOXYRIBONUCLEIC ACID DNA see pages 22 and 23

DEPENDENT VARIABLE see page 3

DESERT Land in which annual rainfall is low and irregular and therefore vegetation is sparse.

DESSICATION The drying out of tissue.

DETRITUS Dead organic matter.

DIEBACK A disease caused by fungal attack on the roots of a plant, eg. Jarrah Dieback (which affects many different species) is caused by the fungus, *Phytophthora cinnamoni*.

DIFFERENTIATION The development of specialised cells as they mature.

DIFFUSION The movement of particles from an area of high concentration to an area of low concentration in a fluid.

DIGESTION The breakdown of larger more complex organic matter into simpler compounds so that they can be absorbed by an organism.

DIPLOID The possession of two of each chromosome type eg. in human cells the diploid number is 46.

DISEASE A malfunction of the organism caused by injury, microorganisms or incorrect biochemistry.

DISTRIBUTION The area over which a species can be found.

DIURNAL An organism which is active during the day is diurnal. (cf nocturnal)

DIVERGENCE The evolution of two or more populations as they adapt to different environments and become different.

DOMINANCE A trait expressed by a heterozygote which hides or masks another trait.

DORMANT A condition in which an organism ceases its activity and growth in order to survive adverse conditions. (eg. hibernation and aestivation)

DYSFUNCTION When normal function does not occur.

ECDYSIS/MOULTING The shedding of an arthropod exoskeleton, for growth, caused by a hormone called ecdysone.

ECOLOGY The scientific study of the inter-relationships between communities and their environments.

ECOSYSTEM The living community in a particular area, together with its non-living surroundings and the interactions that occur between the two.

ECTOTHERMIC see poikilothermic

EFFECTOR The part of an organism which responds to a stimulus.

ELECTRON MICROSCOPE A microscope which uses electrons to magnify the image of an object. (cf light microscope) It has higher magnification (up to 500,000×) and greater resolution than a light microscope.

ELIMINATION/ DEFAECATION / EGESTION The removal of undigestable body wastes from the alimentary tract.

EMBRYO The early stages of development after the zygote begins to divide and before the organism can be recognised as a particular species.

ENDOCRINE GLAND A gland which secretes its product, a hormone, directly into the circulatory system in animals. Hormones may use the phloem for transport in higher plants. An endocrine gland has no duct and targets cells which are generally well removed from it.

ENDOCYTOSIS The process whereby a cell's membrane either folds inwards to absorb a fluid (pinocytosis) or protrudes outwards and engulfs a larger solid particle (phagocytosis).

ENDOPLASMIC RETICULUM (abbreviated as ER) A network of membranes which form channels within the cytoplasm of a eukaryotic cell. Used to transport materials about the cell.

ENDOTHERMIC see homoiothermic

ENERGY The capacity to do work.

ENVIRONMENT An organism's biotic and abiotic surroundings. All the factors which affect an organism during its life.

ENZYME A protein which acts as a biological catalyst. see page 24

EPICORMIC SHOOT A bud growing from the trunk of a tree usually after a bush fire.

EPIDERMIS The outer layer of cells which covers an organism.

EQUILIBRIUM The state of stability in an ecosystem.

ETHANOL see alcohol

EUGENICS Applying the principles of genetics to improve the inherited features of human populations.

EUKARYOTE A cell which has membrane bounded organelles, including a nucleus, eg. amoeba, human cells.

EUTROPHIC A body of water with adequate dissolved nutrients for its community. (cf oligotrophic)

EUTROPHICATION The action of increasing levels of nutrients in lakes and rivers. Usually this results in increased algal growth which upsets the stability of the ecosystem.

EVAPORATION The change from a liquid to a gas, eg. water to water vapour.

EVERGREEN A tree which keeps most of its leaves all year. (cf deciduous)

EVOLUTION The gradual change in a species which occurs over millions of years due to the cumulative effect of mutation and natural selection.

EXCRETA Faeces. The solid waste of undigested matter produced by animals.

EXCRETION The removal of metabolic wastes. These include CO_2, urea, uric acid. (cf elimination)

EXOCRINE GLAND A gland which empties its product into a duct, eg. salivary glands, lacrimal glands, gastric glands. (cf endocrine)

EXOCYTOSIS The removal, by means of a vacuole, of wastes or products via a cell's membrane. (cf endocytosis)

EXOTIC An introduced plant or animal.

EXTINCT A species which has not been sighted live for fifty years or more.

EXTRACELLULAR FLUID The fluid which surrounds a cell inside a multicellular organism.

FAECES Solid wastes produced by the digestive system eliminated via the anus.

FAT A compound consisting of glycerol and three fatty acids called triglycerides. Soft greasy solids.

FAUNA The animals that live in a particular area.

FEEDBACK The effect which a response may have on a stimulus. If the response reduces the stimulus it is called negative feedback. If the response increases the stimulus it is a positive feedback.

FERAL Domesticated animals that have become "wild" or gone back to a natural way of life.

FERMENTATION Anaerobic respiration of sugary fruit juice in yeast cells which produces alcohol and carbon dioxide.

FERTILISATION The fusion of two gametes to produce a zygote during sexual reproduction.

FILAMENT A long chain of connected cells which forms a thread-like structure, as in filamentous algae.

FILIAL Offspring produced by two parents in a particular study. The first generation is called the F1 or first filial generation. When the F1 are crossed their offspring are called the second filial generation, F2.

FISSION When a single cell organism divides into two during asexual reproduction. Often called binary fission, eg. bacteria.

FIXATION When cells are killed and preserved in order to prepare a microscope slide.

FLACCID Condition of cells when they lose water and become soft and limp.

FLORA The plants that live in a particular area.

FLORIGEN A hormone which induces flowering, believed to be produced in the leaves of angiosperms.

FOLLICLE STIMULATING HORMONE (FSH) A hormone released by the pituitary gland which targets the ovaries and promotes the development of ova and their associated follicle cells.

FOOD CHAIN A diagram which shows simple feeding relationships involving a plant (producer) which is eaten by an animal (first order consumer) which is eaten by another animal (second order consumer) and so on. Arrows link each organism to the next showing the direction in which the energy and nutrients move.

FOOD PYRAMID A diagram which shows the mass of producers, first order consumers, second order consumers and so on in the food chain in a community. The plants are drawn at the base. see page 74

FOOD WEB A diagram used to show the many interacting food chains in a community.

FOREST An area over which trees are the dominant plant. A large percentage of sky is obscured by leaves in a forest.

FOSSIL A trace of an organism that has previously lived on the earth, generally found embedded in sedimentary rock.

FUNCTION What an organ or structure does in carrying our its normal activities.

FUNGI (singular fungus) A plant-like organism which lacks chlorophyll, eg. mushrooms, toadstools, yeast. They are important in decomposition.

GAMETE A mature sex cell; sperm, ovum, pollen grain and ovule. Gametes are haploid.

GAMETOPHYTE A plant which produces gametes.

GENE A section of a chromosome which codes for a particular protein.

GENE FLOW A movement of genes from population to population through interbreeding.

GENE FREQUENCY The proportion of a particular allele in a population.

GENE LOCUS The position on a chromosome where a particular gene is normally located.

GENE POOL The total set of genes in a particular population.

GENERALISATION A statement which applies to many cases, eg. living things are made up of cells.

GENETIC ISOLATION Reproductive separation, when two populations cannot interbreed because of a barrier between them.

GENETICS The scientific study of heredity.

GENOME One complete set of chromosomes and their genes.

GENOTYPE The genetic makeup of an organism for a particular trait, eg. Tt.

GEOGRAPHICAL DISTRIBUTION The range over which an organism lives on the earth.

GEOTAXIS The response of a whole organism to gravity.

GEOTROPISM A plant's growth response to gravity, eg. positive geotropism involves roots growing down towards the centre of the earth.

GERMINATION When a plant seed or spore begins to grow.

GESTATION The development of an organism internally within the uterus before birth.

GIBBERELLIN Plant hormones which promote growth (in conjunction with auxin), sometimes stimulate flowering and are involved in the germination of seeds.

GLAND An organ or tissue which secretes a substance used somewhere else in the body. See exocrine and endocrine glands.

GLUCAGON A hormone which is released by the pancreas when the blood's glucose level is low and increases the breakdown of stored glycogen in the liver to glucose, thus increasing the blood's glucose level.

GLUCOSE A simple sugar (monosaccharide) formed by photosynthesis and used as a source of energy in respiration (formula $C_6H_{12}O_6$).

GLYCOGEN A carbohydrate (polysaccharide) made up of a long chain of glucose molecules. Animals store glucose in this form in the liver and muscles. It is convenient in this form as it is not as soluble as glucose and therefore exerts less osmotic effect. It is readily converted to glucose and is a convenient source of energy.

GLYCOLYSIS Anaerobic respiration in animals. Lactic acid is formed and two molecules of ATP produced for each molecule of glucose.

GOLGI BODY/APPARATUS An organelle found in eukaryotic cells which "packages" the substances (eg. enzymes) which the cell secretes.

GONAD An organ which produces the gametes, eg. testis, ovary.

GONDWANALAND The southern land mass consisting of Australia, India, Africa, South America and Antarctica which existed before tectonic movement separated these continents.

GRADIENT A gradually changing environ-mental condition, eg. the concentration of salt may gradually increase in the water from the bottom of a lake.

GRANA (singular granum) The flattened sacs in chloroplasts which are stacked in layers and contain chlorophyll.

GREENHOUSE EFFECT see page 85

GROWTH HORMONE (GH) A hormone released by the pituitary gland which stimulates body growth. Sometimes called somatotrophin.

GROWTH RING A concentric ring found in the trunk of a tree which is due to one year's growth.

GUARD CELL A specialised epidermal cell which paired with another similar 'sausage' shaped cell forms a stomatal pore.

HABITAT The place in an environment where a particular animal or plant lives.

HAEMOGLOBIN An iron containing protein which carries oxygen (and some carbon dioxide) in blood.

HALF-LIFE The length of time it takes for a radioactive substance to lose half of its radioactivity through radioactive decay. The half-life of carbon-14 is 5730 years.

HALOPHYTE A plant which is adapted to live in a salty environment.

HAPLOID One complete set of chromosomes containing one of each homologous pair. In humans the haploid number is twenty three (23).

HEATH Land which is covered by shrubs which have small leaves, are tough and often wind and drought resistant.

HERB An angiosperm with a green non-woody stem.

HERBICIDE A chemical which kills plants.

HERBIVORE A plant eating animal. (cf carnivore and omnivore)

HEREDITARY Capable of being passed on through gametes from parents to offspring. An hereditary trait is controlled by genes.

HERMAPHRODITE An animal with both testes and ovaries or a flower with both stamens and a pistil.

HETEROTROPH An organism which cannot make its own food, but relies on the organic matter produced by other organisms, eg. animals, fungi, bacteria (other than blue-green bacteria and chemosynthetic bacteria). (cf autotrophs)

HETEROZYGOUS An organism with two different alleles for a particular trait.

HIBERNATION Becoming dormant during the coldest season of the year. (cf aestivation)

HIRSUTE Having a covering of hair or hair-like bristles.

HISTOLOGY The study of tissue structures and tissue functions in organs.

HOMEOSTASIS The maintenance of stability within the body of an organism.

HOMEOTHERMIC / HOMOIOTHERMIC / ENDOTHERMIC The capability of maintaining a fairly constant internal temperature regardless of the temperature of the environment, eg. mammals and birds.

HOMOGENEOUS Organisms and objects all of the same type.

HOMOLOGOUS CHROMOSOMES Paired chromosomes which are similar and have the same type of genes although they are not necessarily the same alleles. Diploid cells have a pair of each chromosome type. Human cells have twenty three (23) homologous pairs of chromosomes.

HOMOZYGOUS When two alleles are the same, the organism is described as homozygous (or pure) for that particular trait, eg. TT or tt.

HORMONE A chemical released in small amounts from special tissue which brings about change in another part of the organism. Endocrine glands produce hormones in animals.

HUMUS Organic matter found in the soil due to decaying plant and animal matter.

HYBRID A heterozygous organism, eg. Tt.

HYBRID VIGOUR The increased strength of an organism which is due to its being a cross between different varieties or races.

HYDROPHILIC A particle or that part of a particle which is attracted to water. (cf hydrophobic)

HYDROPHOBIC A particle or part of a particle which is repelled by water. (cf hydrophilic)

HYDROPHYTE A plant which is adapted to live in damp or aquatic conditions.

HYDROTROPISM A growth response in plants towards water.

HYPERTONIC A solution which because of its higher concentration gains water by osmosis from another solution less concentrated through a semi permeable membrane. (cf hypotonic)

HYPOTHALAMUS A small section of the underside of the brain connected to the pituitary gland. The hypothalamus is sensitive to changes in the temperature and the osmotic pressure in the blood. It contains temperature receptors and osmoreceptors. It therefore controls both the body temperature and the level of water in the blood. It controls the release of pituitary hormones.

HYPOTONIC A solution which being less concentrated loses water to another more concentrated solution by osmosis through a semi-permeable membrane. (cf hypertonic)

IMMIGRATION The movement of organisms into a population.

IMPULSE The electro-chemical message which travels along nerve cells or neurones.

INBREEDING The crossing of individuals of close relationship or within a small population.

INCLUSION A particle of non-living material within the cytoplasm, eg. starch grains.

INCOMPLETE DOMINANCE see codominance

INDEPENDENT ASSORTMENT When the chromosomes pair at metaphase I of meiosis their arrangement is random. Therefore the combinations of various genes in the gametes are random.

INDEPENDENT VARIABLE see page 3

INDIGENOUS Naturally occurring native animals and plants are indigenous as are the Aboriginal people.

INGESTION The taking in of food and water by an animal.

INORGANIC Compounds which do not contain carbon (except carbon dioxide, carbon monoxide and carbonates).

INSECTICIDES Chemicals used to kill insect pests.

INSEMINATE To introduce sperm into the female reproductive tract to fertilise ova.

IN SITU Occupying a natural place.

INSPIRATION To breathe air into the lungs.

INSULIN A hormone which is produced by the pancreas, when blood glucose level rises. It stimulates the liver to convert glucose to glycogen for storage and causes body cells generally to absorb more glucose. Therefore insulin reduces the blood's glucose level.

INTERCELLULAR SPACES Gaps between cells either fluid filled as in most organs or air-filled as in the leaves of terrestrial plants.

INTERNAL ENVIRONMENT The factors which create the surroundings of cells within a multicellular organism. This consists of intercellular fluid which surrounds the cells.

INTERNEURONE A nerve cell which connects a sensory neurone to a motor neurone. (Other names include connecting, association, relay and intermediate neurone.)

INTERPHASE A stage during the life of a cell when it is actively carrying out its normal functions and not dividing (by mitosis or meiosis). DNA may replicate during the interphase.

INTERSPECIFIC Between species. Competition for resources between two species is described as interspecific. (cf intraspecific)

INTRACELLULAR Inside a cell. Organelles are intracellular structures.

INTRASPECIFIC Within a species. Competition between two animals of the same species is intraspecific. (cf interspecific)

INVAGINATION An infold which occurs in a membrane during pinocytosis or in a line of cells to form a cavity.

INVASION When an organism expands its distribution into new areas.

IN VITRO "In glass". This Latin expression is used to describe experiments or processes carried out in test tubes and in other laboratory equipment.

INVOLUNTARY An action carried out which is not under conscious control, eg. peristaltic contraction of the muscles of the intestines.

ION A negatively or positively charged atom or group of atoms, eg. Na^+, CO_3^{2-}.

IRRITABILITY The capacity to respond to changes (stimuli) in the environment.

ISOTONIC When two solutions have the same concentration of dissolved solutes they are said to be isotonic. (cf hypertonic and hypotonic)

ISOTOPES An atom which has a different number of neutrons than normal in its nucleus is an isotope of the atom. Although the chemical properties are the same, an isotope has a different mass than the normal atom. It may be unstable and therefore radioactive, eg. carbon-14.

JARRAH (*Eucalyptus marginata*) A eucalypt which grows very tall and is indigenous to Western Australia. Noted for its fine hard timber and slow growth.

JOULE The unit of energy in the S.I. see page 7

JUVENILE Young organism which is not sexually mature.

KARRI (*Eucalyptus diversicolor*) A eucalypt which grows naturally in the south west corner of W.A. and which like jarrah is excellent building timber.

KARYOTYPE The total number and general appearance of chromosomes within the nucleus of a cell.

KRILL Small crustaceans which are the main food for baleen whales in the Antarctica.

LACTASE An enzyme produced by the intestine which digests lactose (a disaccharide found in milk).

LACTIC ACID An organic acid produced during anaerobic respiration in animal cells.

LAMARCKISM The discredited belief that characteristics acquired during the life of an organism can be passed down via gametes to offspring.

LAND BRIDGE Land connections which occur between land masses when sea levels fall during Ice Ages. These allow organisms to migrate more freely from one area to another otherwise isolated area.

LATENT HEAT The heat absorbed by a liquid when it changes into a gas or released by the gas as it condenses into liquid form.

LAURASIA The northern land mass consisting of North America, Europe and Asia which existed before tectonic movement separated these continents. (cf Gondwanaland)

LEACHING The removal of soluble substances from the soil as water flows through it.

LEAF That part of a terrestrial plant which carries out most of the plant's photosynthesis.

LEGUME A family of plants particularly important because their roots often have nodules which contain nitrogen-fixing bacteria. see Nitrogen Cycle, page 75

LICHEN A terrestrial plant consisting of a symbiotic association of a fungus and an alga.

LIGNIN An organic compound which is a major component of wood.

LIGNOTUBER An enlarged base of plant stem which is fire-resistant.

LIMITING FACTOR A variable in an organism's environment which restricts its growth and reproduction.

LINKAGE Genes which occupy loci on the same chromosome and because they are generally inherited together are described as "linked" genes.

LIPASE An enzyme which breaks down fats.

LIPID A fat or an oil, which is composed of fatty acids and glycerol.

LOCUS (plural loci) The place occupied on a chromosome by a particular gene.

LONG-DAY PLANT An angiosperm which flowers when the nights are short. They will not flower if they have a long period of darkness.

LUMEN The opening through a tube, eg. in digestive tract or in xylem vessel.

LYMPH The fluid in the lymphatic system.

LYMPHATIC SYSTEM The system of vessels which drains fluid from tissues which empties into veins at the base of the neck.

LYSIS The process whereby a cell absorbs water to such an extent that it bursts or when a cell is destroyed by antibodies rupturing its cell membrane.

LYSOSOME An organelle which is involved in intracellular digestion.

LYSOZYME An enzyme which breaks down the cell walls of bacteria.

MACRONUTRIENT A substance which is required by an organism in large amounts, eg. oxygen, nitrogen, hydrogen, carbon.

MACROSCOPIC Visible without the aid of a microscope.

MAGNIFICATION The extent to which an object is enlarged by a microscope. It is expressed as the ratio of the image size to the actual size. When using a light microscope it is calculated by multiplying the magnifying power of the objective by the magnifying power of the ocular.

MALE Organism which produces gametes which move to fertilise another less mobile gamete. In animals the male is the organism which produces sperm. In angiosperms the male produces pollen.

MALLEE A form of plant which has multiple stems arising from a large underground root.

MARINE Living in the sea or ocean or associated with them.

MARSUPIAL Mammals which give birth to their young in a relatively immature stage of development and which have a pouch in which the young develop further, eg. kangaroos, possums, koalas, chuditch.

MASTICATION The grinding mechanical digestion of food.

MATURATION The developmental process culminating in an adult stage capable of reproducing.

MEGA Prefix meaning one million, eg. a megajoule (MJ) means one million joules.

MEIOSIS A type of cell division which results in gametes. The number of chromosomes in the original cell (parent/germ cell) is reduced to half, ie. the cells become haploid.

MELANIN A pigment which occurs in the skin, hair and iris giving them their colour.

MERISTEM A region within a plant where mitotic cell division occurs for growth, eg. apical meristem.

MESOPHYLL Layers of chlorophyll containing cells found in the leaf, eg. palisade and spongy mesophyll.

MESOPHYTE A plant which favours moderate water conditions. (cf hydrophyte and xerophyte)

MESSENGER RNA (mRNA) A nucleic acid formed in the nucleus of a cell which carries a code from a DNA molecule through a nuclear pore to a ribosome and from which a particular protein molecule is assembled according to the code which it carries.

METABOLIC RATE The rate at which chemical processes occur within the body of an organism.

METABOLISM The chemical processes which occur within the body of an organism. These include both anabolic and catabolic processes.

METAPHASE The stage in cell division at which chromosomes are aligned along the equator of the cell.

METHYLENE BLUE A stain used in microscopy to highlight the cell nucleus. The nuclear material turns blue with methylene blue.

MICROBIOLOGY The scientific study of microorganisms.

MICROCLIMATE The abiotic conditions which exist in a microhabitat.

MICROFILAMENT A thin thread of protein present in the cytoplasm of cells.

MICROGRAPH A photograph taken with the aid of a microscope, eg. electron micrograph and light micrograph.

MICROHABITAT A very small habitat, eg. in the bark of a tree.

MICROMETRE (μm) One millionth of a metre, (often called a micron).

MICRONUTRIENT A nutrient required in very small quantities, eg. vitamins, trace elements. (cf macronutrient)

MICROORGANISM A microscopic single celled living thing, eg. bacteria, protozoa, viruses, some algae and some fungi.

MICROTOME A device used to cut very thin slices of tissue to use in microscope slides.

MICROVILLI (singular microvillus) Very small projections of cytoplasm from some cells which increases the cells' total surface area for absorption, eg. epithelial cells of the intestine.

MIDDLE LAMELLA A thin layer which joins two plant cell walls together.

MILDEW A fungal growth found on plants which is white and powdery.

MILLILITRE (mL) One thousandth of a litre.

MIMICRY The imitation of another species which may give protection or reproductive advantage, eg. the stick insect mimics a stick for camouflage.

MINERAL Inorganic substance required for plant and animal life. Plants obtain minerals by absorption through roots. Animals generally obtain them in their food.

MITOCHONDRION see pages 11 and 12

MITOSIS A cell division in which the two cells produced are identical to the parent cell. (cf meiosis) Used for growth and repair.

MODEL A scientific idea in which a process is represented by a diagram or a physical structure in order to develop a better understanding of the process and test predictions based on the idea, eg. the fluid mosaic 'model' of the cell membrane.

MONOCULTURE A crop in which only one plant species is grown, eg. a field of wheat.

MOTILE An ability to move independently by using cilia, flagella or amoeboid movement.

mRNA see messenger RNA

MULTICELLULAR Many celled organism.

MUTAGEN Any agent which induces mutations, eg. radiation, synthetic auxin (2,4-D and 2,4,5-T).

MUTANT An organism which has a mutation.

MUTATION A sudden change to genetic material which makes an organism notably different from its parents. Where the change is due to a change in the genes in gametes it may be inherited by offspring.

NANOMETRE (nm) One thousand millionth or one billionth of a metre (10^{-9} metre).

NATURAL SELECTION The process which leads to differential survival and reproduction of organisms which are better suited to their environment. It results in those better suited contributing proportionally more offspring to subsequent generations.

NEGATIVE FEEDBACK see 'feedback'

NEPHRON The microscopic functional unit of the kidney which filters unwanted materials and wastes from the blood and controls the osmotic pressure of the blood by reabsorbing water.

NERVE A collection of nerve cells or neurons and associated connective tissue which conveys impulses to and from the central nervous system.

NERVE IMPULSE The electro-chemical message which is transmitted along a nerve cell or neurone.

NERVOUS SYSTEM The network of nerve cells which transmits impulses from receptors to effectors. It functions to control and coordinate activities in the body of most multicellular animals.

NEURONE A nerve cell. Most neurones have long extensions of the cytoplasm which convey electro-chemical impulses.

NITRATE A soluble compound containing the NO_3^- group, eg. sodium nitrate, $NaNO_3$. Nitrates are very soluble and are an important source of nitrogen for plants. They are absorbed by the roots from soil.

NITRIFICATION The conversion of ammonia from decaying organic matter into nitrites and then nitrates by nitrifying bacteria. Nitrates can be absorbed by plants through their roots.

NITROGEN An unreactive, colourless, odourless gas which makes up 78% of our atmosphere.

NITROGENOUS BASE Organic substances containing nitrogen which make up the genetic code in DNA and RNA molecules (eg. cytosine, guanine, adenine, thymine and uracil).

NITROGEN CYCLE see page 75

NITROGEN FIXATION The conversion of atmospheric nitrogen into nitrates. This is carried out mostly by nitrogen-fixing bacteria which either live in the soil or in root nodules of legumes (eg. beans, peas, acacias).

NOCTURNAL An animal which is active at night. (cf diurnal)

NODULE A small bulge. Nodules found in the roots of legumes contain nitrogen-fixing bacteria.

NON-DISJUNCTION When homologous chromosomes fail to separate during the anaphase of cell division. Some resulting cells have extra chromosomes some fewer chromosomes than the normal haploid number.

NUCLEAR MEMBRANE see pages 11 and 13

NUCLEIC ACIDS Long chains of nucleotides which form DNA and RNA molecules in the cell. see page 22

NUCLEOLUS A dark staining area within the nucleus of a cell where RNA is synthesised.

NUCLEOTIDE see page 23

NUCLEUS (plural nuclei) Large cell organelle bounded by a nuclear membrane which is double layered and has pores. The nucleus contains nucleoplasm with DNA and RNA.

NUMBAT A marsupial which feeds mainly on termites. It is restricted to small areas in the south-west of W.A. and is the State's animal emblem.

NUTRIENT A substance which supplies living things with the raw materials for growth and/or energy. see macronutrients and micronutrients

OBJECTIVE The lower microscope lens on a light microscope which is closest to the object under view.

OLFACTORY To do with the sense of smell, eg. olfactory receptors in the nasal cavity.

OLIGOTROPHIC Nutrient poor water body. (cf eutrophic)

OMNIVOROUS An animal which eats both plant and animal food. (cf carnivorous, herbivorous)

OOCYTE A cell which divides to produce ova.

ORGAN A collection of tissues which together carry out one or more major functions in an organism, eg. leaf, kidney.

ORGANELLE A small structure within the cytoplasm of a cell which carries out a particular function, eg. mitochondrion.

ORGANIC A relatively complex chemical compound which contains carbon (exceptions include carbon dioxide, carbon monoxide and compounds of carbonates).

ORGANISM A living thing, eg. plant, animal, microorganism.

OSMOREGULATION The maintenance of suitable concentrations of water and dissolved salts in an organism's body cells. This is achieved in a variety of ways depending on the organism's environment. Osmoregulation may involve contractile vacuoles, kidneys, impermeable body coverings, special gill cells which secrete salts, the production of dry wastes (e.g. uric acid) and various behavioural adaptations including burrowing and nocturnal activity.

OSMOSIS The movement of a solvent (usually water) by diffusion through a semi-permeable membrane.

OSMOTIC PRESSURE The pressure which is due to osmosis. Where a cell has a high concentration of dissolved solutes its osmotic pressure will be high. Water has a strong tendency to enter the cell if the extra-cellular solution is less concentrated.

OVARY The organ which produces female gametes.

OXYGEN A colourless, odourless and tasteless gas produced during photosynthesis and required in aerobic respiration. The Earth's atmosphere is 21% oxygen by volume. Chemical formula is O_2.

OZONE A form of oxygen consisting of three linked oxygen atoms; formula O_3.

OZONE LAYER see page 85

PARENCHYMA see page 46

PELAGIC Organisms which drift or swim in the open ocean and lakes, unattached to the bottom or shore.

PENTADACTYL LIMB A limb which has five digits common to most vertebrates.

PEPTIDE BOND The chemical link between two amino acid molecules in a peptide, polypeptide or protein molecule.

PERMEABLE A property of a substance which allows others to pass through it freely. (cf semi-permeable)

PERSPIRATION The combination of water, urea and organic salts which is excreted by sweat glands. It is produced in order to lose heat.

PETIOLE The stalk which attaches many leaves to a branch or stem.

PETRIFIED A fossil which has become stone. Left in suitable alkaline soils, minerals in the soil replace the organic molecules of which the organism is made, forming a stone replica of the original organism.

pH The acidity or alkalinity of a solution. It is dependent on the concentration of H^+ ions. Acid solutions (with higher H^+ ion concentration) have a pH of less than 7, alkaline solutions have a pH greater than 7. A neutral solution has a pH of 7.

PHAGOCYTOSIS see page 18

PHENOTYPE The expression of a particular genotype. Phenotype may also be influenced by the environment.

PHLOEM The tissue in vascular plants which carries sucrose and other organic compounds from photosynthesising leaves to the roots and from the roots to other parts of the plant.

PHOSPHATE A compound containing the phosphate (PO_4^{3-}) group. It is an important constituent of ATP and nucleotides.

PHOSPHOLIPID A complex lipid which contains phosphate. The lipids which make up the cell membrane are phospholipids.

PHOSPHOPROTEIN A protein which contains phosphate.

PHOTOMICROGRAPH A photograph taken through a microscope. Often called a micrograph. An electron micrograph is obtained using an electron microscope.

PHOTOPERIODISM A response by plants to the length of the day or night. see long-day plants, short-day plants

PHOTOSYNTHESIS The manufacture of glucose by green plants, using light, chlorophyll and enzymes and the raw materials carbon dioxide and water. A byproduct of photosynthesis is oxygen.

PHOTOTROPISM A growth response to light, eg. when green plants grow towards light this is called positive phototropism.

PHYLLODE A flattened stem or petiole which photosynthesises and therefore functions as a leaf but with fewer stomata. This is an adaptation possessed by xerophytes, eg. acacia (wattles), in which the leaves are often reduced to spines or prickles.

PHYSIOLOGY The way in which an animal or plant functions. (Also used to refer to the study of animal and plant function i.e. how they work.)

PHYTOPLANKTON Microscopic plants which drift in the ocean and lakes. (cf zooplankton)

PINOCYTOSIS see page 18

PIT A thin section of the cell walls between two adjacent cells. Pits in xylem vessels provide an alternative path for water flow.

PITH The cells which make up a soft core in plant stems.

PITUITARY The "master" endocrine gland in vertebrates. It is attached to the underside of the hypothalamus and produces several hormones; some of which control other endocrine glands. Hormones released by the pituitary include ADH and oxytocin from the posterior lobe and TSH, FSH, LH and somatotrophin from the anterior lobe. see hypothalamus

PLASMA MEMBRANE see cell membrane

PLASMODESMATA Cytoplasmic threads which pass through the pits of cell walls thus connecting two adjacent plant cells.

PLASMOLYSIS The shrinkage of the cell membrane away from the inside of a plant cell or bacteria cell due to water loss.

PLASTID A membrane bounded organelle found in plant cells which contains chlorophyll (chloroplasts), pigment (chromoplasts) or starch (leucoplast).

POIKILOTHERMIC (ectothermic) An animal whose body temperature depends on the temperature of its surroundings. (cf homoiothermic)

POLLUTION Addition of materials, noise, or heat to the environment which reduces the likelihood of the natural flora and/or fauna surviving there.

POLYPEPTIDE A long chain of approximately one hundred amino acids. (cf protein)

POLYPLOIDY Having additional sets of chromosomes beyond the normal two sets in a diploid cell.

POTASSIUM A nutrient element essential to living things as a co-enzyme, in nerve impulses and in maintaining osmotic balance within the body's fluids.

POTOMETER A device used to measure the rate of water loss from a terrestrial plant.

PREDATION To kill another animal for food.

PRODUCER An organism which makes its own food by photosynthesis (or chemosynthesis). An autotrophic organism, eg. green plant.

PRODUCTIVITY The increase in the total organic matter in a population or community in a given time. This is a measure of the difference between the rate at which organic matter is synthesised and the rate at which food is respired.

PROKARYOTIC Referring to an organism which has cells that have no membrane bounded organelles, eg. bacteria and blue-green bacteria (algae). (cf eukaryotic)

PROTEIN An organic compound containing carbon, hydrogen, oxygen, nitrogen and sometimes sulphur. Proteins are made up of long chains of amino acids joined by peptide bonds. Proteins are essential components of cells being used for structure and enzymes.

PROTEIN SYNTHESIS The making of proteins which occurs on ribosomes by joining amino acids together to form a long chain.

PROTOPLASM The nucleus and the cytoplasm (including the cell membrane) of a cell. The cell wall of a plant cell is the only part not included in the protoplasm.

PUTREFACTION Decay or decomposition carried out by bacteria and fungi.

QUADRAT An area of study. Quadrats are usually definite areas (eg. 1 m²) selected at random in order to estimate the average density of a particular organism in a particular region.

QUALITATIVE Refers to data which has no numerical values associated with it. eg. To describe the production of heat energy by active animals as **high** is to assign a qualitative value to the production. (cf quantitative)

QUANTITATIVE Refers to data which has numerical values. eg. To express the heat energy released by an organism as 15 J/hour is to assign a quantitative value to this variable.

RACE Subset of a species.

RADIATION A type of electromagnetic energy flow which occurs in waves, eg. x-rays, light rays, UV rays. Radiation may also refer to a movement of radioactive particles such as α or β radiation.

RADIOCARBON DATING see carbon dating

REACTANT A substance which is chemically changed during a chemical reaction.

REACTION TIME The period of time between when a stimulus is detected by a receptor and when the corresponding response occurs.

REAGENT A chemical used to test for the presence of another. eg. Iodine is a reagent used to test for starch.

RECEPTOR A special cell, tissue or organ which is sensitive to specific changes in the environment and reacts to that change. eg. Some nerve endings are sensitive to changes in temperature and when stimulated send impulses via sensory neurones to the central nervous system.

RECESSIVE Refers to a trait which is not expressed in the heterozygote. A recessive trait is hidden due to the expression of the allele for the dominant trait.

RECOMBINANT GENE A gene (or genes) which is inserted on a chromosome to which it does not normally belong.

RECOMBINATION This occurs when genes which are not normally inherited together, **are** inherited by offspring because of crossing-over during meiosis. Genes which are normally linked become separated, while others are recombinant.

RECYCLING Using materials more than once, eg. used glass bottles melted down to form coloured windows, many elements and compounds in a natural ecosystem.

REDUCTION DIVISION see meiosis

REFLEX A rapid response which occurs without thought. Nerve impulses travel from the receptor to the effector via the spinal cord without the brain's intervention.

REFLEX ARC The path, usually comprising a receptor, sensory neurone, connecting neurone, motor neurone and effector, over which an impulse travels in bringing about a reflex.

RELIC Refers to a small group of **animals** which are the survivors of a once greater population with wider distribution, eg. numbats in the S-W of W.A. (cf remnant)

REMNANT A small area of native bush or forest which has been left undisturbed. (cf relic)

REPLICATION The copying of DNA which may occur in cells in the interphase.

REPRODUCTIVE ISOLATION The separation of populations such that interbreeding between them cannot occur, due to barriers such as oceans, rivers, deserts. see allopatric

RESOLVING POWER The capacity of a microscope to visually separate two objects which are close together. The resolving power of an electron microscope is much greater than that of a light microscope, so that the former instrument enables much finer detail to be observed.

RESOURCE A factor in the environment which is used by an organism.

RESPIRATION The chemical breakdown of organic matter, often glucose, in order to release energy, which takes place in cells.

RESPONSE The reaction or change which occurs in an organism brought about by a particular stimulus.

RETRANSLOCATION The movement in phloem of stored nutrients from the roots, stems or leaves to other parts of a plant for use in those parts. (Especially movement of stored sugar in the roots or stem to the site of growing tissue in the leaves before they become photosynthetically active.)

RIBOSE A sugar which has five carbon atoms and is a component of RNA molecules.

RIBOSOME An organelle, which is either attached to the endoplasmic reticulum or free in the cytoplasm, on which protein synthesis occurs.

RNA Ribonucleic acid. A nucleic acid made up of a chain of nucleotides which have ribose sugar molecules (unlike DNA where the sugar molecule has one less oxygen atom).

ROOT That part of a vascular plant which is normally under the soil and which absorbs water and mineral nutrients for the plant. It also anchors the plant and may store food and minerals.

ROOT HAIR see page 44

ROOT NODULE see nodule

SALINE A solution containing salt, eg. sea water.

SALINITY A measure of the salt concentration.

SALT Usually an ionic inorganic compound, eg. sodium chloride (which is commonly referred to as 'salt').

SAP The fluid contents of the phloem.

SCLERENCHYMA see page 46

SECTION To cut through an organ or tissue. Usually thin sections are cut using a microtome in order to produce microscope slides. It may be a transverse, oblique or horizontal section depending on the direction of the cut chosen.

SEDIMENTARY Refers to rock which is usually formed by the settling of sediments under water. Over time different layers are formed. These layers often trap the remains of animals and plants which die in or near the water and thus form an important source of fossil material.

SELECTION see natural selection

SELECTION PRESSURE A factor present in a species' environment which affects its survival.

SEMI-PERMEABLE Permeable to some particles but not to all, eg. cell membranes.

SENSE An ability to detect particular stimuli, eg. receptors in vertebrate ears provide a sense of hearing.

SENSORY NEURONE A special nerve cell which transmits impulses from receptors to the central nervous system in vertebrates.

SEX Classification which indicates the type of gamete produced. If motile small gametes are produced the organism is referred to as male, larger non motile (ie. cannot propel themselves) gametes are produced by females.

SEX CHROMOSOMES Those chromosomes which determine the sex of the individual organism. In mammals one pair of chromosomes determines the sex. A female has two X chromosomes while a male has an X and a Y chromosome in each body (somatic) cell.

SEX LINKED Refers to genes which have their loci on sex chromosomes. In mammals this refers to genes on the X chromosome only.

SEXUAL REPRODUCTION Reproduction which involves the fusion of two sex cells called gametes. The resulting cell is called a zygote. The zygote gives rise to the new organism.

SHORT-DAY PLANTS Flowering plants which only flower after a long period of uninterrupted darkness. (cf long-day plants)

SIEVE ELEMENT A living cell which helps form the vessel in phloem tissue through which sugar and other organic materials are transported. It does not contain a nucleus but does contain other organelles. It is connected to cells above and below by cytoplasmic strands which pass through pores in the cell walls they share. A cell attached to one side called a "companion cell" contains a nucleus which is believed to control the sieve element's activities.

SIEVE PLATE The common wall between adjacent sieve elements which contains pores through which cytoplasmic strands pass from one sieve element to the next.

S.I. UNITS see page 7

SOIL The layer of smaller weathered particles of rock in which plants grow. It contains organic matter (humus) formed from the remains of dead organisms, water, minerals, air and microorganisms.

SOMATIC Refers to cells in the body other than gametes.

SOMATOTROPHIN Growth hormone released by the pituitary.

SPECIALISED Structurally developed to carry out a particular function.

SPECIATION see adaptive radiation

SPECIES A group of organisms which are interbreeding in their natural environment and producing viable offspring or a group of organisms that are structurally and functionally very similar.

SPERM Male gametes of animals.

STARCH A carbohydrate consisting of a long chain of glucose molecules. Starch is sparingly soluble and therefore is a form in which glucose is stored in plant cells. It does not increase the osmotic pressure in the cell to the extent that glucose will.

STEM That part of a plant which supports the leaves and contains vascular tissue for transport between the roots and leaves. The stem may be woody or herbaceous.

STIMULUS A change in the environment of an organism which can be detected by it and induces a response in the organism.

STOMA (plural stomata) An opening or pore for gas exchange in the epidermis of a leaf or stem which is created by two guard cells.

STRATUM (plural strata) A compressed mineral layer which makes up sedimentary rock or a layer of plant vegetation which makes up several levels within a forest (eg. grasses may form one stratum, shrubs another and tall trees a third higher stratum).

STROMA That internal part of a chloroplast which surrounds the grana.

SUBSPECIES see race

SUBSTRATE A molecule which is chemically changed by an enzyme. The substrate fits temporarily into the active site of the enzyme to form a substrate-enzyme complex.

SUCROSE A disaccharide consisting of the two monosaccharides glucose and fructose. This is the sugar often added to tea and coffee to sweeten their taste. It is also the form in which glucose is normally transported in the phloem.

SUGAR A sweet tasting carbohydrate, eg. sucrose, glucose.

SULFUR An element which is a part of many proteins and is responsible for their three dimensional shape.

SWAMP An area of land covered either permanently or periodically by still water.

SWEAT see perspiration

SYNTHESISE To make. see anabolic

SYSTEM A group of organs which together carry out a major function (or major functions) within the body.

TACTILE To do with the sense of touch.

TAPROOT A single dominant root which normally grows vertically down. The taproots of some native trees descend many metres to tap water deep below in the water table, eg. Jarrah. Taproots have lateral roots branching horizontally from their sides.

TASTE BUD A chemo-receptor usually in the tongue which enables vertebrates to distinguish between food types.

TAXIS The response of the whole organism in moving away from or towards a stimulus, eg. chemotaxis, phototaxis. (cf tropism)

TELOPHASE The last stage in meiotic or mitotic cell division, when new nuclear membranes enclose the separated chromosomes and the cytoplasm divides into two daughter cells.

TEMPLATE A mould from which a copy of something is made.

TERMINAL Something which forms the end of a structure, eg. a terminal bud is new growth at the end of a stem (lateral buds are at the ends of side branches).

TERTIARY STRUCTURE Refers to the three dimensional shape unique to a particular protein. In an enzyme this shape creates its "active site".

TEST CROSS The cross between a **homozygous recessive organism** and an organism which shows the dominant phenotype. The resulting F₁ can reveal whether the organism with the dominant phenotype is homozygous or heterozygous.

THEORY A hypothesis for which supporting evidence has been obtained but which needs more evidence for it to be accepted generally as a law.

THIGMOTROPISM A plant growth response to contact. An epiphytic plant which grows around another supporting plant shows thigmotropism

THRESHOLD The strength of a stimulus that is just sufficient to induce a response.

THYROXINE A vertebrate hormone released by the thyroid gland which increases cell metabolism. Increased metabolism involves an increase in oxygen use and a greater release of heat energy.

TISSUE A group of similar cells which together perform a particular function. Organs are composed of various tissues.

TOLERANCE The extent to which an organism can survive change in an environmental factor. eg. A particular bacterium may only live in water which has a temperature range of 10° - 30°C. Outside this range is beyond the tolerance of this bacterium.

TONOPLAST The membrane which surrounds the vacuoles in cells.

TORPOR A condition in which the metabolic rate of an animal slows down to produce inactivity of the organism. Occurs when an animal hibernates or aestivates.

TOUCH The sense involved in detecting objects which contact an animal.

TOXIN A chemical which poisons cells. Many microorganisms produce toxins.

TRACE ELEMENT see micronutrient

TRACHEID A specialised dead cell which together with other tracheids forms a tube through which water passes from the roots to the leaves in ferns and gymnosperms. Tracheids are elongated cells with tapered ends which overlap. Where they overlap pits occur which allows water to pass from cell to cell.

TRACHEOPHYTA The plant Division which has vascular tissue, eg. angiosperms, conifers, ferns.

TRAIT A feature or characteristic possessed by an organism.

TRANSFER RNA (tRNA) A nucleic acid which transports free amino acids in the cytoplasm to the ribosomes where the amino acids are linked to form proteins. Specific tRNA molecules lock onto each amino acid and transport it to a particular part of the mRNA, on the ribosome, which has a codon matching the anti-codon on tRNA.

TRANSLOCATION The movement of sugar and other materials from the leaves to other parts of the plant (roots or stem) via the phloem vessels.

TRANSPIRATION The loss of water by evaporation from the leaves (or stem) of a plant.

TRANSPIRATION STREAM The flow of water in xylem vessels from the roots through the stem, into the leaves (and out through the stomata).

TROPHIC LEVEL The position of an organism in a food chain, eg. the trophic level of a producer is a the beginning of the food chain.

TROPISM A growth response towards or away from a stimulus, eg. phototropism.

TURGID Refers to a cell which is filled with water. (cf flaccid) Plant cells become turgid when surrounded by distilled water but do not lyse because their cell wall prevents this from occurring.

ULTRASTRUCTURE Parts of a cell which **cannot** be seen with the aid of a light microscope but only become visible if an electron microscope is used, eg. double membranes and pores of the nucleus.

ULTRAVIOLET LIGHT (UV) Electro-magnetic radiation with a wavelength which is shorter than visible light and therefore cannot be detected by human eyes.

UNICELLULAR Single celled, eg. amoeba, bacteria.

UREA An organic compound, formula CON_2H_4, which is a waste product of the breakdown of excess amino acids in mammals. This nitrogenous metabolic waste is toxic and is excreted by the kidneys. It is soluble in water.

URIC ACID An important nitrogenous waste formed in birds and reptiles from the breakdown of excess amino acids. It is sparingly soluble in water (formula $C_5H_4O_3N_4$).

URINE The liquid waste produced by the kidneys. Urine generally contains water, urea, uric acid, excess minerals, salts and hormones.

VACUOLE A membrane (tonoplast) bounded sac found in the cytoplasm which stores water and minerals, pigments, starch, sugars or wastes. Animal vacuoles (called vesicles) are smaller than plant vacuoles.

VARIABLE A factor which can change, eg. temperature. see dependent and independent variables, page 3

VARIATION A feature or characteristic which is different within a species. Variation in the offspring of sexually reproducing organisms is greater than that found in the offspring of asexually reproducing organisms.

VARIEGATED A leaf which has areas of mesophyll tissue which do not contain chlorophyll. These leaves often have a yellow and green pattern and are sometimes grown for ornamental reasons. Only the area with chlorophyll produces glucose (and starch) by photosynthesis.

VARIETY see race

VASCULAR Referring to the tubes which carry materials within the organism, eg. the circulatory system in vertebrates is vascular tissue and the phloem and xylem vessels in plants are vascular tissue.

VASCULAR BUNDLE A group of xylem and phloem vessels clustered together with fibre cells found in the roots, stem and leaves of higher terrestrial plants. Sometimes referred to as veins in the leaves.

VASCULAR SYSTEM The circulatory system in vertebrates or the phloem and xylem in plants.

VASOCONSTRICTION The reduction in the diameter of blood vessels which reduces blood flow through them.

VASODILATION The increase in the diameter of blood vessels which increases blood flow through them.

VASOPRESSIN Alternative name for ADH. see antidiuretic hormone

VERTEBRATE/VERTEBRATA Any animal which has a backbone. e.g. fish, amphibians, reptiles, birds and mammals

VESICLE A small vacuole found in animal cells.

VESTIGIAL ORGAN An organ which has little or no apparent use but which may have been functional (and usually larger) in an ancestral organism, eg. coccyx and appendix in humans.

VIABLE Having the potential to mature and produce healthy offspring.

VITAMIN A small organic molecule needed in small amounts to promote health in the organism. Plants produce all their vitamins. Animals must eat vitamins produced by plants.

WASTE A substance which is present in the body but which is not required and may become harmful if allowed to accumulate. It is therefore eliminated in the urine, faeces, expired air or sweat.

WATER CYCLE The flow of water through an ecosystem, eg. water may evaporate from the sea, form clouds, be precipitated as rain onto the land, flow back into the sea. However it may take other pathways. see page 77

WILDERNESS Unspoilt areas which are inhabited by animals and plants in their natural environment.

WILTING An herbaceous plant which is dehydrating and therefore losing its turgidity. The cells in a wilting plant are becoming flaccid.

WOOD Old lignified xylem vessels which make up the bulk of a tree or stem of a shrub.

X-CHROMOSOME One of two sex chromosomes found in human cell nuclei. Females have two X-chromosomes in each nucleus (apart from ova which have one). Males have an X and Y chromosome in each somatic cell (sperm have either an X or a Y chromosome).

XEROMORPH A plant which is adapted to survive almost total dehydration, eg. some plants which live in very dry areas.

XEROPHYTE A plant which is adapted to live in a dry environment. It may have reduced leaf size, phyllodes instead of leaves, stomata only one side of the leaf, water storage cells, leaves reduced to spines, thick waxy cuticle, extensive root system, mallee form of growth. (cf halophyte and xeromorph)

XYLEM see page 44

Y-CHROMOSOME see X chromosome

ZOOLOGY The scientific study of animals.

ZOOPLANKTON The microscopic animals which together with phytoplankton live and drift near the surface of the water in oceans and lakes.

NOTES

NOTES

NOTES

NOTES

TEE STUDENTS

DOES YOUR STUDY PROGRAM NEED A BOOST?

Academic Associates can help you gain that extra confidence and understanding so essential for success at school.

✓ **Study skills courses**

Academic Associates' short courses on study skills will give you the techniques that will help you realise your full potential.

You will:
- improve your study skills
- be more organised and successful
- learn to set goals and achieve them
- be better prepared for examinations
- gain greater confidence.

Need a little extra help?

✓ **Exam preparation courses**

Master your subject with the help of experienced TEE teachers. Their easy to follow step-by-step approach will really help you to understand.

- Saturday classes or holiday courses
- Small groups - not lectures
- Exclusive worksheets/TEE style questions
- Subjects available: English, Literature, Calculus, Applicable Maths, Discrete Maths, Physics, Chemistry, Biology, Human Biology, Accounting, Economics & Geography.

Make success a reality

Reserve your place in our next series of courses.
Complete the form below for more information.

Student Name: _____ Date: _____

Address: _____ Postcode: _____

Phone: _____ Fax: _____

School: _____

Please send me the latest information on courses being conducted by **Academic Associates**.

❏ Study skills courses   ❏ Examination preparation courses

List subjects: _____

Mail or Fax to:

▲ ACADEMIC ASSOCIATES 13 Levey Rise, Winthrop WA 6150. Phone/Fax: 9310 4490

TEE Biology Study Guide